Rob Drum
Plays with Pai

Rob Drummond
Plays with Participation

Bullet Catch

Wallace

The Majority

Top Table

Eulogy

Rolls in Their Pockets

Edited with Introduction by
DAVID OVEREND

methuen | drama
LONDON • NEW YORK • OXFORD • NEW DELHI • SYDNEY

METHUEN DRAMA
Bloomsbury Publishing Plc
50 Bedford Square, London, WC1B 3DP, UK
1385 Broadway, New York, NY 10018, USA

BLOOMSBURY, METHUEN DRAMA and the Methuen Drama logo are trademarks of
Bloomsbury Publishing Plc

First published in Great Britain 2021

A catalogue record for this book is available from the British Library.

A catalog record for this book is available from the Library of Congress.

ISBN: HB: 978-1-3500-9538-0
         PB: 978-1-3500-9528-1
         ePDF: 978-1-3500-9531-1
         eBook: 978-1-3500-9529-8

Typeset by RefineCatch Limited, Bungay, Suffolk
Printed and bound in Great Britain

To find out more about our authors and books visit www.bloomsbury.com and sign up for our newsletters.

Contents

Foreword

Within the world of theatre-making, we often talk about 'risk-taking'. It has become something of a fashionable, catch-all phrase that sums up both the inherent risk taken by artists when their work is new, as well as a celebration of bravery from audiences and curators in taking a chance on that which is untested. What strikes me about Rob and David's work together is that by creating theatre that can only happen – can only be completed – through the audience's participation, there is a different type of risk, an unpredictability and a real unknowability of outcome.

At the time of publication, we are experiencing a particularly turbulent, divisive political moment. In difficult times we look anew at what might be the wider purpose and value of theatre and the arts. The best theatre delivers a shared, visceral experience amongst the audience. An awareness of a communal heartbeat. It is these moments of feeling intensely alive – palms sweating, shivers down the spine – that can bring people together and create new communities. Rob often uses the framework of the text to build improvised conversations around political issues, or to ask moral and philosophical questions. In the face of an atomised and polarised world it simply feels useful to be part of these exchanges. Perhaps the most important function of theatre is its unique capacity to create empathy, and never more so have I felt this than in Rob and David's projects.

This collection is a celebration of collaboration. Just as Rob is more than any one type of artist – he is at once writer, performer, facilitator – so is David more than simply the director. Often Rob takes physical risks as he explores his theatre-making, and the act of creating and holding intimate revelations from the audience-participants takes a mental and emotional strength that requires particular support. The success of their partnership in turn enables the audience to feel as though they can collaborate in the creation of the work. When Rob invites them onto the stage, they feel safe enough to do so, held carefully in a co-created stage world.

What is thrilling about the works collected here is the way that each of them connected to their audiences in multiple ways. On one level there was the excitement of feeling lucky enough to be witnessing something truly innovative and boundary-pushing. But there was always huge heart and generosity towards the audience – a desire to create that which is most celebrated in Scottish theatre: a good night out.

Jackie Wylie
Artistic Director
National Theatre of Scotland

Introduction

David Overend

Dodging the bullet . . .

The magician selects his assistant from the audience. Tonight, she is an elderly producer from New York. Over the course of an hour, he builds her trust, correctly predicting events from her past and asking her about her life. Towards the end of the performance a gun is brought onto the stage. She will be asked to aim at the magician's mouth and pull the trigger as he performs the infamous 'bullet catch' – a stunt that has allegedly caused the death of twelve people. The assistant wavers and she cannot be persuaded to take the weapon. It is immediately clear that this relationship can go no further.

From the back of the seating bank, I shudder with apprehension. This is unchartered territory. I have been working as a director on this production for almost a month and have seen numerous assistants fire a practice shot at a ceramic plate before raising the gun and nervously shooting Rob Drummond directly in the face. We knew this might not happen and had talked about ending the show without the final gunshot, but we never thought the assistant would refuse *before* the practice shot.

Rob turns to his mother who is watching the show that night. Having previously rejected her as a volunteer, he hesitates before asking her to join him on stage to complete the show. She agrees and he hands her the weapon. The tension in the room is palpable and as she holds the cold, heavy gun, which she is being asked to point at her son, she has a change of heart, apologises and returns to her seat. It is not clear how to proceed. Rob addresses the audience, 'this hasn't happened before . . . I've never had nobody willing to do it'.

Ostensibly, the show had gone wrong. This was only the fourth public performance of what turned out to be a three-year international tour, and the climax of the event was in jeopardy. However, as I looked around the auditorium, I realised that the tension had not been lost. People literally sat on the edges of their seats, apparently unsure what was going to happen, willing Rob to find his way out of this situation. The performance had veered off track and weeks of script development and rehearsal could not bring it back. Rob was not stalling for time while he worked out what to do next; he was genuinely appealing to the audience for help. At this point, a voice piped up from the shadows, 'I'll do it'.

Plays with participation

This book contains six plays by Rob Drummond that I directed between 2011 and 2018. These texts represent a short period of time in an ongoing collaboration that started much earlier – when we met as students at the University of Glasgow in the first year of the new millennium. But the productions that we made during these seven years strike me as particularly important examples of our work. We began to take more risks and to worry less about occasionally getting things wrong. Consequently, we learned a lot about the kind of theatre we wanted to make. These scripts document an important period of artistic development and growing confidence in our methods. They also, it seems to me, speak to wider themes and trends in our collaborations with other people in other theatres. As such, they can be read as a sort of testing ground for some of the ideas and formal experiments of our wider practice.

In several of our shows (*Bullet Catch* and *Wallace* are the examples in this volume), there is a point early on when the entire audience are asked to raise their hands. This usually starts hesitantly, but with some additional pleas from the stage – accompanied by the growing realisation that everybody is actually going to play along – even those audience members who are the least willing to participate get on board and their arms go up. I always sense that there is a lot going on in these moments. The simple, playful action is proposed by a performer and taken up by the audience. It is an offer and response dynamic, which is the key to every good improvisation. This encourages a spirit of openness and a commitment to the success of the show. It also creates anticipation about how much the audience will be asked to do, and a hint of risk in accepting the participatory premise of the performance. For the briefest of moments, hanging in the air is a shared commitment to collaboration between the audience and the performers in the live moment of the event. It is a performative action of volunteering, of being counted and of accepting an invitation to participate (White 2013). This is a state of active involvement, which everyone in the room has adopted as their default position. We then invite anyone who does not wish to participate to simply lower their hand.

In this work, participation is never expected, demanded or forced on unwilling audience members. I am sure that this can sometimes be a useful approach, and indeed I have often valued the experience of being pushed outside my comfort zone in a theatre, to do things that I was not keen on. But a sense of trust and collaboration is frequently sacrificed by the shock tactics of non-consenting participation; and we are concerned with preserving such a relationship. We aim to get to know our audiences, to build a relationship with them and to create something together. In my experience, the audience will go a long way with you if they know that you have their best interests at heart. If the intention is to challenge preconceptions and offer alternative perspectives, then a shared ownership of the common ground is a good place to start.

All of the plays collected here use participation to a greater or lesser extent. *Bullet Catch* and *The Majority* are the most interactive: one invites an individual audience member onto the stage to take part in a series of magic tricks and improvised conversations; the other uses electronic voting handsets to stage a series of referenda throughout the show. Act One of *Wallace* casts the audience as viewers of a live televised panel debate and invites them to ask questions of the panel members. The two-part family saga *Top Table* and *Eulogy* uses less direct interaction with the audience, but the notion of *casting* the audience – as guests at a wedding and a funeral respectively – is another form of participation, which expands the setting from the stage to the auditorium. *Rolls in Their Pockets* is set and staged in a bar and the drama emerges from the audience's situation: drinks flow on and off stage and the lack of direct participation becomes clear as the division between the characters and the audience takes on an existential quality and is understood to exceed that of their location on either side of the performance space. The diversity and formal divergence of this selection of texts is reflective of our approach. We are not participatory theatre makers: we are theatre makers who often *play with participation.*

In this Introduction, I want to explore the dramaturgy of collaboration in these plays: the ways in which participation functions as a structural and aesthetic strategy; and the kinds of relationships that emerge from its use. This will be of value to those wishing to produce these plays, or to develop their own work in a similar mode. It will also be of interest to those seeking a deeper understanding of our working methods and the principles informing our practice. It is followed by a *conversation* between playwright and director, which aims to capture something of the reflective, inquisitive nature of our process. All this is a precursor to the play scripts themselves, which we have presented here along with a running commentary combining both of our voices into footnotes that include anecdote and analysis. These explain and interrogate some of the choices we have made, as well as offering an insight into how these texts were performed with their audiences.

Models of participation

To make sense of this work, I start with three propositions: first, that in buying in to the construct of the theatrical experience and negotiating the often blurry distinction between truth and fiction, the audience are not passive or misguided – they are engaged investigators in the artistic structure, making meaning along with the performers and playing a vital role in the whole experience; second, that the notion of participation in experimental, 'interactive' theatre is really not that different from the active, critical role of the audience in the most *traditional* 'text-based' performances; third, that the difference between the fixed, scripted elements of our plays and the open improvisational sections is only a temporary loosening of the framework (but again, this is not that different from 'immersive' and 'participatory' theatre). Catherine Love considers the 'varying balances of determinacy and indeterminacy' that are in operation in play texts (2018, pp. 106–108). This is a useful model for our practice, which allows for a spectrum of textual qualities, helping us to understand how these plays move between degrees of scripted text and improvised interaction, without ever being wholly defined by either.

There is now a general recognition in contemporary theatre scholarship that agency cannot be simply aligned with participation, and that a refusal or unwillingness to 'join in' can be every bit as active and engaged as enthusiastic compliance. For example, Anna Harpin and Helen Nicholson reject 'sharp distinctions between participation (active, rebellious, critical) and non-participation (passive, receptive, docile)' (2017, p. 4). As such analyses of participatory theatre acknowledge, spectatorship is already an active process (Rancière 2011). The current trend for immersive and participatory theatre forms should therefore be understood as a novel framing of this dynamic, rather than a corrective to a supposedly passive relationship with performance.

It is easy to make these claims on an abstract level, and there are various scholars whose theses give them critical weight: the most notable being Jacques Rancière. Published in English in 2011, Rancière's book *The Emancipated Spectator* was particularly influential in its articulation of the agency and artistry of the audience. Rejecting the assumption that seated, silent audiences are necessarily 'passive', Rancière posits an active role comprising observation, selection, comparison and interpretation. The suggestion is that spectators 'compose their own poem, as, in their way, do actors or playwrights, directors, dancers or performers' (Rancière 2011, p. 13). This has been a useful concept that helps to free up an understanding of the traditional theatre audience from assumptions about inherent or inevitable passivity. But these lessons are best learnt in the unpredictable, risky space between the stage and the auditorium. It took years of moving between the two to realise that audiences had to be considered as part of our work, not just as witness to it.

While there are various types of participation in operation in these plays, the important thing to note is that the role of the audience is in constant motion: shifting from overt interaction with performers and each other to quiet contemplation of the ideas explored through the narrative. The continual movement between these modes is central to the work. For every time we invite the audience to join in with a rendition of 'When you're smiling' (*Eulogy*), play their own drinking game (*Rolls in Their Pockets*) or fire a loaded pistol at the performer (*Bullet Catch*), there are also moments when characters or performers ruminate on philosophical quandaries, espouse political stratagems or recount autobiographical anecdotes. We are always actively searching for the right form to carry the moment that we want to create, or to communicate the idea that we want to share or hold up for scrutiny.

Expecting the unexpected

Since that nerve-wracking opening of the *Bullet Catch* tour, there have been numerous instances of objects and events taking us by surprise. We have contended with bungled magic tricks, temperamental firearms (a lot), missing props, angry hecklers and unusually introverted or extroverted volunteers. We have learnt to embrace the unexpected and have relaxed into the unpredictability of interaction with the audience. Not only have we realised that we can get away with the vast majority of such instances, but we have also learnt that they usually add a great deal to the sense of vulnerability, honesty and openness that we are trying to foster. Nonetheless, there is a high degree of mitigation built into the performance structure. There are several ways in which we manage expectations and limit possible outcomes: *rehearsing with the audience, casting the audience, using a 'gatekeeper', working with plants* and *improvised response*.

First, our collaboration with the audience begins early in the process, and we regularly invite audiences into the rehearsal room to contribute to the development of our performances (Overend 2018). We have developed a structure for 'testing out' ideas with small groups of volunteer audience members, who each visit us just once in the process (thereby maintaining the fresh perspective of the uninitiated). These are valuable opportunities to see how far we can push things and whether our strategies are effective. Rehearsal audiences challenge us, offer exciting suggestions and help us to understand the power dynamics of collaboration. For our more explicitly participatory works, we then continue to make changes and rewrite sections once the public audience is in attendance. When shows tour or run for a long time, they tend to be evolve significantly over the course of their existence (the differences between the published pre-rehearsal script of *The Majority* and the latest version, included in this volume, are testament to this (Drummond 2017b)).

Second, we regularly cast the audience in a specific collective role. For example, the audience are the guests at a wedding (*Top Table*) or a funeral (*Eulogy*), the audience at an Edwardian magic show (*Bullet Catch*) or a televised studio debate (*Wallace*). The process of casting the audience often begins pre-show, using an immersive set (wedding tables and orders of service), or seeding the construct in the programme, which may invite the audience to prepare in some way (for example, considering questions to ask the *Wallace* panellists). This strategy of literally giving the audience a role encourages participation because even by sitting silently, watching a play in a darkened auditorium, the audience are collectively playing along. Ideally, this leads to a willingness to play a game with the performers. When more demanding activities are suggested, there will always be individuals who have embraced the role enthusiastically and are more than happy to leap up on stage.

Third, we regularly rely on the role of a gatekeeper (compère, chairperson, master of ceremonies, minister or magician) that is afforded by direct address. There are moments in these plays when the call to participate is made explicit, sometimes in a very direct manner, as in the opening lines of *Wallace* when the chairwoman entreats 'this won't work without your help'. The opening scenes of these plays are often concerned with setting up a sort of contract, in which rules are established and the audience's role is explained. The gatekeeper then carefully navigates the path between scripted dialogue, improvised debate and unsolicited or pre-arranged prompts from the auditorium. These sections are generally very clear, as illustrated in *The Majority* when Rob asks the audience to vote on the following proposition: 'This community understands and accepts the voting system for the show.' We have found that when we are honest about the structure of the show from the start, the invitation to participate is taken up far more readily.

Fourth, we do occasionally work with plants (Wallace Williamson and Andy Hammer in *Wallace* are clear examples), although this technique is not usually our preference and when we do, we tend to be open about it. For example, in *Wallace*, while the initial encounter with these characters has the dramatic impact of an unexpected intervention from the audience, their subsequent delivery of scripted dialogue makes it obvious that they are actors. It has always surprised us, therefore, how frequently reviews of our work assume the use of plants when there are none. Reviews have referred to 'questions brilliantly planted among the audience' (McMillan 2009), speculated as to whether we have planted our volunteers (Fisher 2012) and insinuated the rigging of votes (Sierz 2017). In fact, unless there is a very specific reason to pre-prepare an audience member, it has proved far more interesting to leave open the range of possible responses.

Finally, and perhaps most importantly, we respond to the unexpected elements of the performance through the improvisational skill of the performers. Different actors take different approaches, but the time taken to prepare for multiple possible scenarios is always vital. For example, when Gaylie Runciman prepared to play Scottish National Party politician Sarah Bailey in Act One of *Wallace* – a part that would require a politician's response to unsolicited questions from the audience – she thoroughly researched the key issues of the independence debate and was able to recall numerous facts and statistics to support her position; and for *The Majority*, we rehearsed various alternative scenarios to accommodate the possibilities of the audiences' votes. For one early vote on whether or not to admit latecomers, we had a live video feed, welcome music, scripted dialogue and alternative lighting states all on standby depending on the audience's decision and the arrival of any late audience members. In all cases, one of the key skills is the ability to transition between essential plot points and open improvisation.

Much of our rehearsal and development work is focused on preparing for a range of possible outcomes and events. However, there are always surprises that must be dealt with in the moment of performance. For example, in *Bullet Catch*, a table-floating magic trick is revealed to those audience members who vote to find out. Over the course of the tour, this moment came to the attention of a passionate and committed community of stage magicians, who strongly objected to this flagrant defiance of the code of the Magic Circle (Magic Café Forum 2013). This was a decision that we had considered carefully, but the dramatic experience was indisputably stronger for its inclusion, providing what Chris Megson described as 'a remarkably complex and affecting moment of theatre [that] makes the experience of loss, or "profound" melancholy, central to its meaning' (2016, pp. 39–40). Many of these magical men (and they were always men) attended the performances with the explicit intention to declare their disapproval. Rob was frequently heckled – 'Shame on you!' – and, surreally, groups of magicians often waited at the stage door at the end of the performances to demand that this section was removed. On several occasions, our stage manager had to issue a warning over the theatre's comms system, so that Rob could leave by an alternative exit.

While we were entirely unprepared for this small-scale magical protest (and could have done without the socially mediated vitriol), there were also numerous opportunities to address the tension in the auditorium directly, allowing a brief discussion to take place in a spirit of generosity and respect for alternative viewpoints. This allowed us to reassert an ethical responsibility to our audience, and consequently to emphasise the play's humanist message, as 'through the audience's involvement, the piece instantiates a set of social relations defined by mutual ethical responsibility' (Megson 2016, p. 41). Megson notes the final words that are spoken to the volunteer: 'There is a point to all of this isn't there? And it's each other.' In fact, this final line was regularly changed in the moment to make an even more explicit connection to something the volunteer had offered earlier in the performance.

By bringing the audience with us in an enquiry into truth, belief and illusion, negotiating ethical dilemmas and arriving at a point of human connection, the journey of *Bullet Catch* was clearly mapped out from the beginning. Despite a high level of open discussion, the performance progressed through a series of scripted sections and 'set piece' magic routines, before arriving at a predetermined endpoint. In a sense, like the tricks that structured the performance, we were creating the illusion of indeterminacy as we moved towards our carefully scripted and rehearsed conclusion. Over the next few years, such theatrical resolution began to feel limited as an artistic and political strategy.

Performing agonism

As global politics shifted aggressively to the right, we became interested in theatre as a space of productive antagonism (or, more accurately, what political theorist Chantal Mouffe (2000) refers to as *agonism* – the struggle between *adversaries* rather than *enemies*). In radical democratic theory, contemporary politics is positioned as a dynamic and conflicting force that constantly shifts the boundaries of any given collective and requires a continual openness to new configurations. The theory suggests that some forms of conflict should be avowed and incorporated into our democratic structures, so that difficult or opposing ideas are engaged with, debated and challenged, rather than dismissed or attacked. In the emerging isolationist rhetoric of demagogues on both sides of the political spectrum, we saw little of this approach. Could we develop a performance that enacted an *agonistic* form of audience participation? How might we move from the restrictive binary choice of voting to a productive and generative mode of engagement that does not preclude disagreement?

Emboldened by our ability to respond constructively to moments of disagreement or tension in the theatre, we wanted to make a new performance that could incorporate the sort of disagreement that we had avoided at the *Bullet Catch* stage door, the dramatic potential of which we had only just begun to realise. *The Majority* proved a difficult show to make and we worked on it for almost four years of development workshops, work-in-progress performances and complete conceptual overhauls. Part of the reason for this was the alarming rate of political change: when we created a show about Scottish independence, the No vote cut further development short; when we thought we were making a show about referenda, David Cameron called one for real (Drummond 2017a). In 2017, the National Theatre of Great Britain committed to a production in the Dorfman Theatre in London. We took a different approach and worked very quickly rewriting the script and going into rehearsal soon after the completion of the first draft, which continued to evolve even into the public performances.

This commission offered an opportunity for the liveness of our work to respond in the moment to unfolding political events. A key turning point in the play's development came when Rob realised that the divisive binary vote of the referendum could be used in the theatre to generate a productive frustration at the limited options of a series of propositions. Through electronic handsets, the device of the referenda offered the option to affirm, deny or abstain from voting. However, the 'either/or' logic of these mini referenda is problematised by the 'both/and' logic of the play's narrative and the wider theatrical experience, which is better placed to hold a multiplicity of divergent opinions and ideologies (Frieze 2015, p. 224). This mode of participation is problematised from the beginning, and its limitations prompt an alternative dynamic as, in the final moments, the audience are invited to engage directly with the performer (Overend and Heath 2019):

please don't think this is the end of the show. This should continue.

I'm going to go down to the foyer now. Let's put down our voting pads and just ... talk, shall we? Come tell me why I'm right. Come tell me why I'm wrong. I promise, either way, I'll listen.

Following this invitation to continue the debate initiated in the performance, many audience members joined Rob in the foyer to reflect on their votes and debate the provocation to 'disagree better!' These discussions were often well attended and highly charged, and many responded passionately to the subject of the final vote, arguing against the reductive binary of the referendum on the value of 'attacking someone for holding an opinion', or defending their decision to vote positively on this proposition.

As indicated by Rob's account of these encounters in the footnotes on the script, this was a challenging and exhausting task for a performer who had just completed 90 minutes of interactive solo performance in front of 400 audience members. But we saw this opportunity – for those who wished to debate – as central to the performance. In terms of timing, these sections, which always lasted 30 minutes or more, comprised a full 25 per cent of the show. It was interesting, if not disappointing, that not one of the reviewers mentioned it.

In many ways, this section of The Majority was our purest form of participatory theatre: no scripts, no structure, no agenda; just a group of people in conversation. But a great deal of training, rehearsing, collaborating and experimenting underpinned it. Noting that 'participation is a new aesthetic within a diversity of theatre practices', Rebecca McCutcheon argues that 'the capacity to observe shifting affective dynamics, to hold and sustain a porous openness to one another, seems desirable in performer training' (2019, p. 66). While we have 'trained' as participatory practitioners in rehearsal rooms and theatres more than conservatoires, we recognise the need to hone and develop such skills of openness and responsiveness in the moment of the encounter. In relation to our work on The Majority, which set out to connect these principles of participation to wider discussions about democratic societies, we follow Nikolas Kompridis (2011) in our belief that an effective democratic politics also requires us to work on ourselves. Democratic participation requires an ongoing process of collaboration: of listening to and learning from each other. It is a practice that has to be continually practised.

Playing *with* the audience

The plays that we have selected for this collection range from tightly scripted, character-based dramas to those that have very different outcomes in every performance. Even within these plays, there are often several modes of engagement in any one scene. This relies on the audience's acceptance of a continual slippage between fixed, prewritten dialogue and open, improvised discussion. This really doesn't work without the audience's help.

We not only provide narrative *content* in these dramas: we also provide a *context* for conversation (Kester 2013). It is a context for shared creation, for collaborative exploration and for collective participation. When these performances go as planned (and perhaps just as often when they do not), there is a sense in which everyone in the room – audiences and performers alike – have come together to ask difficult questions, experiment with new ideas and engage in serious play. To make all this happen effectively, the audience has to want us to succeed. This may seem obvious, but the importance of the audience's will for the whole thing to go well cannot be overstated. Importantly, however, we do not assume a unified response or unanimous support. Rather, when dissenting voices do emerge and challenges are raised, we feel it is possible to create a space for disagreement in the theatre. As we continue to develop our participatory practice, this has emerged as a key concern.

Over the course of these six productions, we have experimented with new forms of participation that support a range of enquiries into truth and fiction, faith and science, family and mortality, and democratic politics. We ask these questions in our everyday lives, but we really grapple with them in the theatre. This is a space where it is possible to try out alternative scenarios and to play around with different ways of doing things. Our hope is that we will take something away from these performances that can inform the way we participate in the world beyond.

References

Drummond, R. 2017a. Author's Note. In *The Majority*, 3–4. London: Bloomsbury Methuen Drama.

Drummond, R. 2017b. *The Majority*. London: Bloomsbury Methuen Drama.

Fisher, P. (2012) Review: *Bullet Catch*, Rob Drummond. *British Theatre Guide*.

Frieze, J. (2015) Beyond the Zero-Sum Game: Participation and the Optics of Opting. *Contemporary Theatre Review*, 25, 216–229.

Harpin, A. and H. Nicholson. 2017. *Performance and Participation: Practices, Audiences, Politics*. London: Palgrave Macmillan.

Kester, G. 2013. *Conversation Pieces: Community and Communication in Modern Art*. Berkeley: University of California Press.

Kompridis, N. (2011) Receptivity, Possibility, and Democratic Politics. *Ethics & Global Politics*, 4, 255–272.

Love, C. 2018. Are We On the Same Page? A Critical Analysis of the 'Text-Based'/'Non-Text-Based' Divide in Contemporary English Theatre [thesis]. Royal Holloway, University of London.

Magic Café Forum. 2013. https://www.themagiccafe.com/forums/viewtopic. php?topic=507505&start=0

McCutcheon, R. (2019) Towards an 'ever more wordly sensitive interface': the Affective Turn and Site-based and Participatory Performance Training – a Practice-led Perspective. *Theatre, Dance and Performance Training*, 10, 51–67.

McMillan, J. (2009) Theatre reviews: Arches Live! 2009/Clara. *The Scotsman*.

Megson, C. 2016. Beyond Belief: British Theatre and the 'Re-enchantment of the World'. In S. Adiseshiah and L. LePage (eds), *Twenty-First Century Drama: What Happens Now*, 37–58. London: Palgrave Macmillan.

Mouffe, C. 2000. *The Democratic Paradox*. London: Verso.

Overend, D. (2018) Essais: Training the Audience. *Theatre, Dance and Performance Training*, 9, 125–129.

Overend, D. and O. Heath (2019) 'The Majority has Spoken': Performing Referenda at the National Theatre. *Studies in Theatre and Performance*.

Rancière, J. 2011. *The Emancipated Spectator*. London: Verso.

Sierz, A. 2017. Rob Drummond's New Solo Show about Democracy – 'The Majority' at the National Theatre.

White, G. 2013. *Audience Participation in Theatre: Aesthetics of the Invitation*. Basingstoke: Palgrave Macmillan.

In conversation

Towards the end of the 2019 Edinburgh Fringe Festival, **Rob Drummond** *and* **David Overend** *are in an office at the University of Edinburgh, overlooking Arthur's Seat.*

David   Let's start by talking about our more overtly participatory work, shows like *Bullet Catch* and *The Majority*, and the first act of *Wallace*. It seems really important to me that even though we might ask quite a lot of our audience at times, they are always willingly involved; in the sense that you, or the performers in the bigger shows, are working with them and supporting them so that they get the best experience possible. And I think that requires a commitment on both sides, like a shared creative process. There's an aspiration towards equality and genuine collaboration in that relationship. But ultimately, you're in control; literally writing the script and dictating the pace and the degree of openness of the text at any given moment. How honest do you think we are about that?

Rob   Well, when I first wanted to do *Bullet Catch*, I went to Jackie Wylie, who was the artistic director at The Arches arts centre in Glasgow at the time, and she asked me what show I wanted to make, and I said I wanted to make a show where I could create a genuine relationship with an audience member in an hour. And at that point, I kind of thought it might be a magic show, but I didn't know I was going to be asking them to shoot me in the face. I just knew that I wanted to have an hour where the audience could watch something absolutely, genuinely real, a relationship developing between two people. So, from the very get-go of all of this type of work that I started making, that was the goal, to have a genuine relationship. Now, how you achieve that is by telling a combination of truths and lies, like we all do in every situation in life. You never are honest talking to someone you've just met for the first time, but you're negotiating a kind of truce where you both can be a version of yourselves to each other that's acceptable in the moment.

David   And I think behind that there's a really strong and careful consideration of the ethics behind it, the choices that are made.

Rob   Yes.

David   We actually spend a great deal of time in our rehearsal, very often working with invited rehearsal audiences, testing out our material, interrogating the terms of participation, and thinking through the implications of what we're asking of our audience or of the individual audience members that we bring up on the stage in some cases. I'm interested in how you feel that that ethical commitment relates to the way that we treat facts, autobiography or documentary 'evidence' in the shows. And what I mean by that is that in your writing and in the stories that you tell on the stage, you make up a lot, and we often present that to the audience as though it really happened to you. In *The Majority* particularly: you weren't arrested for punching someone; Eric never existed; you never went to prison. This is all a huge web of deceit, isn't it?

Rob   Well, yeah. I think in all of the work we're talking about, there's usually a moment where I say to the audience in some form, 'look, some of this is true and some of it isn't'. But always, the heart of the piece is true. What I'm trying to get at is telling little lies to get to a big truth. And I think that as long as you play nicely with them, then it's alright. I've seen shows done where audience members get dragged up on stage against their will, and things about their personal life get shared, when they were explicitly told that that was not going to happen. That to me just seems like bullying. But from the very beginning, it was always important that we created a situation whereby we were kindly misleading people, and we were doing it with a wink so that they knew. And also, after the show, in *Bullet Catch* and even *The Majority* we have a big section at the end of the show where I meet audience members face-to-face; that is part of the duty of care of me making sure I can look the audience in the eye and see if there's any real problems that they've got from the show. In *Bullet Catch*, we met every single volunteer after the show, and I made sure that they were happy and left the theatre in a good frame of mind. And in *The Majority*, if someone had a problem with the show, they could literally come up and tell me to my face what the problem was.

David   And *The Majority* was a bit different because it was about, in a sense, provoking disagreement. Really pushing at the boundaries of that relationship.

Rob   As a metamorphosis in my own personality: when I was doing *Bullet Catch*, the magicians who came to see the show were the last thing I wanted. I would tell Deanne Jones, our stage manager, to tell me when they were there so I could avoid them. And it strikes me as quite indicative of my own personality changing over doing these shows that in *The Majority* I asked to meet those magicians, if you will. I literally asked to meet those dissenting people.

David   There was a sense of unease about avoiding those confrontations at the stage door that *The Majority* kind of stepped up to.

Rob   It was my way of growing as a person and as a performer to go 'look, I've done this provocative show, and it's unethical of me now to run away'. I've got to look the audience in the eye and see how they were affected by it and negotiate with them the exit from that building. Everyone's got to leave, if not happy, heard.

David   You mentioned Deanne, who we've always very much enjoyed working with, and I felt we could talk about collaboration. Because I think some of the principles or concerns that we've mentioned so far – that commitment to looking after our audiences and our careful consideration of the relationship between play and authenticity – those also inform who we choose to work with as collaborators, as designers, stage managers, dramaturgs, to develop and rehearse those performances. So, collaboration isn't just something that happens, you don't just turn up to rehearsals on day one and get a cup of coffee and a new team together and start collaborating. And we've worked together for a long time, but we're old friends and we've always made theatre together, but we also increasingly work with the same core team, like Deanne and like Scott Twynholm, the sound designer. What keeps a company like this together over time, and what do you think we've worked out by doing it collaboratively?

Rob   Well, I remember when we first met Deanne in the room for *Bullet Catch* and she was going to be our stage manager, and it became very quickly apparent that she was going to be really good in the room. And I was trying to work out what that was, and I think it was just a complete openness and willingness to not be afraid of problems, and to treat a problem like an opportunity. Every artist is different, but some artists like certainty and they like absolute precision, and I've realised that I don't like that. I like roughness, and I like people to be brave enough to not mind problems.

David   For me, *Bullet Catch* was a really important production in my career as a director, because it's a magic show, magic tricks are all about creative problem solving. I was quite anxious about directing a magic show. I didn't know anything about it, but then I found out that it's just exactly the same skillset. It's about this constant grappling with difficulties and problems and finding and creating solutions.

Rob   It's a great metaphor for theatre, because the magic has to be absolutely precise to work, but you pretend it's not precise by muddying the edges. And it's what happens in between the magical techniques that sells the trick. And that's the bit that you can get muddy and kind of improvise a little bit. It's like all our work, there's a very precise core but then we surround that with just muddiness and vagueness and the chance to go off-piste and make stuff up. And I think that's what's successful, and that's why we work with the people we work with, because they all enjoy responding to things as they happen, rather than being in any way afraid of it.

David   Responding to things as they happen. I've referred to *Wallace* before as a time-specific piece of theatre for that reason. We talk about site-specific work, but that felt very much like it was for that week.

Rob   Yeah.

David   And, in fact, the last night of the performance was the day of the referendum on Scottish independence, wasn't it?

Rob   That's right, yeah.

David   A real palpable tension in the room that came from that.

Rob   There was, and it was great, and that's why I think a lot of my work doesn't get reruns. I hope that's the reason [*laughs*]. Because a lot of it is so time-specific and I pride myself on writing quickly and writing so that it's relevant to the moment of the zeitgeist in a very, very specific way.

David   And that's particularly the case for some of the plays that we've been referring to so far. But along with those more open and improvised and interactive performances, we've also included in the book three plays that are closer to more conventional scripts with characters and stories and set actions, and limited interaction with the audience. Those are *Top Table*, *Eulogy* and *Rolls in Their Pockets*, all of which were first produced at Òran Mór in Glasgow. In those performances, participation is very different, it operates very differently. And we work with broader ideas like casting the audience in a particular role, like the guests at a wedding. And we also, in those plays, respond to the pub venue, the Òran Mór, and the context of older Glasgow audiences who are part of that particular culture and tradition. I think they relate in a different way to the theme of participation, but I'm just wondering what your thinking is about the reasons for including those in this volume.

Rob   Well, for me, I grew up not watching subsidised theatre in black-box venues, I grew up watching Glasgow variety like Francie and Josie (which if you're reading this and don't know them, google them; they're fantastic), and they were very instructive in what I thought theatre was, growing up. It's Glasgow variety, the audience are expected to join in to a point and they're expected to play their own role, and the show does not work without that audience reacting in the right ways at the right times, and they know the rules. So, when I first went to Òran Mór and I saw that audience, I thought 'this is a Francie and Josie audience, I know these people, I know I can write for these people', and I got tremendously excited about writing for them, which is why I keep going back to Òran Mór and writing. The audience is like my aunts and uncles and grandparents when I was growing up. I know exactly who they are, and what they'll laugh at and what they'll like. I know their personalities. In *Top Table*, they are there for a wedding, an old Glasgow wedding, which I know very well (my dad's a minister, I've been to these things). *Eulogy* is a funeral; likewise my dad's done hundreds of funerals over his life. And in *Rolls in Their Pockets*, we cast the audience as drunks in a bar, basically. Which, I'm not casting aspersions, a lot of them would be. I know that room.

David   Us included.

Rob   Yeah, us included. My Uncle Norman is a great example: there's a character in that play called Norman, and he sadly died from alcoholism. I know these local problems and I know that audience, and when you're asking them to watch the shows like that, you're not merely asking them to watch, you're asking them to participate as who they are cast as, and they relate to the show in a very, very personal way. I wouldn't have written those three shows for any other audience.

David   What I also like about including these plays in the book is that we don't *always* use participation and we don't always use it in the same way. We look for the right form to suit the idea that we're trying to communicate. And sometimes that's about getting an individual audience member up on stage to interact with you, and sometimes that's about extended moments of a story playing out in front of the audience. So, we use participation in a way when it helps us, rather than feeling like that's what we're about.

Rob   It's about the right balance, isn't it? For *Top Table* and *Eulogy*, there was no fourth wall, the actors were genuinely talking to that room of people and they were cast as a slightly different version of who they were. In *Rolls in Their Pockets*, there was a fourth wall; it's the only one in this collection that's got a fourth wall. But in many ways there wasn't that fourth wall really because they were in a pub drinking beer at lunchtime, and were talking about an old Glasgow problem of alcoholism. So, they were really in that play, more so than it might even appear just reading it; that room was electric in those performances because they all understood the implications of what we were saying to them.

David   I think this whole project has been a really useful opportunity to take stock of where we're at with ongoing collaboration and our work over the last few years, and to think critically and reflectively about what it is that we're trying to do, rather than just doing it. What do you want to do next?

Rob   Well, I'm very interested in doing a show that is kind of like the last twenty minutes of *The Majority*, where I spoke to the audience in the foyer but extended for an hour and a half of just inviting that level of disagreement into a . . . what do you call those talks that presidents do when they're running for president? Town-hall meetings.

David   Yeah.

Rob   A kind of town-hall meeting with an audience. And what we do is try and pick out audience members who are on absolutely irreconcilable positions on an issue, for example, pro-life and pro-choice. And we invite them on stage in some way, whether that's literal or figurative, we invite their opinions on stage, and we see if we can have what never happens in real life, and that is a constructive conversation. Not a debate, a conversation. About the differing opinions and why they hold them, and whether or not they're willing to move even slightly on those. And I just think it would be wonderful to watch.

David   So, let me ask why you think that that makes good theatre, because you could do that in an actual political town-hall meeting. But what is it about framing that artistically that allows a different relationship to that project?

Rob   Well, in a town-hall meeting, there's all sorts of political motivations behind it, like you're never quite sure whether it's real because they're running for office. If we can set it up in a theatre where we've all got the contract of nobody is trying to win an election, the contract is not 'come and vote for me', it's 'come talk to me', and when you go into that building, you know why you're there and it's for one reason only: to see if you can politely disagree, and what that means.

David   But also by inviting the audience into that show as theatre audiences, you're asking them to take a step outside it and think about *how* they're having that conversation, rather than just being in that moment.

Rob   Right, yeah. You're facilitating a very dangerous thing in a safer way, which is what we try and do in most of our work. Like, for example, in *Eulogy* when we ask an audience member to go up on stage and read a poem that they've never, ever seen before in the moment, with a microphone, in front of two hundred people. That's a dangerous thing we're asking them to do, relatively speaking. We're putting them in a dangerous situation, but because of the camaraderie in the room, it feels safe and lovely and warm and wonderful. In a similar situation, this proposed show would be putting people in an extremely charged situation, because people don't like having these arguments and debates, and actually facilitating a very constructive and useful version of that.

David   And hopefully in these shows, what we're ultimately aiming for is for the audience to leave the theatre taking something away that they can then reflect on and apply to real-life situations.

Rob   Absolutely, yeah, it's not about trying to persuade anyone to the right opinion. Because I don't know if my opinion's right until I will listen to them telling me why it's wrong. It's just about people going in there, and perhaps they budge by 2 per cent on what they thought was true, and that's fine. It's kind of just opened them up a little bit.

David   Creating a forum for the audiences to reflect and to explore and to think together.

Rob   Yeah. And, as always with our work, it's about finding . . . I don't enjoy theatre with no story whatsoever, so there has to be some sort of narrative sewn through that, which will probably end up being a story of an argument or a difficult disagreement from my own life, which will just be the narrative thread running through it all. But, yeah, that might not be the next show, but it's certainly what I want to do; I want to tackle disagreement.

Bullet Catch

Dedicated to our friend Ross Ramsay

Rob Drummond and David Overend perform *Bullet Catch*

Bullet Catch was first performed by Rob Drummond at The Arches, Glasgow, in 2009 as part of the Behaviour Festival.

William Wonder   Rob Drummond
Charles Garth   Random Audience Member

Co-director   Rob Drummond
Co-director   David Overend
Stage Designer   Francis Gallop
Lighting Designer   Alberto Santos Belido
Music and Sound Designer   Ross Ramsay
Stage Manager   Deanne Jones
Arches Production Manager   Abby McMillan

Scene One: Black Ball

Charles Garth *enters wearing a large overcoat. He nervously surveys the crowd.*

Garth   A kind, mild-mannered man with no history of violence or mental illness walks into a room full of people. Not knowing anyone and not knowing what to do with himself, he takes a seat.

The man places his overcoat on the back of the seat. He becomes **William Wonder**.

Wonder   One hour later he is surprised to find himself the centre of attention, and as the crowd look on in silence, he is persuaded to shoot a man in the face. How did this happen? Is it possible to persuade someone to do something they do not wish to do?

He smiles at the audience.

Ladies and gentlemen, I require a volunteer.[1]

But I don't want anyone up here against their will so could *everyone* please put their hands into the air.[2]

And now if the idea of coming up on stage tonight makes you want to kill yourself please drop your hand to your side. Thank you. If you are not comfortable talking about yourself, your life, or reading out loud in front of a group of people, please put your hand down. If you are under eighteen, for legal reasons, please put your hand down. Thanks. Being honest with yourself and – no judgement – if you've had maybe one too many drinks today then but please put your hand down. I can't have anyone up here who is even a little bit inebriated. And lastly, if you are at all uncomfortable handling live snakes then . . . don't worry because there's none in the show.[3]

Now, I'm going to walk around the audience and make eye contact with everyone who still has their hand in the air.

---

[1]   This is very early to select a volunteer. While this had the benefit of immediately establishing the need for participation, we would now be more inclined to build up to this moment to ensure a sense of trust before asking someone to commit to taking part in this way.

[2]   Around the same time as *Bullet Catch*, Rob created a show for young people called *Mr Write* (National Theatre of Scotland, 2010). This performance used a similar format to *Bullet Catch*: Rob got an audience member up on stage and interviewed them about their life. It became very evident during that show (which is totally unpublishable as it was almost entirely improvised) that the audience member, especially a young one, needed to be taken care of and not exploited. We have always tried to avoid coercion in our theatre, and here it became a rule very early on that we would never include anyone who didn't want to be included. That is not to say that we always go easy on them once they are up there – only that they are there of their own free will (which *Bullet Catch* brings into question). For *Bullet Catch*, we had a general rule, which Rob made sure to repeat during the show on multiple occasions, that the volunteer didn't have to do anything they didn't want to do, so they could sit down at any time, they weren't asked to divulge anything they were uncomfortable with, and they understood that, as far as possible, they were in control – it was their show. Of course this was only true to a point as we carefully controlled what happened, but we were confident that we treated the participants in the right way. Rob also met them after the show – each and every one – to make sure they were leaving in a good frame of mind. He often spent a significant part of the evening with them, which introduced a dynamic that we developed further in *The Majority*.

[3]   This is one of those lines that has remained in the script, but which may have been dropped in the performances. The semi-improvised nature of the text means that it was significantly edited throughout the run, with some lines coming and going in response to the pace of the show and the audiences' reactions.

Please take this quite seriously and hold my gaze because it's important I get the right person up here.

He prowls the edge of the stage making eye contact with the willing volunteers. He stops occasionally. Looks deeply into some eyes. Glances at others. Smiles at some faces. Puzzles at others. The process is careful. Deliberate. Never rushed.

He selects three volunteers from the crowd and thanks the others for their enthusiasm. He wishes he could have used them all.

He turns his attention to one of the three and picks a velvet bag from a table.[4]

Could you please confirm this bag is empty?

I have two white balls and one black ball.

He puts the balls into the bag.

I want each of you to put your hand into the bag and pick out a ball, but make sure to keep your hand held tightly around it until I tell you to look at it.

They remove one ball each.

Now I'm going to turn my back and when I do, you all have five seconds to hold your ball up so everyone can see it.

He turns his back and begins a countdown from five. When he is finished he turns back. He is now the only one in the room who does not know the location of the black ball.

Now, I'm just going to start by asking you all a very simple question.

He turns to the first volunteer.

What is your name?

They tell Wonder their name. Wonder then immediately asks them if this is indeed their name. They respond, 'Yes.'.

Ok, so what I've done there is found a kind of a base reading – I now know what you look and sound like when you are telling the truth. Assuming of course you have given me the right name.

Now, what I want you to do next is extremely simple. No matter what question I ask you, your answer will be 'yes', even if that is a lie. Do you understand?

---

[4]   The selection of the volunteer was random to an extent (we only ever used a plant in São Paulo, but this was for a very specific reason which we discuss below). The magic trick that we used here was very easy to perform, and Rob knew instantly which individual had the black ball and was therefore the natural or narratively logical choice for the assistant. However, it quickly became evident that he could alter this if the person with the black ball seemed difficult or unpredictable in any way. In these cases, Rob relied on intuition and would choose as his assistant the person who he could 'read' most easily. This became a genuine mix of the trick just working and Rob genuinely doing what he said he was doing – reading the person. We all do this intuitively – at parties or whenever we are introduced to a new person, we size them up very, very quickly indeed and decide whether or not their personality is compatible with ours. This was no different, only Rob was deciding if the personality of the person was compatible with the show. Someone who is overtly confident and desperately wants to be up there is every bit as bad as someone who is desperate not to be up there, in terms of the ability to control the show.

They all say 'yes'.[5]

Good start.

Lighting change.[6] *The answers to the following questions will always be yes. The person with the black ball will usually be* **Garth**.[7]

Wonder   Is your name Charles Garth?

Are you forty years old?

Are we in London?

Is it 7.30 p.m. on 6 June 1912?

Are you a labourer in a ship yard on the Thames?

Do you have a wife and a young son?

Does your son leave a lemon drop on the dresser each night for you to find when you return from work?

Have you come to watch a magic show?

Are you on your own?

You've come to a magic show on your own?

He turns to another volunteer.

Is your name William Henderson?

Are you the most exciting young magician in the commonwealth?

Are you performing a bullet catch tonight?

In front of an audience of two thousand?[8]

---

[5]   On one occasion, an audience member replied 'No'. It was late in the run and Rob was feeling cocky so he decided to take a risk and made sure that he became the assistant. That particular show went very well, but in general it is best to avoid comedians.

[6]   David is keen on these sudden shifts of register and they are a common feature of our work. *The Majority* also uses this format. With more overtly participatory texts, this offers an opportunity to be open and direct in the way we move from improvised dialogue to scripted monologue. On other occasions such as *Wallace*, we use a more fluid movement between modes.

[7]   In Brazil the gun laws did not allow us to have a volunteer fire the weapon without going through safety procedures first, so we had to get them trained up in advance, which was less than ideal and involved the use of plants. These participants were selected by our hosts at Cultura Inglesa, and were told as little as possible – only that they were going to fire a gun. We regret this. It meant the tension of the show was almost non-existent because the volunteer knew where it was all leading with a certainty that simply did not exist elsewhere, which clearly translated to the audience. We rarely use plants because even if the audience has no idea that they are planted, the plant does and so do the actors, which makes performing with honesty much more difficult.

[8]   A big part of Rob's practice is taking an existing genre or event – a wrestling match (*Rob Drummond: Wrestling*, The Arches, 2011), a quiz show (*Quiz Show*, Traverse, 2013) – and using that construct as a starting point, from which we can all get on the same page as to what is meant to happen in such a setting. We are united in our understanding of the call to play without any effort at all. We know why we are in the room. Implicit in this is the idea that the audience are playing a clearly defined role. They play the part of a quiz-show audience, clapping when told by the applause

Have you got a bad feeling about the show tonight?

Do you wake up with a bad feeling most days?

Do you find it hard to connect with people?

Do you believe that free will is an illusion?

He addresses the final volunteer.

Are you William Henderson's wife?

Do you love him?

Do you find him devastatingly attractive?

Are you pregnant with your first child?

Are you scared to watch his shows?

Are you fearful one night he will not return?

Is tonight that night?

Ok, ladies and gentlemen, I now have a good idea of what they look like when they are lying. So, one last question and you must answer yes.

Are you holding the black ball?

They all answer yes and **Wonder** *finds the person with the black ball.*

They are his assistant, unless of course he chooses to go with someone else, with whom he feels 'a stronger connection'.

Scene Two: Context

The audience member is selected.

Wonder   Now, it was [Assistant], wasn't it?

[Assistant], my name is William and I don't have a gun. Comforting words I'm sure to hear. [Assistant], I don't have a gun but do you have an item on you that we could use to represent a firearm?

An item is taken from the assistant.

And now would you please join me on stage? I'm sure everyone will give you a warm round of applause as you make your way up.

---

boards, or they play the part of a wrestling audience – whooping and cheering and booing. In this case they were being asked to play the part of a magic-show audience – participating, applauding tricks, encouraging volunteers, guessing how tricks are done, gasping and helping the magician out, rather than trying to sabotage him. Within this there may or may not be another layer of casting – in this case we were asking three audience members to pretend to be people from the past as we set up a historical narrative. And of course, the volunteer then becomes Charles Garth (as well as playing themselves) for the entirety of the show.

Don't worry.

I hate it when people are asked on stage and then made a fool of – I'm not going to do that to you. And please don't feel awkward – no one is looking at you and thinking you're standing weird or anything – they're all too concerned with themselves – we're all the same and we're all in this together with you, aren't we?

Would you mind just slipping this jacket on?

The assistant puts on a jacket – they now represent **Garth**.

Wonder   Does everyone know what a bullet catch is?

The bullet catch is really pretty simple. A bullet is marked and loaded into a firearm. The firearm is given to an assistant, whether predetermined or newly acquired from the audience.

He gives the 'gun' to the assistant.

The assistant, carefully, takes the weapon and stands on a designated spot.

The magician takes up their position.

. . . and encourages the assistant to aim at his mouth.

He encourages the assistant to aim the item.

And when the magician gives the signal – sometimes verbally but in Henderson's case by lowering his arm from above his head to his side – the assistant squeezes the trigger, sending a bullet hurtling at 500 mph towards the magician's head with a loud bang.

He waits to see if the assistant will take the initiative and make a 'bang' noise.

Usually this is followed by the magician staggering backwards before revealing the marked bullet between his teeth. But it doesn't always happen this way. In 1613 the inventor of the stunt, Coullew of Lorraine, was accidentally shot in the head when his assistant – who also happened to be his wife – decided to down half a bottle of absinthe before the show. Arnold Buck in 1840 died when a volunteer secretly loaded nails from his pocket into the barrel of the gun. And Raoul Curran forty years later successfully accomplished the stunt only for an audience member to stand up, take out his own pistol and shout 'Oi, Curran, catch this'.

There's a reason this is known as magic's riskiest stunt. When William Henderson declared he was going to attempt it in London using an audience member to pull the trigger his friend and mentor Houdini wrote to him:

Now, my dear boy, this is advice from the heart, DON'T TRY THE D—N bullet catching, no matter how sure you may feel of its success. There is always the biggest kind of risk that something will go wrong. And we can't afford to lose Henderson. You have enough good material to maintain your position at the head of the profession. And you owe it to your friends and your family to cut out all the things that entail risk of your life. Please, William, listen to your old friend Harry who loves you as his own son and don't do it. You have too much to lose. You are free to choose not to do this.

Of course, Henderson ignored this advice and one hundred years ago was killed instantly in front of two thousand people at the London Palace Theatre when kind, mild-mannered labourer Charles Garth shot him in the face.

Garth is reported to have stood stock-still for a good two minutes after the shooting, presumably waiting for Henderson to get up. When the police arrived he was still clutching the weapon. They took it from him, secured it in a lock box (*He puts the item into an empty box and closes it*) and took him in for questioning.

Over the next few months Garth writes a series of letters to his sister in Manchester.

(Now here's where I need you to help me out. Please could you read this clearly loudly and slowly so everyone can hear – don't worry about acting too much, just read it.)[9]

Garth   Dearest Bette

You'll have read by now what happened – the damndest thing. Please do not worry, I'm fine and well – after all it wasn't me who got hurt so I've no cause to complain. The Rozzers asked me all sorts of questions after the show. As if I had shot the poor bugger on purpose. It was just a horrible accident, that's all. There's one thing I can't help wondering though. Would it have turned out differently if I hadn't picked the word 'SAVE'?

Scene Three: Kill, Save, Love

Framed pictures featuring the words 'KILL', 'SAVE' and 'LOVE' are now highlighted.

Wonder *is looking at the word 'SAVE'.*

Wonder   Freud said that when we meet a new person – hello my name is William – three questions instantly, in the merest of nanoseconds, register in our minds. Can I kill it, can it kill me, can I shag it? Every time we meet someone new. Do I fight, flee or make love. Every time. Kill, save, love. Don't feel guilty – we all do it. We have no control over this. We have no control whatsoever.

You see these questions are built into our DNA – they echo back in time to the days when we were little more than animals and every encounter with another living being was life, death or procreation and nothing else. Think about that. How important would it be to pick the right person to connect with if you knew your life depended on it?

---

9   Here, we are doing something that many people advised us not to do: expecting an unvetted audience member to read aloud a piece of text they had never set eyes upon before. Our instinct was that this would be great if they managed it and endearing if they did not. This proved correct. The very few occasions when one of them simply could not manage it – short sighted, bad sight-reader, nerves – Rob simply stepped up behind them and helped them with the bit they were stumbling over, which endeared both Rob and the volunteer to the audience all the more. This taught both of us something very important: the audience want you to succeed – they are not (apart from the angry magicians) baying for blood. This is why being real up there is the only sure-fire way to succeed. Mistakes are allowed, insincerity is not. And the harder a task you ask an unprepared volunteer to do, the more sympathy and good will they receive. The end of this show is testament to that, believe us.

He points to the back of the stage where we see the words 'KILL', 'SAVE', 'LOVE'.

[Assistant], I'd like you now to think carefully and when you are ready, speak one of these three words aloud.

They choose and the word is lit up.[10]

Ok. We'll come back to this later.[11]

I can see we've already started to develop some sort of connection. Let's see if we can test this connection to see if it's real.[12]

I'd like you to stand up now and pick one of these books – look at the titles and covers and maybe one will jump out above the rest – and when you've done that please sit down with it on the edge of the chest there.

What book did you choose?

Why?

Ok.

I'd like you now to turn to any page and pick any word.

Try not to pick something too long or complicated – pick something that you know the meaning of and that everyone in the room is likely to know – try to work with me here not against me. And when you've done that please close the book.

Now, I don't want this word spoken aloud so could you please write it down on this post-it in nice big clear capital letters so when we pass it into the audience they will be able to read it.

Thank you. And when you've done that could someone from the far side please step onto the stage and just take the post-it and you keep a hold of the book.

Now you don't need to all look at it individually, just show it to a few people at a time and let it work its way round the audience being careful not to flash it towards me.

He sits nearer the assistant.

Have you ever fancied someone at a party and made a right mess of chatting them up? Here's a handy hint – instead of going right up to them and saying, 'Hey, I really like you so, eh, how's about it?' – hold off, get yourself within eyesight of them and using your peripheral vision start to mimic their body language. Before long, they'll feel an

---

[10]   The selection of the word is genuinely free each night but only two assistants have ever selected 'KILL' at this stage. No matter the selected word, Rob always reacts like it means a lot. 'KILL' is the rarest but easiest word to react to.

[11]   The next line always depends on the selected word. If they pick 'KILL', it is, 'I can see we have some work to do in order to make a connection'.

[12]   Rob recalls that this was the original premise of the show, way back in 2007/8 when he first conceived it. At that early stage, he knew two things: first, an audience member would shoot him in the face; second, he wanted to meet, befriend and connect with them in real time. While we didn't always achieve this, the vast majority of the shows felt emotional to Rob in some way. He attempted to be genuine at all times with the volunteers and encouraged them to do the same. In this way Rob didn't really feel like he was performing at all at some points, a quality that was reflected in some of the reviews.

inexplicable connection to you. And when you do eventually go up and talk to them they'll feel like they've known you for years, but they won't know why. This works. I wouldn't be married otherwise.

I used to tell people that I got into magic because I wanted to be able to amaze other people. Affect them. But I have come to realise that that is not true at all. It was so they could affect me. So they would think I was special. So I could make a connection that I found hard to make any other way.

Now, I'm going to go through the alphabet and when I hit the letter that your word begins with I want you to scream 'YES' inside your head.

He guesses the letter.[13]

Now I just want you to visualise this word as an image.

He responds to their reaction to this challenge and works out if the word is a noun or not.

Ok so hold that word in your mind, let it flow through you and without moving or miming just embody that word and feel whatever it means to you. And do that while I talk.

I think the need for the acceptance and love of fellow human beings is a powerful determinant of behaviour and some believe that it is this need that keeps humanity alive. Without it there would be no point to life. If you lose that need for human connection then you lose hope and ultimately there is no meaning to anything.

So pulling someone at a party shouldn't really be that tough.

He guesses the correct word.

Thank you – it appears we have begun to make some sort of connection – so maybe we're going to be ok.

He asks the assistant to read again from the diary.

Garth   Dearest Bette

I appear to be famous. I was stopped in the street today by one of Henderson's fans. He called me a murderer. The silly thing is that I know I'm not to blame – I was only doing what I was bloody well told – but I still can't shake the feeling that there was something wrong that night. Something in Henderson's eyes that I should have recognised. This morning Samuel gave me a lemon drop and said, 'Why are you never happy, Daddy?' Always looking after me that one – he takes after his aunt.

---

[13]   It may be possible to substitute the magic tricks for future productions of *Bullet Catch*. However, there are a couple of rules regarding the tricks to bear in mind: they have to be jaw dropping and they have to build in danger and spectacle. Aside from that, we themed the tricks to match the themes of the show. In fact, the tricks sometimes dictated the text and sometimes the text dictated the trick. It was a two-way thing and the show evolved practically (*what tricks are just awesome and how can we make them fit?*) and thematically (*what trick best speaks to the idea of free will?*). The general journey was this: connect with the audience member in a small, funny way; connect with them in a big, meaningful way; share something with them (how a trick is done); then ask them to do something dangerous, before finally asking them to trust you enough to shoot you in the head. Other tricks could be substituted in as long as this general journey is met (but the bullet catch at the end is kind of vital!).The tricks used in this show were Odd Ball by Marc Oberon, Word in a Million by Nicholas Einhorn, Emotional Intelligence by Luke Jermay, Losander's Floating Table by Dirk Losander, Shattered by Scott Alexander and Bullet Catch by Derek Lever.

Scene Four: Emotional Intelligence

Wonder   Why are you never happy?[14]

Sorry – it's unfair of me to put you on the spot like that. It's just, you read that so well. I've read these extracts hundreds of times but it's only when someone else reads them, and reads them well, that I can really hear them and understand them and get a sense of who Garth was, so thank you for that.

I wonder if we might try to experience something that Garth and Henderson experienced that night on stage. You see Henderson was obsessed with a routine that dealt with the formula for happiness.

Do you want to know the secret to happiness?

Sometimes knowing the secret isn't all it's cracked up to be. During the performance that night Henderson gave away the secret to one of his tricks and people were not happy at all.

The theory states that there are seven areas of human life upon which our happiness or contentment depends. It has been demonstrated that if the majority of these areas remain 'in good working order' one feels one's life has purpose. Meaning.

He removes some playing cards.

Now, I am quite happy to talk about these areas because, much like Henderson, my life is pretty much in good working order. So by that logic I should be a very happy person right?

That night Henderson sat Garth down on stage and asked him about his own life. Do you mind if I ask you about your own life so we can get to know each other a little better? You don't have to talk about anything you don't want to.

Could you move up so I can sit next to you?

This is not magic by the way – this is a conversation. In many ways I find this far more difficult.

The seven areas are Travel, Health, Education, Sex, Career, Ambition and Money.

He allows them to dictate what areas could do with improvement and chats about these. There is the option here to link this to **Garth** *and mention what areas he talked about on stage.*[15]

---

[14]   This question was unexpected enough to guarantee a pause, long enough for Rob to continue without expecting an answer.

[15]   Apart from the section in the foyer at the end of *The Majority*, this exchange is probably the purest form of improvisation we have ever done in a major show. (Rob did this in *Mr Write* as well.) Rob found this immensely difficult at first as he had to move between thinking, 'Right, I've got to ask them questions about all these cards and remember at the same time where I'm going next'. As a result, this part was very stilted for a long time. Rob remembers David telling him that he had to listen, really listen to what they were saying, rather than simply pretending to while working out where to go next. This was a watershed moment in our understanding of how to talk to a participant from the audience. It wasn't enough to pretend to care about what they were saying. Rob had to really care. Once he made this change he often got lost in terms of the next line (only for a while, then it became natural) but it didn't matter because it was genuine. Again, mistakes are allowed; insincerity is not.

Imagine there are two people. One is laughing and one is crying. Who do you feel more connected to?

Why?

Are you generally quite a positive person?

No matter what they pick steer them towards happiness.

Pick a card, remember it and put it under your leg or somewhere I can't see it.

Think of a time (associated with that card) when you felt positive and full of hope and sure that there was a point to all this. A time when thoughts of the finite nature of life were far away. A time when immortality seemed possible. Or just a time you were happy.

Is there a time associated with this memory? A month, year, date, time of year?

I'm going to do something 'psychics' won't do and that's make hard and fast, specific predictions, so they might not be spot on.

Just go back to the time associated with this memory and remember what it felt like to be you at that time. And think very specifically of the date or the time period and let the memory run through you and look at me.

He predicts the time and writes this down.

And tell everyone the time period – not the memory itself – just the time period associated with it.

Ok. Not bad.

Now is there a person associated with this memory? Imagine you are looking at them now – remember what it is like to be in their company and look at me and just draw their name on the back of this pad with your eyes. All the time thinking of the memory.

Now, names are difficult because of the different spellings and variants but we'll see how we do.

He predicts the person's name.

And finally concentrate specifically on the word on the card – sorry, could you just let everyone know the name?

Ok. Not spot on but never mind.

Just now concentrate on the word on the card and the whole memory and everything together but most specifically the word on the card.

He predicts the word.

Would you mind sharing the memory?

They share.

That's a lovely memory. Are you generally quite a happy person?

(Yeah. That's pretty much what Garth said too.)

He reveals he got the details correct – possibly some cold reading.[16]

Applause covers the assistant's move back to their original position.

Scene Five: Levitation

Wonder *reads from a piece of paper.*

Wonder   Dear Rob

He looks at the audience and says, 'That's my real name'.[17]

We have carried out a risk assessment and, even though you have assured us you can pull it off and that it is vital to the show, I must advise you against doing an actual bullet catch during the show. There are simply far too many things that could go wrong. Could you just talk about the bullet catch instead of doing it? It's fascinating stuff.

If you still want to do it we won't stand in your way but I will need you to sign a liability waiver. I just think it's not worth the risk.

Hope you are not too disappointed.

Kevin McCallum

Production Manager

[Producing Theatre]

He addresses the audience.

The [producing theatre] weren't the only ones worried about me doing this show. My own parents were horrified when I told them what I was doing. But mainly because they are religious and think that quite a lot of what I do is fairly close to blasphemy.

My dad is a minister actually – as was Henderson's.[18] You know the more I learn about him the more similarities I find. If I believed in reincarnation . . . But I don't. Believe.

---

[16]   Cold reading is simply taking a risk and trying to pretend to mind read based on probability. For example, the magician might guess the volunteer had fallen as a child and had a scar on their knee, or that they knew someone important in their life whose name began with M, or that they are the type of person who is sometimes really down on their self. All of which are true of most people. In this case, once you've already got the information so correct, the cold reading is an attempt to put a bow on top and sometimes with amazing results. Sometimes getting it slightly wrong makes it all the more amazing. When *Bullet Catch* was in New York in the spring of 2013, Rob was bold enough to do this trick in the offices of a theatre producer during a meeting. The woman he was speaking to recalled a memory involving a woman named Cat. Rob deliberately got this wrong and wrote down 'Dog'. When he revealed it, her chin hit the table. All he knew (through the mechanisms of the trick) was the card she drew, the name of the person and the date of the memory. But by getting it wrong and writing 'Dog', he knew something brilliant had happened. He had accidentally got something amazing. This is where the cold reading came in. 'Were you buying a Dog with your sister Cat?,' he guessed, mentally crossing his fingers. He was right and she almost burned him as a witch.

[17]   This is important because it plants the seeds of the performer's reality, which adds another level of danger and tension as we move to the bullet-catch stunt. The performer plays William Henderson, Charles Garth (briefly, at the very beginning), William Wonder and themselves. It is this layering of identity that effectively blurs the lines between reality and illusion.

[18]   This is true, and points to an interesting trope in Rob's work – the covert deployment of autobiography. This is always beneficial. If the audience member doesn't know you or your background they will either believe it or think: is that really true? If they do know you then they *know* it's true and therefore wonder what else might be true in that case. Either way they are questioning reality, which is the aim.

When I was young I used to try to make things move. Float. Just by staring at them. Did you ever do that? We had an old side table in the front room and I remember sitting for hours trying to make it move. I don't know why I did that. I think I remember my dad saying during one of his sermons that anything was possible if you just believed enough. So I guess I was trying to test that out.

Do you believe? In anything. That there is a purpose to all this.

Converse with audience member on this topic.[19]

Would you like to change your mind on the word?

Allow the chance for the word to be changed.

When the table didn't move I just assumed I didn't believe enough. But it was weird because it really felt like I was believing. But the minute I started to think about believing – trying to make myself believe – that meant I didn't truly believe. You shouldn't have to think. It doesn't matter.

The sun is burning out. That is a fact. It's what stars do and no scientist would refute that. It will eventually be gone. And so will everything. It's important to believe in something (God, fate, destiny – as ludicrous as they might sound – I mean I think we all know deep down that this is all there is. It is as simple as it seems). It is important to at least trick yourself into believing in something because if you don't you are in danger of being swallowed up by this fact.

He has lost himself. Music brings him back.

Could you follow me/take my hand.

Thank you for your help so far tonight. Just stand there and take the tablecloth like I do. And look at me.

Wonder *and the assistant perform a levitating table trick.*

It is a thing of beauty.[20]

At one point the box on top of the table is opened up and the assistant is invited to remove a lemon drop.

The table comes to rest as the music fades. **Wonder** *looks at the assistant and the audience.*

You can give that lemon drop to anyone in the audience as a gift.

The table comes to rest – they could come in handy later in firing the gun.[21]

---

[19] This section can take its time. Answers have included people, energy, nature, science and God. No one has said nothing.

[20] It is impossible to do proper justice here to the beauty of this trick. It was designed by master of levitation Dirk Losander. Clips can be found online. It always leaves the vast majority of the audience stunned.

[21] As alluded to in the Introduction, we learned early on (the hard way) that sometimes the person you bring up will simply refuse to fire the gun. In fact, the producer who actually ended up taking the show to New York was such a person. The wrong thing to do in that case is to pick a random person from the audience who has nothing to do with the story. But, by casting multiple audience members throughout the show – including this moment where we get the volunteer to inadvertently select their own back-up – there is a narrative acceptability to bringing them up on stage to save the day (the volunteer gave them something, so now will they give something back?). At the National Theatre in London one volunteer gave the sweet to Stephen Fry. Which would have been interesting to say the least. Thankfully she shot Rob and he didn't need to.

Amazing isn't it? Do you want to know how it's done?

Canvas assistant and audience for their opinions and reasons then take a vote.[22]

I'll tell you what, those of you who don't want to know – those of you who wish to remain in ignorant bliss cover your eyes. For the rest of you just keep watching.

The music replays. **Wonder** *dismantles and packs away the table, revealing the secret. A sad sequence somehow.*[23]

Thank you for looking

Thank you for not looking.

You can say no but . . .

Would you mind if I had a hug?

They hug.[24]

During the hug **Wonder** *gives the assistant their next extract, which includes a short scripted section.*

Garth   I was called into the inquest today – I wore my good suit and bowler hat and someone took a photograph of me as I left. They're saying the shooting might not have been an accident after all. They reckon the daft sod might have planned the whole thing himself – reckon he was suffering from melancholia. You'll think me a right soft clot but I cried when they told me that. Funny thing. Don't know why.

Wonder   Why are you crying, Mr Garth?

Garth   I'm sorry, Your Honour.

Wonder   Had you any indication that Mr Henderson was weak in the mind.

Garth   Weak?

Wonder   That he was planning his own death.

Garth   No.

Wonder   You signed his will did you not?

---

[22]   The majority always want to know. Their reasons mainly fall into the sphere of frustration. 'I simply have to know!'. One of the more beautiful answers involved the phrase 'I believe in truth'. Those in the minority who do not wish to know mainly state that if you know how it works you instantly spoil the beauty. 'Sometimes it's better not to know things'. There are no wrong answers in this section. In this context, any answer appears profound.

[23]   This is the moment that has been a matter of contention among some members of the magic community. We accept fully that revealing the secret to a trick not of our own design is ethically fraught. However, the relationship that this created between the performer and the audience, the comment on the nature of truth and depression, the moment of melancholic and profound theatre that this action makes possible, convinces us that such an act is justified in a theatre show. And anyway, they choose to look.

[24]   When it worked this was the best moment in the show. It worked precisely because Rob and the volunteer had got to know each other a little and shared various activities and discussions. Now was the time for something so untheatrical that it couldn't possibly be faked. A hug. Rob tried to mean it every night. It mostly worked. It was part of the attempt to do what the show set out to do: to try to make a connection with a stranger in one hour and for it not to be faked.

Garth   It was part of the show.

Wonder   You witnessed his will live on stage.

Garth   Everyone was looking at me.

Wonder   In your opinion was Mr Henderson inebriated that night?

Garth   Inebriated?

Wonder   Drunk. Was the man drunk?

Garth   I don't think so.

Wonder   You are quite sure you had never met Mr Henderson before going on stage?

Garth   Never.

Wonder   Because I'm sure you are aware that the use of stooges in these types of variety shows is well documented.

Garth   I did not know that, Your Honour.

Wonder   Are you a nihilist, Mr Garth?

Garth   I don't know what that is, Your Honour.

Wonder   Were you aware that Mr Henderson was a known nihilist?

Garth   I don't know what that is, Your Honour.

Scene Six: Shattered

Wonder   Why would he do it? He had everything. He was a rising star in his profession, wealthy, well travelled, in perfect health, in love and with a baby on the way.

But in the time Henderson was performing, existential nihilism, a belief that life is without meaning, purpose or intrinsic value, was becoming the antidote to religion. And with the growing understanding of the universe, that we were just a drop in an endless ocean, that our sun would one day be gone, that free will is perhaps just an illusion . . . it's easy to see why.

He picks up a bottle and hammer.

So maybe it wasn't a failed trick after all but rather . . . the *ultimate* trick. He made a man, who bore him no ill will, shoot him dead. He took control of his destiny and made an immortal mark on the world.

And maybe that's why they all did it. Risked their lives. So they could achieve some sort of immortality. We all die some time. At least they went out with a bang.

He hits the bottle with the hammer.

Do you believe in free will? That we are free to choose what we do? That we can change the script?

He calmly and scientifically explains how free will is impossible including some of the following arguments.

Can you give me an example of a free choice you have made recently?

Explain that there is always a reason and these reasons lead back to conception/birth.

Did you choose to be created? Did you have any say in your birth? Was your first thought independent of your surroundings? The answer to all these is, of course, no. So – and I don't mean to hurt you with this – I'm just stating the facts . . .

Scientifically, if the first variable in a chain of causality is not free then all subsequent thoughts and choices fundamentally cannot be free either. Cannot be.

This means we can't be held accountable for the 'bad' things we do. But neither can we feel proud or validated by our achievements.

So. Whatever happens next. It's not your fault. It's not my fault. It's just what had to happen.

He breaks a bottle, takes the neck from the bag, puts it on a plinth, spins the plinth, mixing it with three other bags, covering this from the audience so they don't know under which is the bottle, then spins it one more time before turning away himself.

Does anyone need them mixed any more?

He performs 'shattered', an emotional and nerve-shredding trick in which the audience member guides him to safety from impaling his hand on a glass bottle.[25]

He gives the assistant another extract.

Garth   It has been deemed death by misadventure, which is just a fancy way of saying a bloody accident as far as I can tell. His life was perfectly in order so they say suicide is impossible. I suppose they must be right. The thing is, I've been having these dreams, but not during the night, during the bloody day – wide-awake dreams like I'm back there on the bloody stage. And he's asking me if I'm sure I want to go ahead. If I understand what's going to happen. And I think maybe I did understand. I think I know what it was that I saw in his eyes. You see, I've seen those eyes before, Bette.

Scene Seven: Bullet Catch

Wonder *has brought forward the box into which the lipstick was inserted. He opens it up and removes a handgun.[26]*

---

[25] Lots of people described the 'shattered' illusion as the most difficult to watch – even more so than the bullet catch. This is an important lesson in 'selling' to the audience. If you say you're going to die at the end of the show, then the audience are unlikely to believe you. But if you say you might hurt yourself at some point during the show then the stakes are higher because that is conceivable. It's the same when you interact with an audience. If you say that they will be running the show, then they are unlikely to buy it because that's too big a claim. But if you give them small concessions and sell it like they have a degree of control and a degree of ability to ruin it, then the stakes are very high because that's plausible.

[26] Always to an intake of breath in the room. No acting involved on Rob's part really. He knew it was dangerous regardless of the fact we'd made it as safe as possible so he just treated it like he would a 'real' gun.

Wonder   This is a Glock 17, the safety is on and there are no bullets in the handle.

Could you take that in the safety position, please.

Yes, it's heavy isn't it.

The safety position is with your hand around the handle, finger not on the trigger and pointed towards the ground away from your feet. Never point it at the audience, never point it at yourself and only point it at me if I specifically ask you to.

Ok. I think you know what I'm going to ask you now.

Over the past hour I've got to know you. I've got to genuinely like you and trust you. I would very much like you to be the one to fire the gun, and I think you'll be willing to help me with that.[27]

Now if you are going to fire a weapon I need to have something signed.

That always gets a reaction but this needs to be done. This is my liability agreement with the venue – it is my legal document and at no time does it become yours – I simply wish you to insert your details into a clause here that states you will not be held liable should anything go wrong – but it is my document, not yours.

A liability agreement is read and signed by both parties.

I also need you to mark the bullet. Oh.

Wait. We don't have bullets. What was your final decision on the word?

Whatever word she picks bullets are revealed along with a correct prediction card either pinned to the back of the word, in her jacket pocket or under her chair.

It's not your fault – simply a series of events that led you to choose that word above the others. It couldn't have happened any other way.

These are 8 mm rounds – they are small but don't let that fool you. This is the casing – this will eject from the gun when you fire it. This is the ammunition – this will be heading towards me.

Could you examine these?

And now mark one of them on the tip with this marker.

I now need you to confirm I am actually loading them into this magazine. The marked one first and this one on top will be your practice shot.

It's only fair that we give you a practice shot if you'll be firing a gun and this is it.

Magazine switch happens here under cover of target.

---

27   The reactions to this request have been varied. Some immediately agree and some immediately decline. On the two very rare occasions that Rob couldn't convince the assistant to fire the weapon (even at an inanimate plate), he had to pursue other avenues such as asking the lemon drop receiver to take their place. We would never ask anyone to shoot the weapon if they really genuinely don't want to do it.

You'll be firing at this plate.

Position and arm target.

Now, I'm going to make your practice shot quite easy so you can get your aim in.

In a moment I'll encourage you to aim at the target, then I'll go over there and when you are ready you can squeeze the trigger. Could you show me how you intend to aim? Thank you. (Have you any gun-handling experience?). Don't let your hand go above this line.

When you pull the trigger you will feel a kick, the casing will eject from the side and there will be a loud bang. I'll give you some ear and eye protectors. Audience, when I put my fingers in my ears you please do the same.

Ok, so, do you understand the sequence? I'll chamber the round, take off the safety and hand you the gun, then go over there. When you are ready just aim at the centre of the target and squeeze the trigger. Once you've done that the next round will automatically be in the chamber so please go back to safety position. Understand?

Once they are prepped the assistant takes their position and fires their practice round. The plate smashes.

Well done – how do you feel?

Chamber the next round if necessary.

Now, I need you to come and stand here.

The next shot will be the same only I will be standing in front of the target and you will be aiming at my mouth. I will go over there and raise my hand – that's your cue to raise the gun. When I drop my hand that means I am ready – it does not mean shoot straight away, just that I am ready. You shoot in your own time.[28]

Audience, if you didn't enjoy watching the plate and you don't think you'll enjoy this next bit then by all means, with my best wishes and full understanding, you may now leave the auditorium. People have left before, please don't be embarrassed. Ok.[29]

So everyone understands what is going to happen then? And everyone's ok with that? Right.

So. You understand the sequence? I raise my hand, you raise the weapon. I lower my hand, you shoot when you are ready. Audience, put your fingers in your ears when I raise my hand.

---

[28] The performer has to be very sensitive to the assistant at this point. It is possible that they are not able to go ahead with it, which is always allowed.

[29] It was always a delight when people left at this point, which happened more often than not. It meant the show was working (unless they just weren't enjoying it) and it always added to the sense of tension in the room. Questions hovered in the air ... 'Why are you all sitting here watching this? Why does no one stop it?', especially as the implication was that like Henderson, Rob had planned an elaborate suicide. The answer was obvious enough – no one really truly believed he was going to do it. It was a magic show after all? Wasn't it? But the seed of doubt, the pebble in the shoe, is all we needed to make this a truly breathtaking moment. On one occasion someone shouted from the audience, trying to talk Rob out of it, and more than once someone leaving was very unhappy with the direction the show had taken. Presumably some of them thought it was in bad taste, but this all just added to the tension. We loved this moment.

Ear protectors on. **Wonder** *gives them the gun and takes his mark.*

They shoot him. He falls.

He gets up and removes the bullet from his mouth, shows the mark to the assistant and asks the audience to give her a round of applause. She leaves the stage and **Wonder** *puts on* **Garth**'s *jacket.*

Wonder   I know now what it was that I saw in his eyes. I have seen those eyes before, Bette. Each time I look in the mirror. I saw a sadness, deep and rooted. A hopelessness without reason. I saw it in him and he saw it in me. And he thought I would understand. And I do. But I could never put a fellow through what he has put me through.

Tonight after church I found myself looking out over the bloody Thames. Don't remember even walking but there I was. And forgive me, Bette, but, for a second, I thought about how easy it would be. But then I remembered little Sammy. And the lemon drop waiting for me at home.

Why did he not just stop the show and tell me? Why did he not just reach out to me? If I feel like this and if Henderson did then how many more are there out there? I feel like we must look around more. We must find each other. Because really, when it comes down to it, We Are All the Same. There is a point to all this isn't there? And it's each other.[30]

As the lights come down he makes an effort to look every member of the audience in the eye.[31]

---

[30]   The final line of the show is always delivered to the assistant and Rob usually makes an effort to personalise it in some way, for example by adding a reference to what they believe in. 'There is a point to all this isn't there? And it's each other. It's people.'

[31]   After the show, Rob always asks the assistant to wait in the bar for him. It is important to make sure that they are in a fit state to re-enter the real world and are not too shaken by the experience. After a chat and sometimes a drink they have always emerged feeling ultimately glad to have participated.

Wallace

Benny Young as Sir Edward Hammer MP, Moyo Akandé as Petra Lang, and Lesley Hart as Roberta Bishop in *Wallace*

Wallace was first performed in 2014 at The Arches, Glasgow. It was produced as part of the Early Days Festival in the week preceding the referendum on Scottish independence. *Wallace* was presented as a work-in-development commissioned by the National Theatre of Great Britain. It evolved to become *The Majority* three years later.

Journalist/Chronicler/Service Rep   Moyo Akandé
MP's Son/Longshanks's Son/Researcher   Kieran Baker
Wallace   Rob Drummond
Chairperson/Bishop Wishart/Secretary   Lesley Hart
Comedian/Calgacus/Robert the Bruce/Wallace's Dad   James McAnerney
MSP/John Balliol/Receptionist   Gaylie Runciman
MP/Longshanks   Benny Young

Co-director   Rob Drummond
Co-director   David Overend
Assistant Director   Lucy Wild
Lighting Designer   Kai Fischer
Music and Sound Designer   Scott Twynholm
Set and Costume Designer   Neil Warmington
Wardrobe Assistant   Iona Barker
Casting Director   Laura Donnelly
Production Manager   John Wilkie
Deputy Stage Manager   Hannah Nicol
Assistant Stage Manager   Christine Collins

Act One: Political[1]

The Great Cause

A TV studio. The programme is called The Great Cause. *The panel members have assembled and the audience are buzzing.*

Suddenly, the lights dim dramatically and the floor manager shouts, 'And we're live in ten, nine, eight, seven, six, five, four . . .'

Three, two and one are silent.

The intro music plays accompanied by dramatic lighting.

The music fades but continues quietly under the following.

Chair   Good evening, I'm Roberta Bishop and welcome to *The Great Cause.* Tonight's show is a referendum special.[2] Our panel tonight: Scottish National Party stalwart and MSP for Paisley[3] Sarah Bailey, controversial comedian and Yes campaigner Bruce Carrick, Scotland's only Tory MP[4] Sir Edward Hammer . . .

The **Chair** *has to pause momentarily as* **Wallace**, *a man in face paint and full* Braveheart *get-up, boos from the audience.*[5]

Chair   . . . and former *Sunday Herald* journalist, Petra Lang. Please welcome them all.

The audience clap as a final burst of music fills the space.

We want to thank you all for submitting your questions in advance and remind you that these have not been seen by our panellists. If your question was not selected, don't worry, we will accept questions from the floor at regular intervals. Our hope is for a free and open debate in this, the most important week in Scotland's history. So please don't be shy, this won't work without your help.

---

[1]   This act uses an open debate format to deliver a closed narrative. The actors improvise answers while also deploying rehearsed plot points. When Wallace Williamson asks his question, the debate begins to close down, the lighting draws in and we transition into a more traditional play as the narrative takes over. Before the debate begins, the floor manager will invite two members of the audience to ask pre-prepared questions.
　　Despite a general preference to avoid using plants, we have no strong ethical feelings about it – it's all about what's best for the particular show or moment we are trying to create. A plant in *Bullet Catch* would have undermined the whole performance and significantly limited the possibilities, which would have been wrong for that play. *Wallace* was different as we needed to get the balance between creating an environment where audience members could ask whatever questions they liked and making sure we had included the two questions that we absolutely needed for our plot to work, while maintaining the feeling of an open debate.

[2]   On Thursday 18 September 2014 – the date of the final performance of *Wallace* – the people of Scotland voted to remain part of the United Kingdom by the unexpectedly wide margin of 55 per cent to 45 per cent ('Scottish independence referendum (Archived)', gov.uk/government/topical-events/scottish-independence-referendum (accessed 15 August 2019)).

[3]   Member of the Scottish Parliament.

[4]   Conservative Party Member of [the British] Parliament.

[5]   The fact that Rob was in the audience made for an interesting dynamic here as only those who knew him personally or knew his work could be certain that he wasn't just a random audience member who had come dressed as William Wallace. Most people would have had an inkling he was a plant but all you need is a doubt to create a certain atmosphere in a room and there were certainly some people who were suspicious of him.

Before we begin I wonder if we could take a quick poll. Who in the audience tonight is intending to vote Yes? Who is intending to vote No? And who is yet to decide?

The **Chair** *responds to this.*[6]

Let's have our first question tonight which comes from Sam Munro. Sam.[7]

Audience Question One

A 'boom mic' finds the first audience member, who has agreed to play **Sam**.

Sam   Is it ever acceptable to sell your vote for financial gain or should ideology be the primary motivating factor in making your decision?

Chair   This question comes of course in the light of the stories of syndicates of people in Edinburgh putting their votes up for sale on the online auction website eBay.[8] Sarah Bailey.

MSP   Thank you, Roberta. Yes, this is a troubling story. People have become accustomed to their vote not meaning anything. I'm here to say that should you vote Yes on Thursday all of that will change. That's a personal guarantee.

Journalist   Come on, Sarah, you can't even personally guarantee you'll still be around after Thursday. Your coat's on a shoogly peg after Radisson Gate, isn't it?

MSP   There is an internal inquiry ongoing into the incident at the Radisson Hotel so I don't feel like it would be appropriate to talk about it here tonight, Petra.

Chair   Yes, Petra, let's stay on topic please.

Pause.

Sir Edward Hammer.

---

[6]   Perhaps unsurprisingly, given the high degree of support for independence in the Scottish arts community, the audiences were almost entirely comprised of Yes voters. On one occasion, only one audience member admitted to an intention to vote No. This is entirely relevant to the journey towards *The Majority*. We have always been concerned that a major problem (perhaps *the* major problem) with subsidised theatre is preaching to the converted. This was a play written by a left-leaning Yes voter, written for an audience of left-leaning Yes voters. The journey of the maturation of this concept is also the story of Rob's maturation as an artist who now clearly sees his role in the arts as *never* preaching to the converted. *The Majority* challenged the preconception that being on the left meant automatically occupying the moral high ground. While we slightly sent up the jingoistic Yes voters here with the character of Wallace, in hindsight we didn't go far enough as he was still 'correct' in the end. He was still the hero. If we were to make this show again we would make Wallace a No voter. This talks to the conundrum of using audiences in shows in a challenging way whilst simultaneously keeping them on side. It's all about pushing them in a safe way where they know you're never trying to belittle or bully, just challenge them gently. We liken this to sitting your best friend down and telling them a harsh truth in a loving way.

[7]   This was one of the audience members to whom the floor manager had given a pre-prepared question. We used names that were not gender specific so this could be anybody.

[8]   This actually happened: www.independent.co.uk/news/uk/crime/scottish-independence-man-arrested-over-votes-for-sale-on-ebay-9701560.html (accessed 15 August 2019).

MP   Please, please, just Edward will suffice. I cut a pretty lonely figure up here, don't I? After all, there are more pandas in Scotland than Tory MPs.[9] Before I get to my answer I think it's important to extend my good will to both sides of the debate as, whatever happens at the end of the week, we are all going to have to live and work together afterwards.

Comedian   So that's a yes to a currency union then?

MP   We already have a currency union, it's you who wants to put that in jeopardy.

Scotland is a success story in terms of pioneering medical research, education and healthcare. We pay more into the UK coffers than any other nation in the Union. Sounds like we could survive on our own perfectly easily, right? Well, let's think about this. There is a reason we are currently thriving. The UK is the oldest and most successful economic union in the world. Our economy is based on a principle of pooling and sharing risks and resources. We are thriving now. What makes you think changing the situation within which we are thriving will mean we will continue to thrive?

This plebiscite allows you the chance to say no thanks to that risk.

Comedian   Plebiscite?

MP   It's just another word for referendum, Bruce.

Comedian   You really are down with the kids aren't you?

MSP   I find it extraordinary that Edward can sit there and use the fact that we are thriving against us. We've proven what we can do with the shackles on, now let's see what we can achieve with them off.

MP   If we could bring this back to Sam's excellent question. Sam, don't you dare feel guilty about considering finance when you make your decision on Thursday – we *have* to. We'd be fools not to.

But, of course, literally selling votes online is abhorrent – we absolutely cannot allow the monetisation of voting.

Chair   Bruce Carrick.

Comedian   Right. Well I want to start by saying that I'm not totally anti-union per-say. Some unions work fine. In fact the esteemed chairwoman and I are this very night celebrating ten blissful years of union.

*The **Chair** looks embarrassed as he holds up his ring finger and Edward Hammer leads a round of applause.*

Comedian   The problem is, Eddie – may I call you Eddie?

MP   Of course you can . . . Brucey.

Comedian   Eddie, you were saying you were dead against the . . . monetisation of voting. But isn't that exactly what you are doing already?

---

[9]   Remarkably, this was true at the time.

MP   In what way?

Comedian   Well, how much better off will we all be if we vote No?

MP   How much?

Comedian   Yes. If you had to put a figure on it. How much?

MP   I think the current figure worked out independently by economists is around £1000.

Comedian   So you're promising one thousand pounds in exchange for a vote?

MP   No. We're not.

Comedian   Ok, not a promise then, what would you call it? A bid?

MP   We're saying this is our best estimate as to what will happen should someone vote No.

Comedian   And what about you, Sarah? How much are you offering for a vote?

MSP   We are not /

Journalist   / Oh for God sake would you two just admit what's going on? It's pathetic pretending it's not happening. They're valuing independence at around £1400 per year at the moment but no doubt that will change after Edward and his lot raise their offer.

MP   Ridiculous.

Chair   Petra Lang.

Journalist   When the *Sunday Herald* came out as pro-independent I resigned immediately because /

Comedian   / You saw the chance of a media career?

Journalist   Because I could not in all good conscience support a publication that would be so irresponsible as to advocate risking the lives and livelihoods of five million people on nothing more than hopes and dreams.

Comedian   You write for the *Sun* now don't you?

Journalist   I have a guest column.

Comedian   Next to Jeremy Clarkson's.[10]

---

[10]   While this is the sort of thing that Bruce would say, it is also an example of the sort of cheap joke that we wouldn't want to make anymore. It's basically playing to the crowd and virtue signalling (we all hate Jeremy Clarkson, don't we, hahaha). Well, an awful lot of the UK (maybe a majority) love Jeremy Clarkson, so wouldn't it be far more interesting and useful to examine why and to talk to them about that than belittling them in a room full of people who agree with you? In this way, if and when we do another solo show which uses audience members as participants, we plan on exploring the drama of ideological disagreement – the tension involved in inviting an audience into the show and then finding points of disagreement rather than agreement – trying to foster a relationship despite the differences rather than meeting them on safe ground (like *Bullet Catch* did, ironically enough for a show with a loaded gun).

Journalist   The simple fact, which no one can deny, is that moving to independence would be a huge risk. Since when did it become a bad thing to avoid huge risks?

Comedian   The truth is nobody knows whether we'll be better or worse off financially but that doesn't mean we automatically vote No to be safe.

Journalist   Bruce, you are a 'self-employed' (*using air quotes*) 'artist'. You flit from one job to the next with no care or thought for the future. Your lifestyle allows you to think like that. That's why all 'artists' are voting Yes. They don't live in the real world. Normal people with responsibilities, jobs, families, pensions, make decisions based on money and they shouldn't have to apologise for it.

Comedian (*mocking Petra's use of air quotes*)   I might very well lose 'money' if Scotland goes 'independent' but it's not about 'me'. It's not about us in this 'room'. It's about the people on the bottom rungs of society.

Journalist   Since when did you become a champion of the less fortunate?

Comedian   I always have been.

Journalist   Did you not once say that Jimmy Savile /

Comedian   / That was just a joke.

Journalist   / Jimmy Savile did so much charity work near the end so he could be sure of shagging Madeleine McCann in heaven.

Did you say that?

Comedian   My personal history – what I've said or not said in the past – has nothing to do with my ability to rationally discuss the issue here today.

Journalist   It's no wonder you've been on *Mock the Week* so often, Bruce. It's what you do for a living. Why don't you try mocking the strong for once.

Open Debate Session One

Chair   Ok, we now throw this issue open to the floor. Please raise your hand if you have a question and I will try to get to as many of you as possible.

There follows an open debate controlled by the **Chair**.

During this session the following plot points should be deployed.[11]

---

[11]   The performers need to be skilled in moving between open and scripted text. This lies in the actors being absolutely confident and practised in managing to wrangle the conversation back to the script, while truly and wholeheartedly embracing the unknown and letting the discussion go wherever it wants to go in the room. We rehearsed this by throwing a mixture of serious and inane questions at the actors and seeing how long it took them to get back to the next plot point, then refining the length of time they were allowed to deviate for until they had a kind of internal group clock running on proceedings. Every performance worked well in this respect, with the team of improvisors managing to skilfully bring the discussion back around to the script each night in such a way that no one really knew it was happening.

Plot Point A – the Radisson

Journalist   How can we trust you to run a country after the Yes campaign dinner you ran at the Radisson?

MSP   I've already said, we cannot talk about the party until after the inquiry.

Journalist   Ah yes, because of the young man who almost died.

Edward, didn't your son accuse you of having something to do with that?

MP   I will not bite. I will not. I will not get upset no matter how hard you try. I am here to talk about the referendum and nothing else.

Journalist   You did arrange that party didn't you, Sarah? Do you feel you have blood on your hands?

MSP   Listen, it is inevitable that when you assemble a large group of people together some of them are going to let the rest down by /

Journalist   / Murdering people and shagging on balconies?

MSP   What?

Journalist   There's a video on YouTube but no one knows who it is. You can only see arses.

Chair   Can we please stop throwing baseless accusations around.

Journalist   You were there too, Roberta, weren't you? I thought you were meant to be neutral.

Chair   I was there with Bruce. He was performing stand-up.

Journalist   Ah yes, that's when he made the misogynistic, offensive sexual joke about you, isn't it? What was it again? Something about your vagina?

Chair   Petra, shut up!

Our marriage is not the topic of this discussion.

Personally, if you must know, I am undecided on the referendum. I'm hopeful we can go it on our own, but I'm just scared about being wrong.

That is my position.

Ok?

Now, if we've quite finished the mud-slinging . . .

Yes, you sir, in the fourth row.

Plot Point B – Sarah's Ambition[12]

Journalist   So, you have no doubts whatsoever about the financial implications of independence, Sarah? None?

---

[12]   In this case the way to bring the conversation back to the script was simply for one actor to bring up money in response to whatever question they were discussing.

MSP   I am confident that /

Journalist   / Yeah, yeah, yeah, party line, party line. You're ambitious. You want to be first minister, or president, or whatever you're going to call it. But do you not worry that your ambition is clouding your judgement? Is this more about personal ambition than what's best for the country?

MSP   If you want to talk about ruthless ambition, take a look at yourself, Petra. You like to think of yourself as some sort of acid-tongued, no-nonsense reporter when all you really are is a media-hungry rent-a-gob.

Journalist   Is it true that you have been hand-picked by Alex Salmond to be his successor when he steps down as leader of the SNP?[13]

MSP   There is no deal of any sort in place.

Journalist   So you have no ambition whatsoever of being leader of the SNP?

MSP   I stand firmly behind Alex Salmond /

Journalist   / Oh come on Sarah, you lot like to pretend you are a different breed of politician, prove it by actually answering a direct question!

MSP   If you are asking me if, after paying my dues for the last thirty years in politics with the SNP, after being overlooked time and time again, I have earned the right to be talked about as a future leader, then yes. I absolutely have. But that does not mean I am anything less than one hundred per cent behind the current leader!

Plot Point C – Journalist's Tease

Right in the middle of proceedings, a loud, shrill text alert emanates from the **Journalist**'s *phone.*

Journalist   Sorry. I thought it was on silent. I'm waiting for an important message.

Chair   More important than a live televised debate?

Journalist   It's not unrelated.

Audience Question Two

At an appropriate point, the **Chair** *introduces question two.*

Chair   Ok, we go now to a question from Max Smith. Max.

Max   Is it even possible to get to the truth of the independence debate amidst the mire of propaganda and negative campaigning we are subjected to from both sides?

---

[13]   A clear reference to the Scottish National Party's next leader and the fifth first minister of Scotland, Nicola Sturgeon. Sturgeon took office in November 2014 – two months after *Wallace*.

Chair   Bruce Carrick.

Comedian   I sympathise, mate, I really do. I mean, I can't be the only one who can sit and listen to both sides, think they both sound totally plausible and then come out the other side more confused than when I went in. One of them must be either lying or mistaken, they both can't be right.

The truth of the independence debate is this. And you don't need to trust anyone for this to make sense. Forget facts. Forget figures.

Forget lying politicians. Self-governance makes sense.

It is the natural state of a nation.

We're not asking for anything special, just normalcy. If you created a new country, Max, would there even be a question of whether or not it would govern its own affairs? No.

Chair   Petra Lang.

Journalist   Listen, if people really, truly wanted to find out about the intricacies of the issues they would perform a simple google search which would turn up dozens and dozens of peer-reviewed papers on the economical, sociological and political implications of independence. The truth is people don't want to know things. They don't.

MSP   Well, they've come here tonight, haven't they?

Journalist   Debates are not about the free dispersal and exchange of information. They're about convincing through storytelling. If you want facts, don't come to these things, do your own research at home.

Chair   Sarah Bailey.

MSP   We have done an enormous amount to educate the voting public. Our white paper is a comprehensively positive document. What more can we do? The other side is not presenting an alternative model, but using fear-mongering tactics to emotionally sway the public with negative campaigning.

Chair   Edward Hammer.

MP   Our alternative model, Sarah, is the one that already exists, within which, by your own admission, Scotland is currently thriving. See the thing about it is, it is almost impossible to run a No campaign on anything without sounding negative. Your side suggests something new, we tell you why it wouldn't work. The burden of proof is on the side making the claim. We are simply saying your claim that independence would be better is wrong. I fail to see how else we could approach things.

If you see a man heading towards the edge of a cliff you have to negatively campaign to keep him away. You shout, DONT DO IT! You don't shout, it's your choice, we'll see what happens.

MSP   Your entire campaign is based on lies.

MP   Give me one example.

MSP   You claim we'll all need passports at the border, this is a LIE because we plan on joining the EU.[14]

You say we won't be accepted into the EU. Again, a LIE. An independent Scotland will be the fourteenth richest country in the world. Oil rich no less. We will be *welcomed* into the EU.

The pound. You claim we can't have it. LIES. It's as much ours as it is yours. You claim you won't agree a currency union with us when it's patently obvious that you will *have to* if we choose to become independent as it's in all of our best interests and you know it. To say we won't reach an agreement is scare tactics and, again, a LIE.

You say the NHS will suffer if it becomes independent.[15] This is a LIE because Scotland already has an independent NHS and it's outperforming the rest of the UK.

You say *EastEnders* couldn't be shown in Scotland because the BBC wouldn't be in operation up here.[16] Well the BBC is not in operation in the USA but I have plenty of friends over there who watch *EastEnders* all the time. LIES, LIES, LIES.

Pause.

Journalist   Well, Sarah, you know plenty about lies don't you?

MSP   As usual, Petra, I haven't the foggiest idea what you're talking about.

Journalist (*tapping on her phone*)   Oh, don't worry. We'll all find out soon enough.[17]

Silence,

Chair   Let's throw this open to our audience. How many of you feel honestly that when you vote on Thursday you will do so with adequate knowledge of the facts?

Do you feel like enough has been done to make the facts available or do you take some responsibility for this?

Open Debate Session Two

The audience are encouraged to have a free and open debate during which the following plot points are worked in.[18]

---

[14]   European Union.

[15]   National Health Service.

[16]   *EastEnders* is a popular British soap opera produced by the BBC (British Broadcasting Corporation). There was some speculation that it would no longer be screened in Scotland in the event of independence.

[17]   *Wallace* is an example of two styles merging. We love to create live theatre where audience members can alter the show in a genuine fashion, whilst still making sure there is a clear narrative thread. This narrative is often unashamedly unsubtle. In this case it is employed with almost pantomimic promise to the audience that something big is going to be revealed in due course. Audiences love this – subtle is all well and good but people go the theatre wanting to go on a journey with plot points and twists and turns. Along with wanting to challenge our audiences we also want to make theatre for people who think they don't like theatre. People who assume it's all intellectual and slow moving and navel-gazing poetic nonsense. We embrace that too from time to time, but it's all about finding the right form for the ideas you want to share.

[18]   As this play was performed in the run-up to the actual referendum, tensions were running high and, in these moments, it occasionally seemed that the boundaries between fiction and reality were breaking down as some audience members

Plot Point D – Edward's Depth of Hurt

Comedian   Look, the problem is that ordinary folk can't relate to your average politician. Even you, Sarah, to be fair, you have to toe the party line so we never know if we can trust what you're saying.

Edward is a charming man. Course he is. That's his brand. He's setting himself up as an alternative to Cameron but not quite as crazy as Johnson. He wants the leadership. He wants to be PM. I wouldn't be surprised if he actually wanted to lose this referendum so that can happen quicker.

MP   Nonsense.

Chair   If the leadership of the Conservative Party were to become available would you run?

MP   We are here to discuss the matter of Scottish /

Comedian   / Come on, it's a simple question.

Chair   Bruce, do I look like I need your help?

Mr Hammer, would you run against Boris Johnson for leader of the Conservatives?

MP   I fully endorse Mr Cameron as leader of the Conservative Party.

Chair   Will you be running for leader when Mr Cameron steps down?

SNP   Answer the question.

MP   Where did this absurd notion that one must answer any question thrown at one come from? I am under no obligation to answer hypothetical questions. Neither are you, or you, or any of us. And it takes guts to simply say, I'm not answering that. It's stupid and off topic.

Comedian   See. He doesn't care about people. He cares about his own career. He's a career politician straight out of Oxbridge and into Westminster.

MP   Yes, I am. Which means I have devoted my life to politics at the expense of a social life, a family, my wife, my son. I've lost them all and . . .

You know my own son hates me and everything I stand for, yes? Well that's not exactly a secret is it? Petra's written extensively about that. The socialist son of the Scottish Tory. He thinks I'm the devil. He left home as soon as he was legally able. The day of his sixteenth birthday. The same day. Said he wanted to get out of my shadow. It was embarrassing being the son of the only Tory in Scotland. He wanted

---

directed their anger and frustration towards the performers. Perhaps it was testament to their skills as improvisers that they so convincingly portrayed their characters that audiences seemed to forget they were actors, not politicians. Or perhaps people simply needed someone to whom they could vent their disappointment with the real politicians, playing out their own drama on a larger stage. At any rate, when these sections of the play worked as well as was hoped (and this was not always the case), their power seemed to lie in the play's ability to tap into the hunger for argument and discussion that The Arches' audiences brought into the theatre that week.

to make his own way. Make his own mistakes. Said he didn't need me anymore. Sixteen. Didn't need his father.

That was one thing but then . . . he started campaigning against me. Turning up at press junkets. Having his friends follow me.

You know, I could probably win him back by renouncing my politics. My beliefs. Showing him I care more about him than this country and its people. But you know something? I don't. I love him but I care more for this country and its future than for my own son.

So don't you dare sit there and tell me I don't care about this country. Because you don't have the slightest fucking clue.

Plot Point E – Petra's Link to the MP's Son

MP   To suggest that conservatism is unconcerned with social justice is absurd. We want the best for everyone, we believe everyone is equal, we just disagree on how best to motivate people to succeed.

Comedian   Oh really, Edward, you believe in equality. Tell me, what way did you vote on gay marriage?

Pause.

MP   That is neither here nor there.

Comedian   Your son is gay isn't he? How does he feel about your stance?

Journalist   He doesn't really care.

Pause.

MP   How would you know what my son thinks about anything?

Journalist   We've been talking.

MP   What?

Journalist   I gave him a call. I was going to do a story on his nutty conspiracy theories but, you know, a strange thing happened. I started to believe some of them.

MP   That boy is not well, Miss Lang, how dare you /

Journalist   / It's my job, Edward.

MP   Your job is to harass mentally ill young adults?

Journalist   My job is to look out for the best interests of the people by uncovering corruption.

MP   You're not interested in the people, you're only interested in your career.

Journalist   Why can't I be interested in both?

Plot Point F – the Comedian's Announcement

Journalist   This whole thing is a kind of a farce, isn't it? I mean, come on, admit it, you all know it's going to be a No vote, don't you?[19]

Chair   Let's just see, could we have a show of hands again of those of you who will be voting Yes. Ok. And now let's see hands of those of you who expect the *result* will be Yes.

The **Chair** *responds to this.*

MP   You see, even the Yes side concede it's looking unlikely. Or: That's just grandstanding, all the polls show you are behind.[20]

MSP   You know as well as I do that the Yes vote is gaining ground every single day and it is now too close to call.

Comedian   Listen, polls are useless. They only record the views of those people too stupid to avoid a guy in the street with a clipboard.

Chair   I often stop for them. Am I stupid?

Comedian   No. Course not. It was a joke.

Chair   Yeah, you're good at them.

Comedian   Look, I've apologised for making that joke. Are you going to accept it or not?

Chair   You said it's been so long since we had sex that my vagina was haunted!

Silence.

MP   I don't get it.

Journalist   I think it's, like, her vagina died.

MP   If it died, surely that would mean it would be a ghost itself, not haunted by ghosts.

Journalist   Maybe it's haunted by the ghosts of dead sperm or /

Comedian   / It doesn't mean anything, it just sounded good, Ok? It just sounded good.

And it's not even remotely true. I mean, she's a real goer you know /

Chair   Bruce, you're making it worse!

Comedian   It was just a joke.

---

[19]   Many Yes voters genuinely didn't seem to realise this was the likely outcome – perhaps a result of a necessary optimism, or of being in their bubble and not engaging the other side. It was always going to be a difficult referendum to win.

[20]   This vote was always, overwhelmingly, for Yes.

Chair   A joke that the whole of Scotland was laughing at when she printed it the next day.

Journalist   Don't you blame me, he's the one who said it!

MP   I don't think it's funny.

Journalist   Are you kidding? It's really funny.

Chair   Ok. Time for another quick audience poll. By a show of hands, who thinks Bruce is funny?

She responds to the votes.

Right, so it's official then. Bruce Carrick is not funny.

Comedian   Oh fuck off, you didn't count it right.

Chair   We can only apologise for Bruce's use of language.

Comedian   They don't care. They all swear all the time. That's the problem. No one's real up here. They're all just saying what they think they have to say. I'm real.

I'm like them. They've got no one like them looking out for them. You think I don't take this seriously? I do. I take it very seriously. And I'll prove it to you.

I am announcing here and now that I will be standing for my local seat in the next elections for the Scottish Parliament.

MSP   Your local seat?

Comedian   Paisley.

MSP   But that's . . . that's my seat.

Comedian   Yeah, no offence just makes sense to go for my local seat.

Journalist   Oh dear Sarah, that might be a bit of a problem. His last DVD sold twenty million copies. Most normal people couldn't pick you out of line-up.

MSP   Bruce, you are not a politician.

Comedian   Exactly! That's why I'm going to win. And then I'm going to go on and become first minister.

MSP   As an independent candidate?

Comedian   Damn right. An independent first minister in an independent Scotland.

Chair   You're serious about this, Bruce?

Comedian   Very serious. I want to make a difference.

Chair   Oh. Ok.

Well . . .

Good for you, Bruce.

Good for you.

MSP   Good for him? He can't just . . . Bruce, you can't just . . . you can't just waltz in and capitalise on your fame like that. I've worked for this. This is my time. This is my fucking time!

The silence after the outburst is deafening.

Chair   Eh. Maybe we should go to our next question now.

It's from Wallace. Wallace.

Audience Question Three

Wallace (*nervous energy, his hand stuck frozen in the air*)   Eh, hi, my name's Wallace Williamson, and I got a MA in history from Glasgow Uni and I'm now a writer of Scottish historical fiction. I've written a book about the Great Cause actually. It's called *The Meet on the Tweed* and it's available on my website www.wallywilly.co.uk.

Long pause. No one cares.

Chair   Your question please.

Wallace   Eh . . . Yeah. So . . . WHEN Scotland gets its independence . . . (*Waits for applause, doesn't get it.*) When we get our FREEDOM . . . Eh, is the next logical stage taking a leaf from our forefathers and deposing the unelected monarch that represents the hundreds of years of oppression that we have endured under English rule!

Chair   The question I have on the card – you can put your hand down now Wallace – the question I have on the card is should an independent Scotland keep the monarchy?

Edward Hammer.

MP   I might be wrong but I do find the tone of the young man's comments a little racist.

Wallace (*hand back up*)   Hey, woah, that's not fair. I'm not racist against the English. I have lots of friends who are . . . racist against the English. But I'm not.

It's just . . .

See when Longshanks met with Robert the Bruce and John Balliol on the Tweed it was to trick them into a Union that seemed fair but actually favoured him. That was the thirteenth century. And we're still facing the same problem today. Enough is enough.

MP   Are you comparing David Cameron to Longshanks?

Comedian   That would be disrespectful to Longshanks.

MP   Again, barely disguised racism. What has thirteenth-century England got to do with today? This is a baseless appeal to history.

Wallace   History's important!

MP   But not relevant. And not accurate either I may add. Robert the Bruce was a teenager during the Great Cause. It was his father, Robert de Brus, who would have been at that meeting.

Wallace   Aye, well, I knew that but . . . it's just a better scene if the more famous, actual Robert the Bruce is there, you know?[21]

MP   Ah, so facts are unimportant to you. That's good to know.

Chair   Sarah Bailey?

She is still staring daggers at the **Comedian**.

Chair   Sarah.

MSP   What?

Chair   The question.

MSP   Eh, yes. I think what the gentleman there is trying to say is that we are not criticising a race, we are criticising a system. A system that means we have our affairs controlled by an unrepresentative body in a different country. A government that does not reflect this country's values and core beliefs of free education and healthcare, progressive taxation and an acceptance of the duty to look after the most unfortunate members of its society. Bruce, are you really serious? This is a wind-up isn't it? It's one of your jokes.

Comedian   It's no joke.

Chair   Petra Lang.

Journalist   I am sick to death, Sarah, of hearing the dangerous nationalist rhetoric coming out your mouth day after day. 'We have our affairs controlled by an unrepresentative body in a different country?' I mean, this is just UKIP rhetoric on the EU, is it not? You sound more like Nigel Farage than he does.[22]

It's a good thing Bruce will soon be replacing you in parliament.

Chair   Bruce.

Comedian   I can't believe we're still even having to defend ourselves on this one. Yes, we give out a bit of banter, but we get it back in spades – I mean, *Have I Got News for You* as well as being the most toothless, overrated piece of crap on TV,

---

[21]   This speaks to a general liberal approach to the truth in these plays. We are generally comfortable about lying or bending the facts to tell a bigger truth, which is mirrored in our use of plants and generally telling the audience that a story is based on reality when it often is not. This could be argued to be just as problematic in the theatre as it is in the political sphere, but we are in the business of telling stories not creating laws or policies.

[22]   The United Kingdom Independence Party is a right-wing populist party led by Nigel Farage from 2006 to 2016. Farage went on to launch the Brexit Party in 2019.

basically just exists to make fun of the drunk Irish, the sheep-shagging Welsh and the heroin and deep-fried Mars Bar junkie Scots.[23]

Wallace   Yes, exactly, that's exactly what I mean.

Comedian   But I'm afraid, Wallace, you're doing us no favours with the language you're using.

Wallace   It's just a joke. You know, the Scottish sense of humour.

Comedian   We don't have a special sense of humour, mate, that's just made up. It doesn't stand up to any level of scrutiny. We're all more or less the same.[24]

MP   I have a question for the young gentleman himself if I may. Why are you voting Yes?

Wallace   Me?

MP   Yes.

Wallace   Because self-governance is the natural state of a . . . place. We've got a system, right, that means we've got an unrepresentative body in a different country . . . doing our things. Running our . . . A government that does not reflect this country's values and core beliefs of free education and healthcare, progressive taxes and caring for poor folk and that.

MP   I'm sorry, sir, but all you've proven there is that you are at best a mediocre parrot.

Wallace   There's nothing wrong with repeating good arguments.

MP   You are arguing from a position of *zero* authority based on *no* research. All rhetoric and no substance. Which is, I'd imagine, exactly what this book of yours will be like. Under-researched, jingoistic, simplistic, bigoted nonsense where the English are all vicious baddies and murderers and the Scots heroic goodies fighting for justice.

Wallace   Sometimes that's true!

MP   Do you think I'm evil?

Wallace   Well you're a Tory so . . . aye.

MP   Well, that says it all really. I'm done.

Wallace   What? Afraid to debate me?

MP   I would love to engage in a battle of wits with you, sir, but I see you are unarmed.[25]

---

23   *Have I Got News for You* is a British comedy news panel show – just the sort of show on which Bruce Carrick would have appeared.

24   The phrase 'We're all the same' recurs in several of Rob's previous plays, *Bullet Catch* included. Here, it morphs into 'more or less the same', and subsequently it disappears. Here, we are concentrating on the fact that we are different but should engage with those differences more maturely. Rob's work used to be more idealistic.

25   This is one of those lines that is difficult to attribute. We think Christopher Hitchens said it once.

Wallace   And you're a total cock!

MP   You see this is the sort of person you do not even need to argue with. You just allow him to talk and he ends up making your case for you.

Who are you meant to be anyway?

Wallace   William Wallace. The hero of the Scottish Wars of Independence.

MP   You do realise that even if he existed, and there's no concrete evidence he did, he would certainly not have painted his face like a first-century Pict.

Pause.

Wallace   He did exist.

MP   Evidence?

Wallace   Blind Harry.

MP   A poem is your evidence?

Chair   I think we should move on.

MSP   Where are you registered to vote, sir, if you don't mind me asking?

Wallace   Registered?

MSP   Yes. What's your district?

Wallace   I don't know where I'm voting yet.

Pause.

MSP   You do know you need to register to vote, don't you?[26]

Pause.

Wallace   I live here.

Comedian   Oh my God.

MP *starts to laugh.*

MP   And this, ladies and gentlemen, is natural selection in action. Disenfranchisement through idiocy. He has just taken his vote out of the gene pool.

Wallace   You can't talk to me like this, you Tory fucking prick!

Comedian   Woah. Man. You have to leave.

MSP   Yes I think we need to get him out, Roberta.

Wallace   I didn't mean that. I'm sorry.

Chair   Sir. We need you to leave, sir.

---

[26]   Based on the many, many people who were enthusiastic Yes voters but didn't know you had to register.

Wallace   It just slipped out.

Chair   Wallace. Please.

Silence. **Wallace** *knows he's gone too far. Tail between his legs, he leaves the auditorium. On the way out he turns to* **MP**.

Wallace   I'm sorry, sir. I went too far.

He extends his hand.

MP *refuses to shake it.*

Wallace   I said I'm sorry.

MP   I heard you.

Wallace   Are you not going to say sorry back?

MP   Why should I?

Wallace   That's how it works.

MP   I'm not sorry. I did nothing wrong.

Silence.

Wallace   I don't give my consent. For this to go out on air.

Chair   It's a live show, Wallace.

Silence.

Wallace *is well and truly humiliated.*

Wallace   Fuck yous all!

He lifts up his kilt, giving the panel an eyeful, then leaves.

Audience Question Four

Chair   Our next question from the audience is from Andy. Do we have Andy?

An audience member in a cap stands up and just stares at the panel.

Are you Ok, Andy?

Andy *says nothing.*

Chair   Would you like to ask your question, Andy?

It's on the card if you've forgotten.

Andy   I don't need the card.

Chair   Fair enough. On you go.

Andy   This is a question for Edward Hammer.

MP   I hope it's more intelligent than the last.

Pause.

Andy   Edward. What is the select committee for Contingency Strategy?

MP   What?

Chair   The question I have on my card is about the currency union.

Andy   Answer the question.

MP   I'm afraid I don't /

Andy   / Do you not even recognise my voice?

MP   What?

Andy *takes off his cap.* **MP** *stands up in his seat.*[27]

MP   Edward?

Son   Hi, Dad.

They stare at each other.

Journalist   Didn't see that coming did you?

Comedian   Fuck me.

Chair   Bruce!

Eh. The name I have here is Andy.

Son   It's what I go as now. Used to be Edward Junior.

No points for imagination on that one, Dad.

MP   What are you doing here, Edward?

Son   Answer the question, Dad.

MP   Maybe we can talk about this later. Over a coffee and a wee roll and potato scone (*pronounced skone*). You still like potato scone?

Son   Scone.

MP   Skone.

Son   Scone!

MP   Fine. Yes. Sorry. Scone.

The **Son** *puts his head in his hands.*

---

[27]   In this play we had three types of plant: the two audience members with pre-prepared questions; Rob, the obvious plant (although still a lot of people didn't know for sure); and Andy, the deliberately low-key plant who quickly became part of the narrative.

MP   Are you Ok, Edward?

He moves down the aisle to the front.

Son   NO. No I'm not Ok. My partner's in hospital in a coma. What is the Select Committee for Contingency Strategy?

MP   He was your boyfriend? The one they found at the party?

Son   With his head bashed in by the Clyde, yes.

He texted me. Said he had found something. Something to prove what we've been saying all along. He said it proved that you're all in it together. All of you.

What is the Select Committee for Contingency Strategy?

Pause.

Journalist   Answer him, Edward.

MP   We have a lot of committees. I don't know anything about that particular one.

Son   You tried to shut him up.

MP   These are very serious accusations. Think about this before you go too far.

Son   You tried to have him killed!

MP   Nonsense.

Son   You were there that night! He followed you.

MP   And what evidence have you of such a ridiculous claim?

Silence.

None. Exactly. Because I wasn't there at all. Now let's all just calm down and /

/ **Journalist**'s *phone goes off and she grabs eagerly for it.*

Son   Petra. Is that it?

Journalist   That's it.

Son   We've got him?

Journalist   We've got him.

MP   This is ridiculous. I'm not staying here to be /

Journalist   / I have a friend at the Radisson. He's just managed to get me the CCTV footage from the night of the party.

MP   Footage of the attack?

Journalist   No. I got something better.

What room number were you in at the hotel . . . Sarah?

Pause.

MSP   I fail to see how that is relevant.

Chair   Answer the question, Sarah.

MSP   I don't remember what room I was in. What does it matter?

Journalist   You wanted evidence of a conspiracy. I have evidence. Hotel records show you were in room number 327 that night.

MSP   So?

Journalist   So who is this, captured on the hotel's CCTV footage making his way into room 327 on the night of the Yes campaign dinner?

Silence. Sarah's face drops as she looks at the screen.

It's Edward Hammer MP, is it not?

MSP   It appears to be. Yes.

Journalist   What were you doing there? What were you two discussing?

Silence. **MP** *looks up at* **MSP** *who looks horrified.*

As he goes to answer she shakes her head furiously.

MP   We weren't discussing anything.

We were . . .

MSP   No. Edward.

MP   We were making love. On the balcony.

Silence.

Son   What? Is that true?

Hesitation.

MSP   Yes.

MP   The heart wants what the heart wants.

Son   The heart?

MP   Who ever loves, if he do not propose

The right true end of love . . .

Son   Stop it with the fucking poetry!

MP   Edward, I realise you are angry at me for leaving your mother, but really, son, it was the right decision. For both of us. It just wasn't working anymore.

And as much as you would like this to be something more . . . sinister . . . there is no conspiracy, no plot to eliminate your friend, no secret committee, nothing but two people who happen to be on opposing sides of a serious debate, who fell in love. Like Romeo and Juliet.

Journalist   It was just an affair?

MP   Petra, no doubt you imagined this stunt as some sort of live job interview for the US-show circuit but all you've done is reveal yourself as the desperate, self-interested troll that you are.

The **Journalist** *looks crestfallen.*

So maybe we should wrap this up and /

Comedian   / No. We're not wrapping anything up.

MP   I think it would be best.

Comedian   You're lying.

Chair   Bruce, please don't.

Comedian   Come back to me then. Give me another chance.

Chair   You've had chance after chance. You'll never change.

Comedian   I have changed. I'm doing this. I'm being serious. Political. Isn't that what you wanted?

Chair   Wait. Are you running for parliament because you want to change things or because you want to impress me?

Comedian   Can't it be both?

Chair   Bruce. We. Will. Never. Get back together.

We're done.

It's over.

Pause.

Bruce   We need to tell the truth then.

Chair   I know. I know we do!

Me and Bruce were the ones on the balcony.

We were trying to . . . spice up our marriage . . . be all . . . risky. If I had known he was going to go straight downstairs afterwards and humiliate me in front of all those people I'd have pushed him off the fucking balcony.

Journalist   That's your arse on YouTube?

Chair   Yes. That's my fucking arse!

Journalist   Why are you lying, Edward?

MP   I'm not lying.

Journalist   You clearly are. Why?

Silence.

MSP   Because the truth sounds worse.

MP   Now, Sarah, just think about /

MSP   / It's over, Edward.

MP   Just take a moment /

MSP   / Edward and I /

MP   / Sarah, stop /

MSP   / Edward and I were joint heads of a committee /

MP   / Sarah /

MSP   / The Select Committee for Contingency Strategy.

Pause.

MP   Fuck.

Journalist   What was it?

MSP   It was a safety net. For both sides.

Son   A safety net for what?

MSP   For whatever happens.

It's logical. It makes sense. Come on, if we're being honest it's probably going to be a No, isn't it?

Son   With that attitude maybe.

MSP   We've seen the polls. It makes sense to try and get as much out of this as we can. In advance. Use the outside chance of a Yes vote as a bargaining tool. Secure more power.

MP   It's more than an outside chance. We've seen the polls, we're losing ground. A Yes vote is a disaster for us. It makes sense to minimise our loses by negotiating in advance. In case we lost everything. Is that not reasonable?

Son   So, whatever happens everything stays the same.

Pause.

MSP   More or less.

Pause.

MP   I think you'll find that we've actually, technically done nothing wrong here.

Son   What about Peter?

MP   Who's Peter?

Son   My boyfriend!

MP   We have no idea what happened to him.

Do we, Sarah?

Silence.

Sarah?

MSP   It was an accident. You have to believe that.

He broke into my car. Do you know that? He actually broke into it. Now that's a crime right there so . . .

MP   I want it on record that I had no part in whatever she is about to admit. Tell them, Sarah. Tell them.

MSP   He's right. Edward had left by this point. I had locked my copy of the agreement in my car. I was having a cigarette out front when I heard the alarm. I went back and caught him. Peter, is it?

Son   Peter.

MSP   Edward, I caught him red handed. He had broken into my car and was rifling through my briefcase. He had found . . . he had found the agreement.

What was I meant to do? Let him walk away with it. With my career? My future. Scotland's future.

He bolted down onto the path by the Clyde. I ran after him. It had been raining and he . . . he slipped and banged his head. Hard. On the railing – you know the little handrail by the . . . by the river.

I picked up the document. *My* document . . .

Son   And you left him there.

MSP   Not once did I touch him. He made the choice to break into my car.

He made the choice.

I did not touch him.

I have done nothing wrong.

Silence.

It's easy to think of us as monsters – career politicians driven by money and personal glory but that's simply not true. Yes, we are ambitious but most of us also believe that what we are doing is in the best interests of the people of this country.

I mean, why can't it be both?

This deal was necessary and I do not apologise for it. And I do not apologise for trying to keep it secret. There are things that should be secret. There are deals that need to be put in place and only work if they are secret.

Leaving him there. It was . . . It was in the best interests . . .

We were only trying to make sure we were protected.

If we lose.

Is it wrong to safeguard? Is it wrong to be careful?

Chair   Yes. Yes it is.

If you believe something is the right course of action but don't act because you're scared then what are you?

What are you?

Lights fade.

Music.

Smoke fills the space and it transforms into an ancient Scottish glen. The characters transform too as the music plays.

Act Two: Historical[28]

Characters[29]

Chair = Bishop Wishart
Comedian = Calgacus/Robert the Bruce
MSP = John Balliol

MP = Longshanks
MP's Son = Longshanks's Son
Journalist = Chronicler

Introduction

The music fades away and a voice-over begins.

Voice   Northern Scotland, AD 83. A Roman army led by Gnaeus Julius Agricola, having swept through Britain, raping, pillaging, conquering all who stood before them, arrive in the Scottish Highlands in the deep of winter. Waiting to greet them, the last unconquered British tribe, the Caledonians; thirty thousand Pictish warriors led by a chieftain known as the Swordsman or . . . Calgacus. This is the first evidence in recorded history of the people of Scotland.

Through the mist comes **Calgacus**, *wielding a powerful-looking sword.*

Voice   Before the battle Calgacus made a speech to his men.

Calgacus   Whenever I consider the origin of this war and the necessities of our position, I have a sure confidence that this day, and this union, will be the beginning of freedom for the whole of Britain.

To us who dwell on the uttermost confines of the earth and of freedom, this remote sanctuary of Britain's glory has up to this time been a defence. Now, however, the furthest limits of Britain are thrown open, and we are faced with that which is most fearful of all: the unknown.

If you are scared, find safety in the knowledge that your future under Roman rule is far more terrifying than any battle. For obedience and submission offer no escape but rather fuel the fire of oppression.

---

[28]   After an interactive Act One, this sudden and unexpected shift in time and location was accompanied by a change in form to a more traditional, fourth-wall drama. Nevertheless, the numerous parallels with Act One throughout Act Two ensured an active, if not directly participatory, role for the audience.

[29]   The doubling of characters was a key feature of *Wallace*, with direct equivalences between characters from Acts One and Two. This was partly a comment on the cyclical nature of history, but it also points to a metatextual playfulness in these scripts and the keen-eyed reader will find connections between plays as well as within them.

These robbers of the world, having by their universal plunder exhausted the land, they rifle the deep. To robbery, slaughter, plunder, they give the lying name of empire; they make a desert and call it peace.

Think of that which you hold most dear. Your families. Our people. Will you let them be torn from you, conscripted to fight in wars we did not start? Our goods and fortunes collected for their tribute, our harvests for their granaries? Creatures born to slavery are sold once and for all, and are, moreover, fed by their masters; but Britain is daily purchasing, is daily feeding, her own enslaved people.

Let us, then, a fresh and unconquered people, never likely to abuse our freedom, show forthwith at the very first onset what heroes Caledonia has in reserve.

Do you suppose that the Romans will be as brave in war as they are licentious in peace? To our strifes and discords they owe their fame, and they turn the errors of an enemy to the renown of their own army, an army which, composed as it is of every variety of nations, is held together by success and will be broken up by disaster. These Gauls and Germans, and, I blush to say, these Britons, who, though they lend their lives to support a stranger's rule, have been its enemies longer than its subjects, you cannot imagine to be bound by fidelity and affection. Fear and terror, feeble bonds of attachment, remove them, and those who have ceased to fear will begin to hope.

Few in number, dismayed by their ignorance, looking around upon a sky, a sea and forests which are all unfamiliar to them; hemmed in, as it were, and enmeshed, the gods have delivered them into our hands. Be not frightened by the idle display, by the glitter of gold and of silver, which can neither protect nor wound. In the very ranks of the enemy we shall find our own forces. Britons will acknowledge their own cause; Gauls will remember past freedom; the other Germans will abandon them. The forts are ungarrisoned; the colonies in the hands of aged men; what with disloyal subjects and oppressive rulers, the towns are ill-affected and rife with discord.

Whether you endure oppression for ever, or instantly dismiss the very notion, this field is to decide. The choice is yours. Think, therefore, as you advance to battle, at once of your ancestors past and of your descendants yet to come.

He stands triumphantly in the mist. The lighting changes to reveal two other figures behind him. The glen vanishes. They are sitting at a table in a thirteenth-century house.

The Bruce   There. I remembered it. Pay up.

Balliol   You do know it's total bullshit, right?

The Bruce   I don't care if it's bullshit. Pay up.

Wishart   You lost the bet, John. Pay the man.

Balliol *reluctantly passes* **The Bruce** *some coins.*

The Bruce   You don't know it was bullshit. Not for sure.

Balliol   It was written by a Roman.

The Bruce *shrugs.*

Balliol   How did he hear it?

Did the Romans all stand round and listen? Did their chroniclers write it down as he spoke?

In ancient Caledonian?

Or maybe Calgacus spoke Latin.

Or maybe, just maybe, Calgacus didn't even exist.

The Bruce   Yeah, right. Next you'll be saying that there's no evidence for Jesus Christ.

Wishart   You watch your fucking mouth, Robert.

The Bruce   Sorry, Bishop.

Silence.

The Bruce   Why would this Roman make the enemy sound so heroic then?

Balliol *puts a hand on his sword. Stands behind* **The Bruce.**

Balliol   Say I drew my sword right now and ran you through before you could even rise from your chair. Would it not serve me better to say you fought like a warrior but I bested you nonetheless?

Why defeat a lamb when you can vanquish a lion?

The Bruce *spins round, going for his own sword.* **Wishart** *places a hand on his shoulder.*

Wishart   I don't think it serves our great cause to be fighting amongst ourselves now does it?

They stare. Remove their hands from their blades. Sit down again.

Balliol   The stronger claim is mine, Robert. You know this.

The Bruce   I have proximity of blood.

Balliol   Primogeniture has been used since King fucking Edgar.

The Bruce   History and tradition is a weak argument in the face of logic, John.

Balliol   Has the church decided yet?

Wishart   Decided what?

Balliol   Which of us it stands beside.

Wishart   The church stands beside God, John.

Balliol   Why don't you answer the fucking question, Bishop?

Wishart I am a guardian of Scotland and a man of God, you will address me with respect.

Pause.

The Bruce Why don't we just kill him? Longshanks. Decide for ourselves who's king.

Wishart Decide for ourselves? Just like that? Outside of the law?

Like it or not, Longshanks is the only person who has the authority to make this decision.

We need him. He's impartial, legally savvy and more importantly his word makes it legal. And longstanding.

And besides which, he is family /

The Bruce / Oh come on /

Wishart / When Alexander died Longshanks mourned him like a brother, not a brother in marriage. I saw him. I was there. He is not an evil man.

Pause.

Balliol Yes, and if we kill him all we'd be left with is his son on the throne. An effeminate, lisping fourteen-year-old king who rumour has it was banned from jousting *for his own safety*. Imagine it.

The Bruce They say he prefers boys. The prince. Edward found him in his bedchamber 'wrestling' with a young Frenchman.

Balliol I find that hard to swallow.

The Bruce Funny, that's exactly what the prince said.

Balliol *and* **The Bruce** *laugh.*

Wishart Robert if you wish to be taken seriously I suggest you stop making foolish jokes. To accuse the boy of this is not only to accuse him of blasphemy but of heresy.

A noise from outside.

That's them. Give up your swords.

Both men hesitate.

Those are the conditions of the meet on the Tweed.

Balliol *gives up his weapon.*

Wishart I know it's prudent to be careful. That is why we have men surrounding us. They would not dare do anything. It is mutually assured destruction.

The Bruce *gives up his sword.*

The Bruce Who is coming this time?

Wishart Whoever comes? Delegates. Delegates. Delegates.

Balliol   And we are never closer to an answer.

Wishart   You two need to stick together on this. Don't fuck this up.

He exits with the swords.

Without a word, **The Bruce** *brings out a dagger. He looks at* **Balliol***.*

The Bruce   Just in case.

Balliol *nods.* **The Bruce** *hides the dagger underneath a basket on the table.*

Wishart *re-enters looking a little flushed.*

Balliol   What's up with you?

Wishart   They didn't send delegates.

The Bruce   Well, who did they send?

Through the doorway comes a **Chronicler***, a well-dressed young man and, finally, after a pause,* **Longshanks***.*[30]

They stand in shock.

Longshanks   You needn't worry, Robert, we have been thoroughly searched and found to be quite unarmed and my men are waiting outside. With your men. Quite amicably. I think I heard one of yours call to one of mine by name. It seems they have a mutual cousin. If you can fathom it.

The Bruce *stands very close to the basket, under which the knife is secreted. He places a hand on it.* **Balliol** *moves him away.*

Balliol   King Edward. A surprise. But a pleasant one. Isn't it, Robert?

The Bruce   Very pleasant.

Longshanks   May I present my son, Edward, Prince of Wales. He is here to witness how a king should conduct himself. What is expected of him. Who he must become.

We're going hunting later. Going to bag ourselves a couple of grouse. Aren't we, Edward?

Edward *says nothing.*

Longshanks   My chronicler will be documenting the meeting for the public record. His name is . . .

Balliol   Peter Langtoft.

Longshanks   Oh, you know each other?

Balliol   Yes. He wrote about me. What was it you called me again, Peter?

---

[30]   Scott Twynholm's sound design for this scene blended the sound of the regular passage of trains above the venue with the sound of war drums, which built tension here and climaxed dramatically on Longshanks's entrance.

Chronicler Toom tabard.

Balliol Ah yes, toom tabard.

The Bruce The empty coat. Sounds about right to me.

Balliol He used to be Scottish.

Chronicler I am still Scottish.

Wishart But you work for the king of England.

Chronicler We all work for the king of England.

Pause.

Wishart Shall we have some wine?

Longshanks *sits at the table. The rest of them join him.*

Longshanks Raise your glass, Edward.

Edward I don't like wine.

Longshanks Come on, Edward.

Edward I like mead.

Longshanks He has it in his head that he wants to understand the common man. I understand the impulse but he takes it too far.

Drink the fucking wine, Edward. You don't have to like it, it's just the way things are done.

The Bruce Yes, come on, Edward, just open your gullet and let it slide down.

Balliol *snorts.*

Wishart What shall we drink to?

Edward To Britain?

Wishart Yes. Of course. To Britain.

Hesitation.

All To Britain.

Longshanks *stops* **Edward** *from drinking. They wait until* **The Bruce** *and* **Balliol** *have swallowed and then drink.*

Longshanks So, Bishop Wise Heart. How long has it been?

Wishart Years. And Wishart will suffice.

Longshanks I remember consulting with my brother-in-law King Alexander on your appointment as Bishop of Glasgow. Do you remember?

Wishart I have not forgotten your part in my appointment.

Longshanks   I'm glad of that.

The Bruce *begins to laugh.*

Longshanks   I must confess I do not get the joke.

The Bruce   It's just . . . I mean this with respect . . . the balls on you. I mean, to come in here without guards.

Longshanks   But make no mistake about it, if anything happens in here to me my men will make sure that none of you leave this place alive. Nonetheless. Thank you. My balls are indeed . . . rather large.

The Bruce   Still. It's a risk. I could easily have a weapon hidden somewhere.

Longshanks   As a king you have two choices, Robert. Govern carefully and do things as they have always been done. Or govern boldly and take a risk. Now the latter might lead to a shorter life but the former . . . the former leads nowhere.

Balliol   And what of compromise?

Longshanks   Compromise makes losers of us all. You know that, John.

Now. I understand you are both interested in the position of king of Scotland. Unfortunately we only have one vacancy so . . . let's get down to it shall we?

Wishart   Indeed. We are here today to discuss the setting up of a parliament to decide who shall be the next king of Scotland. Present at this meeting are myself, Robert Wishart, Bishop of Glasgow and Guardian of Scotland in the absence of a living monarch. The two claimants to the throne of Scotland, Robert the Bruce and John Balliol, and . . . His Royal Highness King Edward I of England and His Royal Highness the Prince of Wales.

Now, where did we get to last time?

Chronicler   From the minutes of the last meeting it appears you rejected the offer of a parliament in Norham Castle.

It does not say why.

The Bruce   We're not going to decide this in England.

Longshanks   Why not?

Balliol   Symbolically, it does not look good.

The Bruce   We have our pride.

Pause. **Longshanks** *drinks.*

Longshanks   Pride. Ha.

He looks at the **Chronicler** *and nods. The* **Chronicler** *leaves his post.*

Longshanks   Edward, do you remember me telling you the story of King Æthelstadt?

Edward *nods.*

Longshanks   Would you like to recount the story for our friends?

Edward   No.

Longshanks   Edward. You like art. You like music. You like . . . acting.

Well . . . act the part.

Edward   There was a king. Called Æthelstadt. And he wanted to rule the whole of Britain. So he got an army and he marched north to fight King Constantine II of Scotland. Constantine had two options. He could fight or surrender. But he chose a third option. He went and hid. Like a coward. In a castle on a rock.

Longhshanks   Called?

Edward   The Rock Fortress of Dunnottar.

Longshanks   Good boy.

Edward   And he hid there for ages until Æthelstadt made him an offer. He could be king of Scotland but he had to admit that Æthelstadt was the real king. The proper king.

Longshanks   And what did Constantine do?

Edward   He accepted.

Longshanks   Why?

Edward   Because . . . because he wasn't an idiot.

Longshanks   But then . . .

Edward   But then people started calling him names and he didn't like it.

Longshanks   Because?

Edward   Because he was a proud man.

They were saying he was a coward and that he had sold the entire country. So he went and he made a deal with the Viking king and in the year 937 – that's like three hundred and . . . fifty years ago – the Scots and the Vikings marched south to fight the English in the Great Battle.

Longshanks   And what happened to them?

Edward   They were annihilated.

Longshanks   Æthelstadt lost thousands. Constantine, tens of thousands. They went their separate ways to lick their wounds, both with the same thought ringing in their ear.

Fuck. This.

This is not worth it. There were no winners in the Great Battle, only losers.

And all because of pride.

He stares at **The Bruce**. **Balliol**, *exasperated, takes a wander.*

Edward   Constantine ended up living in a cave. Did you know that?

Balliol   I did. In St Andrews.

Pause. The **Chronicler** *is standing by the door.*

Balliol   Expecting someone?

Chronicler   An important message.

Balliol   More important than this meeting?

Chronicler   It's not unrelated.

Back at the table.

The Bruce   Is that story meant to intimidate us?

Longshanks   No. It is meant to teach you. It is meant to teach us all.

Balliol (*to* **Edward**)   Do you know what Scotland used to be called?

Edward *shakes his head.*

Balliol   Pictland.

Edward *smiles.*

Balliol   And the king of the Picts was Constantine's father.

Edward   Constantine. From my story?

Balliol   The very same. His daddy, King Æd, was murdered and dethroned by a man named Giric, so he had to flee to Ireland. He grew in the household of the Gaels, bided his time, grew strong, gained the respect of the Gaelic people, then returned and . . .

Edward   And what?

The Bruce (*glancing at the hidden knife*)   Slit King Giric's throat with a knife.

United the Gaels and the Picts. And created Alba. Scotland.

We were conceived in blood. And we shall spill it to stay alive.

Right, John?

Hesitation.

Balliol   Right.

Wishart (*sotto, to* **The Bruce**)   That story's a myth.

The Bruce (*sotto*)   Aye, but it's a useful myth.

Longshanks   So we seem to have reached an impasse.

What do you suggest we do?

Pause.

Balliol   We could ask the people what they want. Let them decide.

Pause.

They all burst out laughing.

Longshanks   A plebiscite, that's all we need!

Pause.

Edward   Sir John.

Balliol   It's just John.

Edward   John.

Have you seen the Stone of Scone (*pronounced Skon*).

The Bruce   Scone (*Skoon*).

Edward   Skon.

The Bruce   Skoon.

Edward   Skoon.

Balliol   Yes.

I've seen it.

I plan one day to be crowned upon it.

Edward   Is it true that it comes from the Bible?

Wishart   Of course it's true. God told Jacob that stone would witness the coronation of every ruler of God's people until the Lord returns.

Edward   How did it get here?

Wishart   The prophet Jeremiah salvaged it during the sacking of Jerusalem. Brought it with him to Ireland.

Edward   So . . . the king of Scotland is the ruler of God's people?

Wishart   Couldn't have said it better myself.

Pause.

Longshanks   I think the stone might look good in Westminster Abbey.

The Bruce   Over my dead body.

Longshanks   I don't think so. We wouldn't let your dead body anywhere near Westminster Abbey.

He stands up.

Well, it appears we have nothing more to discuss. I have made a generous offer to conduct a parliament at Norham, the other side have rejected. We can go no further it seems.

Wishart   Wait. Wait. We are here to negotiate.

Longshanks   You are here to avoid a brutal and pointless war between the armies of Bruce and Balliol in which thousands of your people would surely die. That was my understanding.

The Bruce *and* **Balliol** *nod.* **Longshanks** *sits back down and sighs deeply.*

Longshanks   I am not an unreasonable man. In return for my choosing of the location I will allow you both to choose forty of the one hundred and four auditors who will sit on the panel.[31]

Wishart   Forty?

Balliol   Each.

The Bruce   That seems fair.

Balliol   So forty will vote for me and forty will vote for him.

Longshanks   You can always persuade people to change their allegiance. With a reasoned argument.

You will not receive a better offer.

Silence.

Wishart   Are we agreed?

Balliol   Yes.

The Bruce   In principle.

Wishart   Good. So may I suggest /

Longshanks   / I'm not finished yet.

I shall also require each of the claimants to the throne to submit to legal recognition that the realm of Scotland be held as a feudal dependent of the throne of England.

Silence.

The Bruce   You want to serve as supreme overlord of Scotland?

Longshanks   I wouldn't call it that but for the sake of avoiding a semantic argument.

Yes.

Please.

Balliol   You have no right.

Longshanks   Oh, I think you will find that the law is firmly on my side on this one.

---

[31]   Significantly, this was very close to the average audience size for these performances.

The Bruce   You come from a long line of kings who thought they could claim ownership of us. How many of them succeeded?

Balliol   The whole idea is a thing of the past.

Longshanks   The law lives in the past. It's only practised in the present.

The Bruce   Sixty years of peace and now this. This is a joke.

Longshanks   No. This world is far too serious a place for jokes. What we are trying to decide will affect the lives of millions for years to come.

Wishart   You say you have the law on your side.

The **Chronicler** *presents papers.*

Chronicler   The Treaty of Falaise decrees Scotland a vassal state of the English crown. English soldiers may occupy Scottish castles and the English crown will have the right of taxation over Scottish subjects.

Wishart   The Treaty of Falaise was vetoed by Richard Lionheart in 1189 in order to fund the Crusades. As well you know.

But the Treaty of Salisbury, which you yourself signed just two years ago, guarantees Scotland remains separate and divided from England according to its rightful boundaries, free in itself and without subjection.

Longshanks   Yes, in exchange for Queen Margaret's hand in marriage to my son the Prince of Wales. And the last time I checked Queen Margaret was dead of a fever. Edward here was quite distraught.

Edward (*under his breath*)   No I was not.

Longshanks   My brother-in-law, God rest his soul, pledged his allegiance to me before he died.

The Bruce   He may have pledged allegiance but he gave me his blessing as king of Scotland.

Longshanks   Well we only have your word for that whereas my claim was actually written down. Wasn't it, Peter.

Chronicler (*finding the document*)   The following is taken from a signed declaration from King Alexander III.

I become your man for the lands I hold of you in the Kingdom of England for which I owe homage.

Pause.

Wishart   Finish the quote, Peter.

Chronicler   What?

Wishart   Finish the quote.

Silence.

No?

OK. How about I finish it for you?

I become your man for the lands I hold of you in the Kingdom of England for which I owe homage . . .

Saving my Kingdom.

He never gave up Scotland.

Longshanks *laughs bitterly.*

Longshanks   And here was me thinking you were on my side, Bishop.

Wishart   I am a Guardian of Scotland, sworn to protect her in the absence of a living monarch. I am on the side of God. And His country, Scotland. I respect the king of England and the process of non-violent arbitration but I will not stand by and watch as our hard-fought-for autonomy is stolen from us through tricksy politicking and bastardy of the law.

The Kingdom of Scotland is not held in tribute or homage to anyone save God alone.

The Bruce *applauds this wholeheartedly.* **Edward** *joins in automatically.*

Longshanks *stares at his son. He stops clapping.*

Longshanks   Rhetoric will not do any good here. This is not a debate it is a legal process and legally I demand you produce evidence to prove that I am not in fact, *already* overlord of Scotland as we speak.

Wishart   I believe you are shifting the burden of proof there, Edward. One cannot prove a negative.

Longshanks   What if I said God does not exist. Would you not wish me to prove such a claim?

Wishart   Are you saying that?

Longshanks   All things desire to be like God, and infinite space is a mirror that tries to reflect His body. But it can't.

Wishart   St Francis of Assisi.

Longshanks   I am not God but legally if you cannot prove my claim false then you must relinquish ultimate authority to me.

Wishart   Legally, Edward, it is only a king who may relinquish a country. Is that correct? By the letter of the law.

Longshanks   Yes.

Wishart   And am I a king?

Pause.

Longshanks No.

Wishart No. I am a guardian. Not a king. And these men here are merely claimants. In the absence of a king we have no one with legal authority to grant what you are asking. Anything we say would be worthless. Legally.

The **Chronicler** *is scribbling away.*

Longshanks Strike that comment from the record.

The **Chronicler** *looks up.*

Longshanks Strike it!

The **Chronicler** *looks from* **Longshanks** *to* **The Bruce**. *Hesitates. But eventually complies.*

The Bruce Integrity is nothing when coins come rattling.

Longshanks Integrity? Do you really think that you are, somehow, *better* than us. That your way is more moral. More ethical. More . . . holy?

The Bruce Yes /

Balliol / No.

Silence.

Longshanks How far would you go?

The Bruce As far as it takes.

Longshanks Would you kill for it?

The Bruce For Scotland.

Longshanks Oh, don't pretend this is about Scotland. It's about ambition. And power. I would rather do this without spilling blood but if it came to it I would hammer every last Scot into the ground to get what I want.

How far would *you* go?

Would you kill John here?

Balliol He might die trying.

Longshanks Would you kill a child?

Balliol Of course not. None of us would.

Longshanks Really? What about Alexander II? Your dear dead king's father? His deeds are recorded in the Lanercost Chronicle, are they not?

Chronicler They are.

Longshanks There was a child. An infant. Not yet even in control of her own head. She was a distant relative to the Canmore line. A rival claimant to the throne. He couldn't take any chances could he? He couldn't take the risk. So he . . . Oh. What was it he did again?

Chronicler   The daughter who had not long left her mother's womb, innocent though she was, was put to death in view of the market place. Her head was struck against a column and her brains dashed out.

Longshanks   Do not sit there and presume to come from more noble, more moral, more principled stock then we. For we are all the same. We all call ambition altruism. We all stink of shit. All of us. I just have the good grace to admit it.

Pause.

You have a son do you not, John? A sole heir.

Balliol   *nods.*

Longshanks   Do you think for one second that if Robert the Bruce becomes Robert King of the Scots he will not dash that child's head on a column to consolidate his position?

Balliol   He would not.

Longshanks   Robert?

The Bruce *does not answer.*

Balliol   Robert?

The Bruce   I would not harm your son.

Balliol   I do not believe that answer.

The Bruce   Believe it or not it is my answer.

Balliol *stands up.*

Balliol   Look me in the eye and tell me you would not harm him.

The Bruce   Sit down, John, you're embarrassing yourself.

Wishart   Gentlemen, please /

Balliol *pushes* **Wishart** *aside.*

Balliol   Look me in the eye!

The Bruce *gets to his feet and goes chest to chest with* **Balliol**.

The Bruce   Sit down.

Balliol   Make me.

Wishart *steps between them.*

Wishart   This is exactly what he wants.

Balliol   Maybe I'll give him what he wants.

The Bruce   What do you mean by that?

Balliol   It's for the good of Scotland.

The Bruce   Giving in to his demands is not in the interest of Scotland.

Balliol   Would you rather war decides which one of us is king? My army far outreaches yours.

The Bruce   And I have the people.

Balliol   This is my destiny, Robert. You may have the fame but this is my life. This is what my life has been leading towards. I have paid my dues. It is my time. This is my time!

He goes for **The Bruce**. *They scuffle.* **Wishart** *separates them.* **Edward** *cowers.*

Longshanks *laughs.*

Longshanks   I do so enjoy watching the children squabble.

The Bruce *looks towards the upturned basket. He places a hand underneath.* **Longshanks** *is not paying attention. Now would be the time.*

A knock at the door.

The **Chronicler** *leaps to his feet and exits.*

Longshanks   It appears our messenger has arrived.

Wishart   With what?

Longshanks   Shall we take a seat?

They all sit in silence.

They continue to sit.

The door eventually opens.

The **Chronicler** *comes in holding a message.*

He gives it to **Longshanks**.

Wishart   What is that?

Longshanks *looks at the seal of the letter.*

Longshanks   Does anyone have a knife?

The Bruce *eyes the hiding place.*

Longshanks *reverts to ripping open the letter.*

He reads it. Smiles. Folds it up again. Sits back in his chair.

The Bruce   Well?

Longshanks   I want to give you one last chance. A parliament in Norham. One hundred and four auditors, forty chosen by each of you, twenty-four chosen by me.

My arbitration on succession to the throne of Scotland dependent on an advance legally binding agreement of recognition of the realm of Scotland as a feudal dependent of the throne of England.

No war. No bloodshed. Everything stays . . . as it is.

Deal?

The Bruce   We've already given you our answer.

Longshanks   John Balliol?

Pause. **Balliol** *is thinking.*

The Bruce   John?

Silence.

Balliol   No.

Scotland's not for sale.

Longshanks *sighs.*

Longshanks   Let the record show that King Edward tried to be reasonable.

He places the letter on the table. **Wishart** *picks it up and reads it.*

Longshanks   Are you familiar with medieval law, Bishop?

Wishart   A little.

Longshanks   Under medieval law if there are more than two claimants to the throne the arbitrator has final say. That is to say, he may take the advice of the appointed auditors, all one hundred and four of them, under advisement. He may make a unilateral decision and, in essence, hand pick the new king.

The Bruce   What's he talking about?

Wishart *has gone sheet white. He drops the papers to the table.*

Balliol   Bishop?

Wishart   He has other claimants.

The Bruce   Others?

Balliol   How many?

Wishart   Thirteen.

Stunned silence.

They have all agreed to his terms.

Pause.

Longshanks   So. The parliament in Norham will happen. If you wish to be considered, you will acquiesce to my terms now. If not, I have plenty of other, loyal claimants to choose from.

*The **Chronicler** slides contracts and quills across the table.*

The Bruce *and* **Balliol** *stare at them.*

But of course, you have your principles. And they're not for sale are they?

The Bruce   Bishop? What should we do?

Wishart   We don't have a choice.

Balliol   What do you mean what do *we* do?

Wishart   The church is backing Robert, John.

Balliol   What?

Wishart   He has made certain guarantees /

Balliol   / You made a deal?

Wishart   We have too much to lose, John. We can't risk going with you.

Balliol   Where's the risk?

Wishart   You're weak, John. Robert has the backing of the people. They believe in him.

Balliol   I'm weak?

Wishart   I'm sorry, John.

He turns his attention to **The Bruce***.*

Wishart   You've always wanted to be taken seriously, Robert. Well, now's your chance.

Sign it.

The Bruce *has frozen.*

Unseen until now, **Edward** *has edged his way towards the upturned basket on the table. He lifts it and finds the dagger. He picks it up.*

Balliol *sees him and lunges for the dagger, grabbing it from his hand and holding it to the child's neck.*

Everyone stops. **Longshanks** *stands up.*

Longshanks   What are you doing, John?

Balliol   I'm weak? Am I? Am I weak?

Wishart   Think about this, John.

Longshanks   I have hundreds of men outside just waiting for an excuse. All I have to do is shout.

Balliol   And all I have to do is slice.

Edward   Daddy.

The Bruce   What's the plan here, John?

Balliol   I have men outside too you know.

Longshanks   Put the dagger down now. We leave. Deal?

Balliol   Or I kill him then you.

Longshanks   Do you think you would have time?

Balliol   Worth the risk.

Longshanks   Is it? Then what? You die along with hundreds of your men.

Pause.

Balliol   You can't just get away stealing a country.

Longshanks   You cannot steal what is yours by law.

Edward *is whimpering now.*

Longshanks   Edward, you are a prince. And one day a king. Kings do not whimper.

Edward   I don't want to be king.

Longshanks   Of course you do. Everyone wants to be king.

Edward   Not me.

Longshanks   Well, what in hell do you want?

Edward   I want to be free! I want to go my own way. Make my own mistakes.
I don't need you anymore.

Longshanks   Edward, you do not get to choose your own future – that is absurd.
Here is what will happen. You will marry, you will bear an heir, you will continue
the history, honour and tradition of those who have gone before you and then you
will die.

Edward   I'm not getting married! I don't even like girls.

Pause.

Longshanks   Do you know what you are doing? You are inviting charges of heresy
upon yourself. You are arming your enemies against you.

Edward   They're not my enemies. You are my enemy. I loved him. I loved him and
you killed him.

Longshanks   Your dead brother spins in the ground to hear these words. How much
would Alonso give to be in your shoes now? And how much would I give that you
were in his grave.

Edward   What?

Longshanks   You heard me. Go on. Kill him. I have other heirs.

Balliol *stops.*

Longshanks   Do it then.

Go on.

Balliol *releases* **Edward**, *who falls to the ground.*

He drops the knife and goes to sign the document.

The Bruce   What are you doing?

Balliol   I still have a chance. With or without the fucking church.

The Bruce   You're selling out.

Balliol   I'm compromising!

Pause.

Longshanks   Looks like we have found our new king. There is no one on this list can come close to contesting his claim. Unless . . .

Longshanks *looks at* **The Bruce**.

The Bruce *looks at* **Wishart**, *who is now standing by* **Longshanks**.

The Bruce *walks to the table. He picks up the quill and signs the contract then slumps down in his seat. Defeated.*

Longshanks   Edward. Come with me.

Edward *looks up at his father. What choice does he have?*

He follows his father out of the room.

The **Chronicler** *gathers the contracts from the table and goes too.*

The Bruce *and* **Balliol** *sit in shame.*

Wishart   I have to journey north to meet the noblemen. What should I tell them?

Balliol   Tell them we did what we had to do.

Wishart *stands to leave.*

Balliol   Will you be travelling to Ayrshire?

Wishart   Aye.

Balliol   There's a landowner up there. Alan Wallace. He has a son.

The Bruce   William. William Wallace.

Balliol   Aye.

The Bruce He must be a man by now.

Wishart Is there a message?

Balliol Just tell Alan . . . tell him we might need to start getting them ready. The boys.

The Bruce Ready for what?

Balliol For what is to come.

Act Three: Personal[32]

Wallace *steps from the shadows.*

He passionately recites a passage from The Wallace *by Blind Harry to the audience. At the end he says . . .*

Wallace   Well, what do you think?[33]

The lights snap up and we see we are in his flat in Partick. An armchair and beer cans pointed towards a television set. A laptop sits on a table next to a copy of Scotland's Future *white paper, which is being used as an ashtray.*

He puts a hand to his ear. He's on a Bluetooth device.

No, I didn't write it. Blind Harry wrote it.

No, he's not a friend of mine. He's a famous poet. From the thirteenth century.

Of course blind people can write.

How? It's simple . . . they . . .

Well, I don't know how they do it but they can.

Look, wait a minute, I'm going to put you on speaker, this thing's pish.

He takes out the Bluetooth device and presses a button on his iPhone.

Secretary   . . . I mean, maybe I can see how the blind could write today but back then, well, it must have been very difficult. Maybe he had a friend who wrote his poems down for him. But, then, that's a lot of responsibility because you couldn't guarantee he was writing it down correctly could you? Until you heard it back.

Wallace   How did we get onto this anyway?

Secretary   You were telling me about your book and how it ended with a mention of William Wallace but you never actually meet him, which you thought was really clever but I just thought was a bit of a middle finger to the reader, and then I said there was no actual evidence that William Wallace even existed and you said /

Wallace   / Right. Yeah. So, you see. There is evidence. That poem.

Secretary   Even if he did exist, how do we know he did all those heroic things? Couldn't it all just be made up?

Silence.

Wallace   Are you going to put me through to Edward Hammer or not?

---

[32] This second shift occurred after an interval.
[33] We left a long enough pause here for the audience to wonder whether a response was expected.

Secretary   I've told you, I'm not.

Wallace   He owes me an apology.

Secretary   Why?

Wallace   Because he made fun of me on national TV and now I'm some sort of laughing stock.

Secretary   Mr Hammer has his own problems at the moment, sir.

Wallace   I don't care about that, I want an apology. And I want it to be made public.

Secretary   That is not going to happen. Is there anything else?

Pause.

Wallace   What should I do? People are laughing at me. There's memes. GIFs. Fucking auto-tuned YouTube clips. Listen.

He clicks on a button on a laptop. We hear part of his speech from Act One set to music.[34]

Secretary   It will all blow over. People forget quickly.

Wallace   I can't even vote. People are out there right now, deciding on Scotland's future without me. How is that fair?

Secretary   Well, you didn't reg /

Wallace   / I know I didn't register. I've lived here all my life. I'm Scottish. No one told me I had to register. I just thought . . . No one told me. Am I meant to guess? I've got proof of address, credit cards, a passport. What more do they need?

Secretary   May I suggest you take this up with your local Electoral Registration office?

Wallace   My what?

Secretary   Google. It.

Pause.

Will that be all, sir?

Wallace   This isn't over. I'm getting that apology.

He hangs up. Grabs a beer.

Stupid English cow. No. No. Not English cow. Just a cow. Who happens to be English. The matter of her Englishness is not related to the fact of her cowishness.

He turns up the volume on the TV and picks up his iPhone. He searches for something on his phone while the TV plays a recording of the debate from Act One. He reacts as he hears himself. A mixture of embarrassment and anger.

---

[34]   Another excellent contribution from Scott Twynholm, who had a lot of fun mixing this track from pre-recorded excerpts from Act One.

Wallace *finds what he's looking for, turns the volume down on the TV and dials a number. He puts down the phone as it begins to ring. Speakerphone again.*

Service Rep   Hello, Glasgow City Council Electoral Registration Service, Tanya speaking how may I assist you?

Wallace   Ah, Tanya doll, so nice to hear a Scottish voice. Listen, love, I've made a bit of a mistake and forgotten to register so I wonder if we can do anything about that, eh?

Service Rep   I'm afraid registration closed at the beginning of the month, sir.

Pause.

Wallace   Right. Yeah. So. What are we going to do about this then, Tanya?

Silence.

Service Rep   You're him aren't you?

Wallace   No. I'm not anyone I just want to/

Service Rep   /Yeah, yeah, you're Wallace.

She sings a little bit of the YouTube song.

Wallace   Listen. Is there anything you can do for me, Tanya?

Service Rep   Would you come to my kid's birthday party. Sing the song for him? He really likes it.

Wallace   It's not my song. I didn't make it . . . Jesus, could you just/

Service Rep   /Are you single?

Wallace   What?

Service Rep   Would you like to go for a drink sometime? I've never met anyone famous before.

Wallace   No. Look. Maybe. But, right . . . You need to get me on that register.

Service Rep   Will you do my kid's birthday?

Wallace   Yes.

Service Rep   And take me out?

Wallace   Yes.

Service Rep   Ok. I'll call you back on this number, yeah?

Wallace   Seriously?

Service Rep   I'm not promising anything but . . . I'll see what I can do.

Wallace   Oh my God, thank you, thank you so much.

Service Rep   No problem, I'll call you right back.

Wallace hangs up the phone. Happy. For now. He opens another can of Tennent's.

His phone goes – The Proclaimers, 'I'm Gonna Be (500 Miles)'.

He answers it.

Wallace   That was fast.

Dad   Your mum's bought a fucking laptop.

Wallace   Oh. Hi, Dad.

Dad   Don't you' Hi, Dad' me. Your sister told your mother you were trending on the Twitter and she went out and bought a fucking laptop. Five hundred pounds that's cost me. And she can't even get the bloody thing open.

Wallace   You saw it then?

Dad   Course I saw it. The whole street saw it. Your mother had friends over. Shortbread and fucking ginger wine was consumed. And then you appear. Dressed as William fucking Wallace. Your poor mother almost died of embarrassment.

I mean what is this obsession all about?

Wallace   You're the one who named me after him.

Dad   So what? If I'd named you Jesus would you have gone on nailed to a fucking cross?

Wallace   I was being patriotic. Like you taught me to be.

Dad   You know what's patriotic? Voting Yes. Are you going to do that? No. Because you didn't even register.

You know what this means don't you?

Wallace   What?

Dad   Your sister and your mother voted No. We were going to cancel them out. Me and you. But now, our family, it's a No family. A fucking No family. If we lose this, how can I ever look anyone in the eye ever again?

Wallace   We won't lose. We have to just believe.

Dad   No, Wallace, believing is like praying – it does fuck-all. If you want something to happen, you have to act. It's no good just believing on its own.

Wallace   I'm sorry, Dad, Ok? I'm sorry.

Silence.

I've finished my book.

Dad   Yeah?

Wallace   Yeah. I think it's pretty good.

Dad   Are the English characters balanced like I told you?

Wallace   Kind of.

Dad   What do you mean kind of?

Wallace   Well, I tried to make them, you know, not just evil villains, but it was . . . well, it's kind of better if they are . . . a bit evil.

Dad   It's too simplistic.

Wallace   No, coz . . . Well, I was doing research, like you said, about Longshanks and he was . . . well he was a total dick.

Dad   Look, son, when you're writing it doesn't matter what the actual truth was, you need to think about your critics. And if you're a Scottish writer and your English characters are too evil, you'll be called a racist. Even if those characters are, in reality, total dicks.

Wallace   I made the Scottish characters dicks too though. To balance it out.

Dad   Oh. Smart move.

Wallace   You think?

Dad   I do.

Wallace   I'm not an idiot, Dad. I just . . . I didn't know you had to register.

I thought it would be funny – to dress like Wallace.

And . . .

And up there, in front of all those people, those . . . proper people, when I was talking, I just got really really nervous, like I wasn't really even me anymore. I've watched it back and I don't . . . I don't even remember half of it. It was like I was there but not there. You know?

Dad   I know. I used to feel the same on book tours. Like I was an impostor or something. Like I didn't deserve to be up there talking.

Wallace   That's it. Exactly. Like I'm not good enough to talk or write about Scotland or independence because I'm not smart enough. I mean, who am I? What do I know?

Dad   Yeah. Exactly.

Wallace   I need people to know I'm not the idiot they think I am. I have to make this right.

Dad   Some things you can't make right. Some things you just have no control over.

Wallace   I don't accept that.

Dad   We like to think we have democracy, son, but really what we have is the illusion of democracy. True democracy cannot exist. Cannot.

Wallace   No. That can't be right.

Dad   Try not to think too much about it.

One vote never makes a difference anyway. See you, Wallace.

Wallace   *hangs up. Melancholy now. But he's had a thought.*

He picks up his phone and searches for something. Finds it. Dials another number.

It rings on speaker.

Researcher   Hello.

Wallace   Hello, is that David?

Researcher   Eh, yeah.

Wallace   This is Wallace Williamson. We spoke last week.

Silence.

Hello?

Researcher   What do you want?

Wallace   I want to come back on TV.

Researcher   To do what?

Wallace   I want to come back on and explain myself.

Researcher   I don't think they'll go for that.

Wallace   Who's they?

Researcher   I'm just a researcher. I'd have to sell it to the producer.

Wallace   We could do a sit-down interview.

Researcher   Interesting. Would you want to wear the costume again or . . .

Wallace   No. I should never have listened to you about the fucking costume.

Researcher   I think if you wore the costume again I could definitely sell them on an interview.

Pause.

Wallace   No. It has to be me. The real me. The man behind the myth. Yeah?

Researcher   I don't think I can sell that.

Wallace   But I'm famous.

Researcher   You're not famous.

Wallace   There's a YouTube clip..

Researcher   There's literally billions of YouTube clips.

Wallace   Mine has like a hundred thousand hits.

Researcher   Toddler licks hedgehog has fourteen million. You're not famous.

Wallace   People are laughing at me. I should get the chance to redeem myself.

Researcher   It doesn't work like that.

Wallace   That's not fair.

Researcher   Life's not fair.

Pause.

Wallace   When we go independent you're not going to even have a job, you know that. The BBC won't exist. Then we'll see who's laughing.

Researcher   Is that all, sir?

Wallace   No. It's not all. I want it pulled.

Researcher   What?

Wallace   The programme. I want it pulled from iPlayer.

Researcher   They're not going to do that.

Wallace   I demand they pull it.

Researcher   Wallace, I think the damage has already been done.

A tone.

Wallace   Fuck. That's my call waiting. You wait on the line, yeah, I won't be long.

Researcher   I'm not waiting.

Wallace   I'll be one minute.

Researcher   Please don't call this number again.

Wallace *switches calls.*

Wallace   Hello.

Service Rep   Hi, Wallace?

Wallace   Tanya?

Service Rep   You remembered my name.

Wallace   Did you do it? Can I vote?

Service Rep   Well . . . no.

Wallace   No?

Service Rep   Not technically, but . . . Listen, how about this. You take me out for dinner, come to my son's party, dressed, you know, in the costume, and in return you can have my vote.

Wallace   I can have your vote?

Service Rep   Yeah.

Wallace   You haven't voted yet?

Service Rep   Nah. Wasn't going to bother.

Wallace   You work for the voting registration service.

Service Rep   I know where I work.

Wallace   And you don't vote?

Service Rep   No point is there.

Wallace   What?

Service Rep   Well, they're all pricks and fannies aren't they? Politicians. All you're ever really voting for is which prick to be shafted by. Or which fanny to be . . . smothered with.

Wallace   What?

Service Rep   One vote doesn't make a difference.

Wallace   Would everyone stop saying that.

Service Rep   It's true.

Wallace   No it's not. What if everyone thought that?

Service Rep   Well, if everyone thought that then, you're right, one vote would make a difference. But they don't. So it doesn't. So. Pick me up at eight?

Wallace   No. Look. You should vote. For yourself. It's important.

Service Rep   I don't think it is.

Wallace   It is.

Service Rep   Why?

Wallace   Because . . . because otherwise you've just admitted that you've given up.

Service Rep   I have given up. And there's peace in that. I've accepted that my situation will never change. So rather than worrying about it, I just keep my head down and try to enjoy my life. Let the pricks and the fannies get on with it. If you don't think about them it's almost as if they don't exist.

What were you going to vote?

Wallace   Yes.

Service Rep   Ok. I'll vote Yes. Come pick me up at eight outside my work.

Pause.

Wallace   Fine.

Service Rep   Oh, and Wallace . . .

Wallace   Yeah?

Service Rep (*sexual*)   Wear the kilt.

The line goes dead. **Wallace** *checks the other line. Nothing.*

Wallace   Hello? David? Are you there? David?

Nothing. Depressed, he wanders around his flat. He picks up another beer.

He plays the YouTube clip one more time. Dances a little. It finishes.

He has another idea. Rushes to his phone. Picks it up, searches, dials.

Receptionist   Yes. What?

Wallace   Eh, is that Sarah Bailey's office?

Receptionist   We're not giving quotes to the press.

Wallace   I'm not press.

Receptionist   You're not?

Wallace   No.

Receptionist   How do I know that?

Wallace   I'm Wallace. From the TV. You know . . .

Receptionist   What? The guy dressed up as William Wallace who forgot to register to vote?

Wallace   Yes.

Receptionist   The same one with the song . . . (*She sings the song.*)

Wallace   Aye, the same one.

Receptionist   That was really silly of you not to register.

Wallace   I know!

Receptionist   I looked up your book you know. I placed an order on your website.

Pause.

Wallace   That was you?

Receptionist   What can I help you with, son?

Wallace   I . . . eh . . . I need to speak with Sarah.

Receptionist   I'm afraid that won't be possible.

Wallace   Not another one. Look, I demand to speak to her.

Receptionist   Well, you'll need to call the Queen in that case.

Wallace   The Queen?

Receptionist   Miss Bailey is currently at Her Majesty's Pleasure.

Wallace   She's with the Queen?

Receptionist   She's in prison.

Wallace   What?

Receptionist   Didn't you watch the end of the debate?

Wallace   No.

Receptionist   The man in the coma died last night, Miss Bailey has been arrested for manslaughter and the MP's son who was the dead man's lover has gone missing.

Wallace   That's ridiculous.

Receptionist   I know, but it's exciting, isn't it?

And that's not all. It was Roberta Bishop's arse on that YouTube clip!

Wallace   What?

Receptionist   And the journalist woman, she had evidence that the Yes and the No campaigns were in cahoots all along.

Wallace   What?!

Receptionist   So you see, this vote isn't really that important it seems. Whatever happens everything's going to be much the same.

One vote doesn't make a difference after all.

Silence.

Wallace   The MP's son has gone missing?

Receptionist   Yeah. It's a sin. They think he might have topped himself over the death of his gay lover. It's like *River* bloody *City*, I swear.[35]

Wallace? Are you still there?

Wallace   Eh. Yeah. Just . . . I need to go.

He hangs up on her. He's had an idea. He dials a number.

Secretary   Hello, Edward Hammer MP constituency office, Martha speaking, how may I help you?

Wallace   Martha, it's me again.

Secretary   Oh Jesus, look, I've told you, Mr Hammer does not accept unsolicited calls.

Wallace   I've got his son.

---

[35]   *River City* is a Scottish soap opera known for its . . . er . . . elaborate plot lines.

Pause.

Secretary   What did you say?

Wallace   I said I've got his son. And if he doesn't talk to me . . . I'll kill him.

Silence.

Martha. I know he's in his office today. Put me through to him. Or his son dies.

Secretary   One moment please.

Hold music. Something comical.

Wallace *waltzes around his flat to the music.*

It stops.

MP   This is Edward Hammer.

Wallace   Halle-fucking-lujah! Do you know how long I've been trying to get a hold of you?

MP   You have my son?

Wallace   Yeah. Yeah, I do.

MP   What do you want?

Wallace   What I want is very fucking simple. I want an apology.

MP   I'm sorry. There. Let him go.

Wallace   No, no, no. I want an apology on TV. Live. A press conference.

MP   Is that all?

Wallace   No. It's not all. I want you to endorse my book. And . . . and I want you to vote Yes.

MP   Vote Yes?

Wallace   Yeah. Vote Yes.

MP   And if I refuse?

Pause.

Wallace   I kill him.

MP   You'll never get away with it.

Wallace   I know. It will be mutually assured destruction.

MP   Ok. I will do everything you ask.

Will you let him go?

Wallace   As soon as you do the press conference.

MP   I have one arranged for this evening anyway.

Wallace   What's it for?

MP   I'm announcing my resignation.

Wallace   Oh.

Right.

Good. Fuckin' . . . good.

Pause

MP   Can I speak with him?

Wallace   With who?

MP   My son.

Wallace   No you can't talk to him. He's unconscious.

MP   Unconscious?

Wallace   Yeah. I hit him. With a . . . rolling pin.

MP   A rolling pin.

Wallace   Yeah.

MP   Do people still use them?

Wallace   I do. I make bread all the time.

MP   Me too.

Wallace   But you don't have a rolling pin?

MP   No. I don't. I use a bread maker.

Wallace   Pussy.

Pause.

MP   Well, I'm not apologising or endorsing your book until I know you've got him.

Wallace *hops around the flat trying to think. He finds a dirty kitchen knife on a plate.*

Wallace   Fine. Right. Well . . . I'll send you a finger then.

MP   A finger?

Wallace   Yeah.

MP   Ok.

Wallace   Ok?

MP   Yes. I suppose that would prove it.

Wallace *is looking at his own hand now.*

Wallace   Fuck. I mean, fine. Yeah.

He puts his hand down and lines up the knife against his finger.

Wait. It would never get to you on time. Your press conference is tonight.

MP   Yes it is. So what are we going to do about this then?

Silence.

Wallace   Aaaargh! All I wanted was just to go on TV and plug my fucking book and you had to make me look like an idiot.

MP   I think your book does that on its own.

Wallace   I was going to write about independence. A political thriller or something but . . . I mean, do you know how difficult it is to write about independence?

MP   I can only imagine.

Wallace   You have to learn so much shit. And it's not interesting shit. It's boring shit. Interest rates and economic strategy and . . . It's just fucking dull.

MP   Well, why do it then?

Wallace   I don't know. Because . . . because it feels important. And I want people to think I'm intelligent. But I'm not. I mean, I'm not an idiot but . . . Maybe, deep down . . . I know. It's all for nothing.

MP   How is it all for nothing?

Wallace   Well, you know, Yes, No . . . it's always going to be more or less the same isn't it?

MP   That's not a very positive message.

Wallace   Yeah, well, I don't owe you a positive message do I?

Pause.

MP   No. If I believed things couldn't change I wouldn't have gone into politics.

Wallace   Why did you then?

MP   To try to help people.

Wallace   Ha. Yeah, good one.

MP   It's true. Somewhere along the line it became a career and then . . . yes, ambition does come into it, I won't deny it, I wanted to be leader but only . . . only so I could have more power to help people.

Wallace   You really believe that?

MP   I think so. Yes.

Wallace   Well, I want to help people too. I want Scotland to be a place that helps people. Not people like me who are basically doing alright . . . but people who need our help. I'm not voting Yes for me. I'm voting Yes for them.

MP   Very eloquently put.

Wallace   That's what I was meant to say last night. On TV. But I got all . . .
flustered.

MP   Well, if it's any consolation, people will have forgotten about you by this time
next week.

Wallace   Aye, well . . . thanks.

Pause.

MP   Why is independence so important to you?

Wallace   I don't know. It just . . . it just seems right. Who doesn't want to be
independent? Make their own mistakes. Have their own successes. Take control of
their life. Like, when I was sixteen I wanted to go out to the pub with my mates but
my dad wouldn't let me and I was, like, I'm old enough to have sex but not old
enough to drink, that's mental and my dad was, like, while you live under my roof
you'll go by my rules. So I left school and got a job as an office junior and I moved
into this flat and the very first night I went out drinking with my mates and I drank
beer and ate peanuts and then I came home and pebble dashed my bedroom wall with
nutty vomit. It was a disaster. But I remember thinking . . . I made this choice. This is
my disaster.

MP   Yes, well, I know something about children wishing to make their own way.

Wallace   And now, ten years later, I've got good at it. Being independent.

I've worked out how to do it. And you know Scotland, right . . . see if the oil does run
out in thirty years or whatever . . . I reckon that's time enough for us to have worked
out how to be independent so that after it does run out, we'll be fine.

Like, you know, before I became a writer. I tried doing other things but I realised very
quickly that writing was my thing. And at first I thought, shit, writing's not like a real
thing, like an important thing or anything, it's just making up stories and that. But
then I made up with my dad and he's a writer and he told me, Wallace, writing is
about capturing the feeling of a nation, writing is giving voice to ideas, writing is
speaking for those who have no voice. So that's what I try to do now. And I'm not
brilliant at it. But it makes me feel like . . . like I'm helping. In some way. In
my way.

See I'm Scottish. And I'm proud to be Scottish. But I don't fucking hate . . . I don't
hate anyone. It's not about anyone else. It's about us. And my therapist says it's ok
sometimes to be selfish.

You need to look after yourself. You are not responsible for other people's happiness,
Wallace. You are responsible for your own.

See, Scottish people, we're different. Not in a major way, I mean, really human beings,
we're all the same aren't we, we all want the same things, but . . . Scottish folk . . .
We're slightly different as well. See, the other day, this wee Japanese tourist was on
my bus and he asked the driver where his hotel was and the driver didn't know so, like,

four or five people on the bus went down to the front and all, like, debated over where
the hotel was and how best he should get there. The wee guy was shocked – he
actually looked frightened at first until he realised . . . this is just Scottish folk! This is
just what they're like. And I've no doubt that other places in the world folk are like
that too but . . . but we just take so much pride in that. In the end one of them got off
the bus – it wisny even his stop – and he walked the wee Japanese guy to his hotel.
Right to the front door. I love that. That's us. We like to take care of people.

Why won't you let us?

MP   You don't have my son do you, Wallace?

Wallace   How did you know?

MP   Because my son is sitting in reception with my secretary.

Pause.

Wallace   Why did you let me go on like that?

MP   I thought it might be funny.

Pause.

Have you ever been divorced, Wallace?

Wallace   Never been married.

MP   If you ever get divorced, do it right. Especially if you have kids. Stay in touch.
Co-operate. Don't make an enemy of her. Make the separation work.

Wallace   Stay friends.

MP   If possible.

Wallace   Have you called the police?

MP   All calls to this number are recorded but . . . no. No police have been called.

Wallace   Thanks.

MP   No problem.

Wallace   You're not going to vote Yes are you?

MP   I already voted, Wallace.

Wallace   Oh.

Silence.

We did this thing at school and I've never been able to get it out of my head. There's
this train, right, and it's hurtling down this track and there's five people up ahead tied
to the tracks and there's a lever that will send the train onto a different track but on
that track there's one guy tied up. Do you push the lever?

MP   Well, obviously you do.

Wallace   Yeah, coz you're saving the lives of the five folk. But you're killing one. One who was originally safe.

MP   You have to make decisions based on the greater good.

Wallace   Right, yeah. But how about this. The train's heading towards these five folk and you're on a bridge with a big fat guy and if you push him off he will stop the train. He'll die but they'll live. Do you push him.

MP   No.

Wallace   Why not?

MP   Because . . .

Wallace   It's the same action as pushing the lever, you're just pushing a guy.

MP   That's not the same then is it?

Wallace   You wouldn't do it?

MP   Wait, who's tied these people up anyway?

Wallace   I don't know, some psycho.

MP   And why have I only got two options. Couldn't I find another solution?

Wallace   No. Those are the options. Do you push the fat guy?

MP   No. I don't believe it's right to kill someone.

Wallace   In any circumstance?

See I was brought up religious, right. I was told there are moral absolutes and that was that. But it's not that simple is it? So this dilemma, it really hurt my head.

I mean, what if they were babies on the track and the guy was like . . . an escaped murderer. Or he was about to commit suicide anyway. Would you push him then?

MP   I don't know. Maybe.

Pause.

Wallace   It's difficult isn't it? It used to keep me up nights. But then I thought of something. How do we know he would stop the train?

See, we can't predict the future with absolute certainty so how would we know? For sure. I mean the train might plough through him and kill the babies so then you've killed someone and saved no one. We don't know what's going to happen. All we can do is act in the way we believe is correct in the moment. Some people would push him, others widny. There's no right or wrong and we'll never know if the road untaken was really the right one because the minute we don't take it, it disappears forever.

All we can do is make a decision based on our own ideological beliefs. Nothing's certain but at least you can look yourself in the mirror that way.

Pause.

MP   Well, Wallace, I'd best be off. I've enjoyed talking to you.

Wallace   Yeah. Me too.

MP   I'll apologise in my press conference if you still want me to.

Wallace   Only if you want to.

Pause.

MP   Goodbye, Wallace.

Wallace   Goodbye.

The Majority

To The Arches Theatre Company

Rob Drummond performs *The Majority*

The Majority was first performed by Rob Drummond in the Dorfman Theatre at the National Theatre of Great Britain, London, in 2017.

Rob   Rob Drummond

Director   David Overend
Stage Designer   Jemima Robinson
Lighting Designer   Michael Harpur
Music and Sound Designer   Scott Twynholm
Associate Video Designer   Mogzi Bromley-Morgans
Stage Manager   Ben Donoghue
Production Manager   Anna Anderson

With thanks to Ben Power, and to Roxy Cook for her invaluable assistance throughout rehearsals.

Originally co-commissioned by The Arches and the National Theatre.

Act One

This play should be performed by one actor. The audience have voting pads by which they can vote only YES or NO.

A swarm of bees fly around the room as the audience enter.

Scene One: March 2016

A mug-shot image of **Rob Drummond** *appears in the space.*

Rob   23 March 2016. I am under caution at Victoria Road Police Station in Aberdeen. My rights have been read, my prints taken and my soul digitally removed by a 2010 Canon power-shot camera.

What I am about to tell you is the truth. More or less. But in deciding which events, quotes and facts to leave in and which to eliminate I am . . . focusing reality for you. For your benefit. You may find yourself thinking, that's too neat to be true. And it will be. I will have moved a pleasing motif, an image, a line, a thought, from one place to another because . . . this is theatre after all.[1]

This mug shot, for example. It happened. But we couldn't get our hands on the real ones so we mocked them up. For you.

So. How did I, a respectable, mild-mannered, law-abiding individual with no criminal record, end up here?

Scene Two: Present Day

Rob   Hello and welcome to *The Majority*. Tonight, I will be telling you a real story from my life and asking you all to think seriously about democracy. I'll also be asking you to vote on a series of propositions, some that will ask you to think and others that will ask you to act. Some of these votes may become a little bit ethically fraught, but please trust me because I need your help here. Together it is my hope that we can reach some sort of agreement and find an answer to the question: how did we get here and how do we get out?

---

[1]   When we tell an audience that a play is 'more or less real' we consider this to be a kind of indirect disclaimer, a nod and a wink that, of course, we made some of this up. It invites the audience into the world – instant stooging them, to borrow a magician's phrase – and we have never had a problem with making stuff up in order to better tell a bigger truth. After this show we found that most people had simply believed the show without question, which did give us pause to think about the ethical ramifications of that as *The Majority*, more than any other we have ever made, was really very far from the truth of Rob's life. In the end, though, the line we draw is in whether or not we believe we are conning our audiences, doing them a harm, causing them grief, or simply playing with them. We like to think we don't cross that line but we are always open to hearing whether and how we may have.

This is how the voting will work. I'll put a proposition to you and it will be your job to press one if you agree with that proposition and two for no. And don't panic. If you don't know the answer, if you don't understand the question, you don't have to vote. Simple.

So let's test the pads out shall we. An easy one to start.

This community understands and accepts the voting system for the show.

That is the proposition. Press one for YES if you agree with this. And obviously two for NO. Vote now.

The audience vote. **Rob** *comments on the result, shown somewhere in the space.*[2]

Who voted no? You are free to leave the theatre at any time if you're not happy with the community decision.

Right then, let's get started with something of vital importance.

The latecomer policy.

Some of you won't mind latecomers shuffling into their seats, disrupting the show, making noise and putting the performer off, taking you out of the carefully constructed world he's created. And others, like me, will find it nothing short of unacceptable. You know the start time of the show, I mean, come on. We all managed it.

So. The second proposition I wish to put before you is as follows.

This community wishes to ban all latecomers.

Vote one for YES and two for NO. Vote now.

The audience vote. **Rob** *comments on the result.*[3]

We've shut the borders.

Or:

We've opened the borders!

---

[2]   Having said that we don't coerce our audiences, this is certainly venturing into that territory. As the show developed, we made this clear, even adding a line that went something like, 'If you vote no the show will end immediately, so be careful. There will be no refunds.' The idea was to playfully ask the audience to be complicit with the entire show, and this wasn't lost on them as they voted. They were allowing the show to go ahead so it also demonstrated a mutual trust – they trusted Rob not to abuse the power they were granting him and he trusted them not to vote the wrong way and stop the show dead in its tracks. Trust between the performer and the audience is almost entirely what good solo shows are based on. If the performer doesn't look confident, easy, happy to be there, then the audience don't trust them and the show fails. Likewise, if audience members play up, shout things out, try to derail the show, the performer doesn't trust them and the whole thing fails. By offering them something and putting your trust in them to give it to you, you demonstrate respect and almost instantly there is a bonding effect you can palpably feel in the room. The performer makes themself vulnerable and so do the audience. And then we're all going on a journey together, needing each other to reach our destination.

[3]   Unlike the free improvisation of *Bullet Catch* and *Wallace*. Rob's comments here were improvised, but much more tightly controlled; effectively rehearsed based on a limited range of outcomes. The more comfortable he got with the show the more licence he could have to go off script and see what happened. In *Bullet Catch* that was ok but here, where the show was much more about communicating a monologue, rather than getting to know an individual audience member, he had to watch not to go too far.

The policy is put in place.

Now, before we continue I'd like to get a rough idea of who today's community is. So, if you could please answer YES or NO to the following propositions as they relate to you personally.

Rob *asks a series of questions which may include some or all of the following:*

I am a liberal.

I am white.

I am male.

I am a social media user.

I believe voting should be mandatory.

I believe violence is sometimes the answer.

I believe in absolute freedom of speech.

I believe I can make a difference.

Rob *collates the results in their entirety and creates a profile for the community. Something like . . .*

We have a majority of liberal, white, non-male, social media users. This community believes voting should be mandatory and violence is sometimes the answer. This community believes in freedom of speech. This community believes they can make a difference.[4]

That is who you are.

The majority has spoken.[5]

---

[4] On the whole 'the majority' was the same in each performance (white, liberal and non-male), though its relative size varied somewhat. Despite being overwhelmingly liberal, there was only limited support for absolute freedom of speech ('very liberal' Rob quipped). This perhaps indicates that audiences were already prepared to put boundaries on what opinions they found acceptable to air.

[5] By asking the audience to mark their identity at the start of the show, a direct statement was made about who would be calling the shots. This was a provocation that highlighted the divisions and the inevitable rejection of minority opinions, but also set up an 'in crowd' that the production then set out to disrupt and challenge. This section also had an important function in its consciously problematic use of subjective terms, presented out of context and put forward for a vote without the opportunity to explore their ambiguity. Terms like 'liberal' are open to interpretation and likely to mean different things to different people. We had a lot of discussions about this section and were at times considering cutting the whole thing. We believe that being provocative and owning it is important and as long as you do it knowingly then it's ok. We are not telling the audience who don't fit the majority description they are not welcome – we are saying, look at what happens when we democratically decide things – we automatically create a minority every single time. And this show is about how we deal with that problem. How we talk to people who fundamentally disagree with us. It's risky, though, because get it wrong and you're not so much playing with the audience as bullying them. Retaining the frustration that this caused, which sometimes seemed to border on anger, was a conscious strategy. The script was worded carefully and the pace and tone of the performance were given a lot of attention. But the temptation to remove this section was avoided as it was considered important to engage the audience directly with the problem of majority rule early in the performance. These were the problems that the play set out to grapple with and by the end the aim was to suggest possible solutions

Scene Three: September 2014

Rob   It's 19 September 2014. The day after Scotland voted against its own autonomy.

I'm in George Square and it's a mess of blue and white flags and vodka and Irn-Bru bottles. The clean-up has begun and all around sit teary-eyed Scots trying to come to terms with what has happened, as No voters celebrate and police keep order and offer hugs.

There are 1,617,989 Scots who need hugs this morning. And 2,001,926 'cunts', as Frankie Boyle helpfully points out on Twitter. Isn't that nice?

A car drives by with a NO sticker on the back window. It stops at a red light. Someone throws a vodka bottle at it. I slip away.

As I say, I'm looking for agreement, not conflict.

England, I'm told, breathed a sigh of relief at the result. After all, communities are stronger together. Unless you're talking about European communities of course.

How many of this community breathed a sigh of relief? Let's see shall we?

This community believes that Scotland should be an independent country.

They vote. **Rob** *comments on the result.*[6]

Selfish fucking bastards.

Or:

It's a shame this counts for nothing isn't it?

A drunk comes up to me and puts his arm around me.

Drunk   Sokaypal. We'll getemanexttime!

Rob   He thinks I'm one of them. He thinks I voted Yes.

When the truth is . . .

The truth I've never told a soul in Scotland is . . .

I didn't vote at all.

The most important referendum of my life, something that would undoubtedly affect my future and . . .

I didn't vote.

Why?

I'm not sure I even know.

---

[6]   70 per cent of the audience voted No to this proposition. The question of Scottish independence does not have the same liberal support base south of the border. While statistics are not available for the same vote in *Wallace* (which was held in the week of the real referendum), the result went overwhelmingly in the other direction.

Maybe it was something to do with the campaign. It had just been so . . . shouty.

And somewhere along the line I had just decided . . . whatever the result, I couldn't see that the shouting would ever end.

I wanted everyone to agree but I knew they never would so . . . Why bother?

But clearly I was feeling guilty. My gesture of remorse? Coming to George Square to offer myself on the altar of the aftermath.

The drunk is still idling nearby. He's a big wee guy with little arms resting on a pot belly. A scrawny beard on a face that launched a thousand Rizlas. He's constantly moving, checking over both shoulders, dancing on the balls of his feet, like an out-of-shape boxer.

I accidentally meet his gaze once more and he launches into a tirade.

Drunk   Fucking No voters, eh? Voting against things becoming fairer. I mean who votes against fairer? Who votes against autonomy? Eh? One point six million people. Ignored. It makes me fucking sick.

Rob   Yeah. Terrible.

Drunk   I take it you voted Yes?

Rob   Yeah. Course I did.

Drunk   Quite right.

Rob   A friend of mine didn't vote at all.

Drunk   Scum. I mean that. Scum. Contemptible. One thing worse than someone who doesn't shout their opinion squarely in the opposition's face and that's someone who doesn't have an opinion to shout.

Rob   The drunk looks over his shoulder as a police van enters the square. He hands me his wallet.

Drunk   Here. Hold this for me.

Rob   And he's off. Bobbing through the square, ducking and diving in and out of the crowd until . . . he vanishes.

I wait there for him. I wait for two hours. But he never comes back.

And I've still got his wallet.

I take a look inside. No money. A few business cards. A bank card. A Scottish Socialist Party membership. Nothing that would even hint at an address. The name on the membership is Eric Ferguson.

And I realise. The reason he gave me the wallet. He didn't want the police to be able to identify him.

Pause.

As soon as I get home I look for Eric on Twitter and find him almost immediately.

I look through his recent posts.

Today is a dark fucking day for Scotland. A socialist country run by capitalist scum. And we just voted to keep it that way. I'll be drinking in Glasgow if you need me.

Look out! Crooked Tory councillors don't care about you. Nazi scum.

How the Illuminati is controlling the banks.

His handle is Eric@SocialJusticeApiarist (that's a fancy word for a beekeeper) and his chosen picture is him standing in a field covered in bees.

Now. I didn't have to make contact with him. It was his fault and there was nothing in the wallet he couldn't replace. But I was feeling . . . lost. Guilty. I should have voted. I want to want to vote. I want to feel like I can make a difference again. Maybe someone like Eric can help me find that.

I sent him the following message.

Dear Eric, you gave me your wallet in George Square today. I imagine you'll be wanting that back. Let me know an address and I'll be happy to send you it.

I don't really know what I was expecting to happen. All I knew was that this was a guy I had to get to know better.

Scene Four: Present Day

The latecomers policy is put into action. Either audience members can be seen being denied access on a screen, or they are welcomed in with a fanfare.[7]

In the event that no audience are waiting to come in **Rob** *just skips ahead to the next part of the show.*

The Trolley Problem.[8]

Rob   There is a runaway train car heading towards five railway workers. There's no time to warn them. They will die if it hits them. You are standing by a lever which, when pushed, will send the train car onto a siding on which there is a single workman. If you push the lever he will die, but the five workers will be saved.

---

[7]   Including audience members in your work and inviting them on stage is always a gamble. You have to simply give up power for a moment and see what they do and how they react. Then deal with it. On press night we had a very dramatic individual who couldn't have looked more like a plant had he been wearing leaves and sitting in a pot. But there is absolutely nothing you can do about that and if you want to genuinely play with the audience you have to accept that sometimes someone is going to knock over your tower. The bargain is that for every ten moments of beauty you get from it you're going to have a couple of ugly moments too. But the way to deal with them as always is to remain calm and smile.

[8]   For these sections, David ensured a dramatic shift in the stage aesthetic, with a signature train sound motif bringing a sense of foreboding into the space, along with a tight spot in place of the 'game-show' lights of the regular voting sections. We also introduced a live-feed camera which picked up Rob in close-up from various corners of the space, projecting his image onto the monitors and the circular hive-like structure suspended above the playing space. Rob delivered the trolley scenarios directly to the camera. This is a common feature of these performances: a sudden shift into a new scene, often with a very different atmosphere and form. We enjoy trusting the audience to catch up and just launching into something new without over explaining. This requires a constant, active process of renegotiating the terms of the performance.

What is the correct decision?

The proposition is this . . .

This community would push the lever.

1 for YES or 2 for NO. Please vote now

The result comes in and hangs in the air.[9]

I can see some of you are anxious to explain your answer. Unfortunately that's not how this works.[10]

Scene Five: May 2015

Rob   15 May 2015. Nine months after I contacted Eric. Without reply. I've still got the wallet. I can't bring myself to throw it away. I'm still clinging to the faint hope that this man will be the key to bringing me out of my political funk.

Unlikely now.

I'm round my mother's house for Sunday dinner and the topic of the wallet comes up. As it usually does.[11]

Mum   So still no reply?

Rob   No, Mum.

Mum   It's just so strange.

Rob   My mum is even more obsessed than I am. It's really unhealthy. She's suggested everything from hiring a private detective to randomly driving round Scotland with the window down shouting, 'Eric!'

---

[9]   The results of these votes suggest a complex negotiation of beliefs and ethical positions, which resulted in a slight increase in abstention over the first four 'trolley problem' questions, as it became increasingly difficult to take a clear stance on the escalating scenarios. We took the decision not to display the number of abstainers for reasons of dramatic clarity, but this was very much an active choice available to the audiences and those votes with high degrees of abstention indicate a rejection of the binary choice available.

[10]   Here, we are deliberately blocking participation in order to generate a productive frustration with the limitations of the voting system. A risky strategy, perhaps, but when the chance to debate comes at the end of the show, it seemed to have had the effect of building dramatic tension. The lack of dialogue at this point is an enactment of the problem that *The Majority* attempted to address.

[11]   This scene initially included Rob's dad, a character who was omitted from the performed version. This is a good example of a common trend: thematic and dramaturgical considerations outweighing any notion of responsibility to autobiographical veracity. Thematically, it's better if these characters are not together, as it's about fractures in unity and the difficulties of maintaining a relationship with those with whom you hold disagreements. And dramaturgically, it was just very difficult for Rob to pull off being three characters and maintain the focus and drive of the scene. We sacrificed comedy for story, which was the right thing to do. Also, the character of Rob's mum is actually nothing like the real thing. She's not a Tory for starters. In another play Rob showed a genuine photograph of her and told the audience 'that's not really her' which was more or less an in-joke for just him, but these small fictions can serve to place a helpful level of doubt in the audience's mind and to encourage attentiveness to the nature of truth and deception.

Mum, it's up to him to reply if he wants it.

Mum   What did you say he did? Sold his vote on the T-Bay?

Rob   eBay.

Mum   That's no right. I mean, my father fought and died so that . . .

Rob   Your dad's still alive! We saw him last week.

Mum   Other people's fathers then! They fought and died so you could vote.

Rob   No. They fought so I could be free to choose whether to vote or not!

Mum   I like voting. Makes me feel like I'm doing my bit. And I always get the answer right.

Rob   What?

Mum   I always get it right. Like independence. I voted No and that was the right answer.

Rob   There's no right answer, Mum.

Mum   Then why do we bother asking people?

Rob   Mum, something doesn't just become right because most people think it.

Mum   Aye it does. That's how it works. We decide what's right by voting on it. Don't we?

Rob   Right! This coming from a Tory voter.

The Tories have just won the general election with a bigger majority than anyone expected. And the SNP have yellow washed Scotland. The map of the UK looks famously like Maggie Simpson.[12]

The country has never been more divided.

Rob   Are you serious about this, Mum.

Mum   All I know is that I voted Conservative and the Conservatives won.

Rob   So let me get this right, Mum. You think that if a majority of people want something, that automatically makes it right?

Mum   Do you have a better way of deciding?

Rob   But people used to think slavery was ok.

Mum   In those days maybe it was.

---

[12]   Google it, it's true!

Rob   What the fuck did you just say, Mum?

Mum   Language!

Rob   Are you really telling me that slavery was once acceptable?

Tell me this. If Northern Ireland had a vote on gay marriage and the result came back No, would that mean it was immoral to be gay in Northern Ireland?

Mum   If that's what those people decided. Otherwise what's the point in asking them?

Rob   Fuck. You're a bigot. You're a total bigot.

Mum   Ocht, don't get all worked up. It's not like it's real anyway. It's all just nonsense.

It would just be nice if everyone could agree, wouldn't it?

Rob   Yes. It would.

Mum   As long as what they all agreed with was what you thought already.

Rob   I silently fume. My mum has a habit of doing this. Stumbling into very good points.

Mum   Maybe you could send him another wee message. About the wallet.

Rob   Mum! It's over. Move on! He's not going to reply!

And would you believe it . . .

At this precise moment . . .

Nothing happened. But then later, as I was getting ready for bed . . .

My phone beeped.

Eric had finally replied.

Scene Six: Present Day

Rob   There is a runaway train car heading towards five railway workers. There's no time to warn them. They will die if it hits them. You are standing on a bridge with a large fat man. If you push this man off the bridge his girth would be enough to stop the train car. He would die but the five workers would be saved.

It's the same as before, but you have to push a human, not a lever.

What is the correct decision?

The proposition is this . . .

This community would push the fat man to his death.

Vote now.

They vote. The result simply hangs in the air. Presumably fewer people have voted to push the man than the lever. In which case **Rob** *can say . . .*

It's different when you have to push a person, right? And I bet we had more abstentions this time. Is that because the question was more difficult?

You can't just not answer the hard ones.

In the unlikely event that more people want to push the man than the lever **Rob** *says . . .*

You have no idea who that man was.[13]

Scene Seven: May–August 2015

Rob   It turns out Eric is from a little town up on the east coast of Scotland. Somewhere between Thurso and Aberdeen. He thanks me profusely in his message and apologises for not replying sooner, explaining that after the Indy result he had decided to spend some time off the grid.

I post his wallet to the address he gives me and a few days later I get another message.

Eric   Hey, Rob. Got the wallet. Smashing. But there was a fifty in it, you fucking dirty thief! Ha. Only kidding. Let me know if there's anything I can do for you comrade. Peace.

Rob   This is the opening I've been waiting for.

Eric   There is something you could do. Tell me who you are.

Rob   And this is where things got a little odd.

Eric   What the fuck is this? Are you media? Police?

Rob   No. I'm Rob. I'm a playwright. I'm just interested.

Eric   Playwright. What, you going to write a fucking play about me?

Rob   No. But if I did I promise I wouldn't use anything you're not comfortable with. I give you my word.

There's a long delay before the next reply. Two weeks in fact. And then . . .

Eric   Rob. I'll tell you who I am. I'm Eric Ferguson and I live in a town that is infested with Nazis.[14]

---

[13] This was a contingency line that was never used. It goes to show how meticulous we have become since *Bullet Catch* at rehearsing the possibilities. *Bullet Catch* was a real learning curve because we hadn't done enough of this and Rob was thrown on multiple occasions.

[14] On 12 August 2017 – the day of the second preview performance – at a far-right rally in Charlottesville, Virginia, a car was driven into a crowd, injuring several people engaged in peaceful protests, and killing thirty-two-year-old civil rights activist Heather Heyer. This incident had a big impact on the play's reception. *The Majority* was intended as a timely

Rob   Fair to say not the reply I was expecting.

Between May and August of 2015 Eric and I exchange countless messages.

He tells me that the three independent councillors representing his town on the local council were all Nazis. How did he know this? Because they were all affiliated with a Nazi group called White Hand, run by a mysterious guy called Ralph Weiss (not his real name). And that organisation does exist because I googled them and found Ralph's website. But from what I could see they were active nearer Aberdeen, not out where Eric lived.[15]

How do you know these councillors are affiliated with White Hand?

Eric   Because I keep my ear to the ground.

Rob   Hardly convincing.

What have they done so far to make you worry, these councillors?

Eric   Nothing yet. But they're taking a vote on an immigration issue in a month's time. And I bet I know what way they'll vote.

Rob   The immigration issue concerned the proposed re-settlement of refugees from Syria. This is around the time that ISIS were really getting a foothold in the country and local councils across the UK were asked to consider taking a hypothetical group of displaced citizens.

So if they vote against it . . .

Eric   Then we'll know for sure.

Rob   Cards on the table, my initial impression of Eric . . . He's a nut-bag. A paranoiac.

But he grew on me. Over those first few months of exchanges.

Here's his response to me mocking the idea of Trump running for office.

Eric   Don't you fucking laugh, it will happen. You'll see. Trump for president. The world's going that way.

---

response to a changing political landscape, but the shocking immediacy of Charlottesville emphasised the liveness of the production and complicated responses to the play's central message. Our focus on white nationalism was emphasised in this context and the play's overall message – a call to debate, rather than attack – was seen by some to imply moral equivalence between activists on both sides. This made the play very edgy in a way we hadn't banked on and we ended up changing a lot of the 'Nazis' for 'far right' or 'right-wing' to soften the impact of this word. Twenty years ago this play would have landed very differently but, and perhaps this is testament to how much we captured the mood of the country, it was very tense in 2017, both during and following the show.

15   If you google Ralph Weiss or the White Hand Gang, you won't actually find anything. For a combination of reasons, this was invented. For us, it's enough that this is 'based on' the truth. There are neo-Nazi groups operating in that area, but would it matter if there were not? The truth that this is all really based on is the perception of the right-wing rising that people on the left can see. It's based on the idea that there is a new right-wing threat (and this is more than likely true) that we need to battle. The question is: how do we battle it? So whether the White Hand actually exist or not is kind of unimportant. Groups like them do. What do we do with that knowledge? We needed a bogey man to focus our audience's attention upon – a representative of the problem that we were asking them to participate in solving. This play was really a think tank on the issue of dealing with extremist views.

Rob   So, clearly not the fool I maybe first thought.

And he was funny too. This is him talking about his bees.

Eric   I fucking love my bees, Rob, they keep me in beer! Honey money baby!

Rob   See, funny.

I found out he had a wife, Lucy, and a child, Morag. They were still together but lived separately, which was odd but seemed to work for them.

And he had a scientific mind, which is something I could relate to. He didn't believe in God. He believed in science.

Which is how he trapped me.

Eric   Let me ask you something, sugar tits.

Rob   I think he'd had a few beers when he composed this message but I'm reading it to you as I received it.

Eric   What's the point of all this, eh?

Rob   All what?

Eric   Life. What do you live for?

Rob   I don't think there is a point. I mean the andromeda galaxy's going to collide with ours in about five billion years. We know that. We know everything's headed to nothing.

Eric   Ah. You're a nihilist. I suspected as much.

Rob   I tell him that I don't consider myself a nihilist, but a realist. That nothing I did would really change anything for the better. He didn't like that.

Eric   Have you ever marched? Ever done anything? To try to change things for the better? No. So you've made a conclusion without testing the hypothesis.

I'm talking about action. Real action. Like what I used to do. Back in the eighties.

Rob   What did you do?

But every time I ask him about this he closes me down.

Eric   Everything I say, on the phone, on here, is monitored by the government. I don't think that, Rob, I know that. All I'll say is, my name wasn't always Eric.

Rob   You changed it?

Eric   Come up and see me. Help me campaign. Test your hypothesis. And maybe I'll tell you all about it.

Pause.

Rob   Go up to the Highlands and visit crazy bee man.

Well, beats doing nothing.

Act Two

Rob *travels north on a train.*[16]

Scene One: September 2015

Rob   As I step off the train in Thurso, which is the northernmost train station on the British mainland, I see a little man with a tweed jacket and a cap pulled down over his eyes sitting on a bench with a sign that reads 'Drummond'. I've arranged a car to take me the rest of the way as there's really no other way of doing it. I approach him only to find he's asleep. I gently place my hand on his shoulder and . . .

Old Man   Fuck you!

Rob   He swipes at me with the back of his hand, catching me on the chin.

I point at his sign.

Eh. I'm Drummond.

At this point you'd expect at the very least an apology. An explanation. I was in a war. I have PTSD. I've been mugged in my sleep before.

But no. He just nods and walks away. I work out for myself to follow him and he leads me to a twenty-year-old BMW. I get inside. It reeks of dog.

The old man gets in the front. He knows where we're going.

Old Man   Fit are you going there fir?

Rob   I'm meeting with Eric Ferguson.

The **Old Man** *laughs.*

Rob   You know him?

Old Man   Oh aye, I ken Eric Ferguson.

Rob   He seems to think there's a Nazi problem up here.

The old man suddenly becomes very serious. And then he says one word, which I'm not sure how to take.

---

[16]   Rob left the stage at this point and a map with a moving route was projected around the space. This was the only moment he got to leave the stage in a ninety-minute performance. For the performer, this show was much tougher than *Bullet Catch* or *Wallace* because it was essentially a monologue with audience participation reduced to pressing buttons. When we realised the audience wouldn't talk in this show, that was a real turning point because it was the perfect fit for the subject matter. Their interaction was reduced to the purest form of democracy – the audience had a collective voice but didn't have individual voices. Making a show with audience participation is all about working out the rules for that interaction. What are they allowed to do and say and what do we restrict? And if the audience understand their role early on everything runs smoothly.

Old Man   Problem?

Rob   I decide to put my headphones in for the rest of the journey. I'd rather not know what this guy thinks about Nazis to be honest. I don't want to risk getting in an argument and being kicked out the car on a country road in nowheresville.

The journey takes us two hours. The town, which I'm not going to mention the name of, is a sleepy little poverty-stricken fishing town. Not exactly where you'd expect to find the base of a burgeoning Nazi resurgence.

Eric's house is modest enough. A semi-detached near the high street with a view of the North Sea. Not bad.

I ring the doorbell and wait for a few minutes but no one appears so I let myself round into the back garden.

And there he is.

Standing at the bottom of a relatively small garden with thousands and thousands of bees buzzing all around him. He's not wearing a beekeeper's helmet. Just a hat. His face is uncovered and so are his arms.

I should make it clear that this garden was way too small for so many bees. And they were buzzing their way towards me now. Almost as if they could sense my fear.

Social Justice Beekeeper just stood there staring at me.

He's set this up. He knew I was arriving now. He's done this for me.

He shouts over at me, but I can barely hear him over the buzzing.

Eric   ROB!

Rob   ERIC!

Eric   YOU'VE CAUGHT ME UNAWARES!

Rob   Aye, right.

CAN WE GO IN THE HOUSE?

Eric   WHAT?

Rob   I DON'T WANT TO GET STUNG!

As I'm saying this, well, alright it was a few months later but it's better for the story if it's now, as I'm saying this a bee stings me. My first ever bee sting. Which Eric finds hilarious.

CAN WE GO INSIDE?!

Eric   ALRIGHT, YOU BIG JESSIE. THE BACK DOOR'S OPEN.

Rob   I leap at the invitation to get out of the bee garden and into the house. And after a legitimate twenty minutes Eric joins me.

He's smiling maniacally. Red bee-sting welts all over. Constant movement. Just like

George Square.

He makes me some tea, toast and honey and I accept all despite liking none. And before I can even properly say hello he launches into one of the most astonishing monologues I've ever heard.

I've tried my best, as with most of this, to remember what he said.

It went something like this . . .

Eric   The Nazis. They sell cocaine to the kids. All over the place. People think I'm on cocaine but I'm not. I'm just naturally energetic. If anything I need drugs to slow me down. A little bit of weed to take the edge off my brain you know. We can do some later if you like. Anyway, Rob, let me tell you, I'm on to them. And they know it. And one day they're going to kill me for it. I'm telling you, if I die, they did it! Most fishing towns they have a drug problem, because, well it's fucking boring here. And a few years back this Nazi group moved in down the road and starting selling. Now, you're going to think this is mental right but bees, they have better smelling than dogs right and they take shorter to train – you just get them to associate the coke with a reward of sugar water and bang, the next time they smell coke their little proboscises shoot out and you know – fuck, that's cocaine. I'm not joking, there will be sniffer bees at airports within the next ten years. So, I thought, fuck me, I can train my bees to sniff out the coke. So I went to the police and asked them for some coke so I could get started on the training and I told them that if they helped me we could uncover the whole thing and get them all locked up. But they were having none of it. And that's when I realised that they were in on it too. All of them. The police, the council. They're all in on it.[17]

Rob   It's at this point I start to question if I have selected the best possible mentor. But something about Eric is undeniably intoxicating. I found myself wanting his stories to be true. I mean they obviously weren't. Or at least there was so much untrue about them so as to totally undermine the truthful bits. But still . . . Nazis. We all hate Nazis right? Little disagreement there.

We spent the weekend together. He took me up to the house he called the Nazi compound. Disappointingly no one was home. He said they had many bases all along the coast. It seemed far-fetched to me. I mean, why? Why move in up here?

Eric   Why not? It's not like this is the only place they are. They're all over the UK now. Part of the far-right resurgence.

Rob   I found myself trespassing that first night. We scaled a fence and went right into the compound. Looking for evidence of drugs. And Nazis. A swastika of coke I think would have sealed the deal . . . but we saw nothing.

On the second night we mainly just hung out down the seafront eating fish and chips. His wife Lucy and his daughter Morag join us. I get the sense that Lucy is reticent to

---

[17]   This was the only extended monologue in character in this play, which demanded a shift in performance style and was an opportunity for Rob to embrace a more traditional acting style, which he was never that comfortable with as a performer.

talk about Eric. I'm desperate to know more about why they live apart but I don't want to ask something so personal so soon.

Eric later tells me that she has something called dissociative disorder. A form of depression that means nothing feels real to her. A kind of defence mechanism against the world he says. Having a discussion with her is like talking to a stoned artificial intelligence. She met Eric shortly after he came up to the community, around fifteen years ago. I ask her about the Nazis and she says . . .

Lucy   Aye, man, Nazis, man. Everywhere.

Rob   Morag wants to go so Lucy kisses Eric and says she loves him and she'll see him tomorrow.

And then they leave. To go to their separate houses.

I ask Eric about the local community. What do they all think about the place?

Eric   There's two types of people. Those who keep their heads down and those who look for a fight wherever they can find one. And guess which one's going to make the difference in the world?

Rob   The second one.

Eric   This place is full of the first type. Like most places. These days I need to go onto the internet to find an argument.

Rob   Do you think we'll ever work it all out? Both sides. Agree with each other. Get along?

He thinks for a long time. But he never answers.

On the third night, Eric offers me some weed. To be honest the weekend has been a little bit dull. He wanted me to come up and 'help him campaign' but I didn't see much campaigning going on at all.

I took the weed.

And I inhaled.

And it was good.

Eric   I've been thinking, Rob. You *should* write about this place. Get our story out there.

Rob   But there isn't much of a story is there, Eric?

He stops short and puts his spliff down.

Eric   You. Follow me.

Rob   And I did. Out into the back garden where Eric picked up some sort of package and then off out down the main street, high as a kite, looking up at the blanket of stars in the sky and thinking, I don't know where we're going but this is fucking exciting!

We arrive in front of a house. Much like any other.

Eric   This is where she lives.

Rob   Who? Lucy?

Eric   No. The councillor.

Rob   Whose name I will not mention.

He tells me that all the local councillors, as he had predicted, had voted against the immigrants coming. But the rest of the council voted them down. So it was still happening. But now he knew for sure. They were Nazis.

He handed me the package from the garden.

Eric   Put this through her letter box.

Rob   What?

Eric   Put it through her letter box.

Rob   What is it?

Eric   It's bees.

Rob   I swear he said this like it was the most normal thing in the world.

I'm not putting bees through her letterbox.

Eric   She's got to know she can't get away with this shit.

Rob   We can't do that.

Eric   Do you think we should take immigrants?

Rob   Well, yes I do but . . .

Eric   Then put this through her letterbox.

Rob   No.

Eric   Fine. I will then.

Rob   No. Wait.

How did I get here? In a small northern fishing town trying to persuade a mad socialist not to drop bees through a Nazi's letterbox.

Let's do something else.

Eric   Like what?

Rob   Here.

And at this point I picked up a big chalky stone from the ground, I got down on my hands and knees and I carved into the ground right outside her house the words . . .

NAZI SCUM.[18]

I wasn't sure she was one. In fact, I was pretty certain she was just plain old right-wing, but, well, fuck her. She voted against helping actually desperate human beings.

---

[18]   Here, we faded up a projection of these words on the stage as Rob mimed writing them.

And I was saving her. From waking up covered in bees. And I was saving myself too. From a potential confrontation. And I was saving Eric, from himself. I was doing the right thing here. For the greater good.

Eric looked down at my handiwork.

She'll see it when she leaves the house tomorrow morning, I say.

Eric   Well. It's a start.

Rob   As we walk away from the house I notice a child's seat in the car on the driveway.

Scene Two: Present Day

Rob   There is a runaway train car heading towards five railway workers. There's no time to warn them. They will die if it hits them. You are standing by a lever which, when pushed, will send the train car onto a siding on which stands . . . your child. If you push the lever your child will die but the five workers will be saved.

It's the same as before only this time it's your child.

What is the correct decision?

The proposition is this . . .

This community would push the lever.

Rob *comments on the result. In all likelihood the number of people pushing the lever will be lower than ever.*

Scene Three: October 2015–March 2016

Rob   I'll be honest, vandalising the councillor's driveway had been childishly exhilarating.

I had felt guilty though and when I got back to Glasgow I googled her and was happy to see she did seem pretty awful. She was independent but really her Facebook page read very much like that of a UKIP candidate's. All union flags and Britain first and British jobs for British people.

I was just relieved to find that the target of my abuse had deserved it.

I was on a high.

Quite literally actually.

Now, I've never really smoked weed but up there, well, it seemed like the right thing to do.

With every trip Eric would tell me more and more about his years in political circles. More and more about the differences he had made in people's lives. The mining strikes he had attended in solidarity. The marches he'd been on, the pressure he had helped put on governments over the years. The political party he had started in the eighties. And it all started to make sense.

And a funny thing was happening to me. I was beginning, for the first time in my life, to feel politically motivated.

I even engaged in my first Twitter feud with Ralph Weiss – the anonymous leader of White Hand.

No one knows what his real name is or where he lives. Eric tells me there are a lot of anti-fascists who would kill for that information.

One night in November, I asked Eric: why did you move here in the first place?

He looks at me for a long, long time. Finally seems to decide I've earned his trust.

Eric   I got in trouble. Went away for a while.

Rob   To prison?

Eric   No, to Antigua. Of course to prison.

Rob   What did you do?

Eric   The party we set up. The Socialist Front. We went bust. Tried to make some money to keep it going. Ended up doing something stupid.

Rob   What?

Eric   What's the worst thing you've ever done, Rob?

Rob   I don't know.

And I didn't. I couldn't think of a single bad thing I'd done. At least nothing that would impress him. Which is what I now realise I was trying to do.

Unless . . .

I suppose the worst thing I've ever done is . . .

And I told him I didn't vote in the independence referendum. And that I was trying to work out why and . . . fix it. I don't know why I thought that would impress him. I was high. I thought we might bond over my honesty.

But instead he just looked at me.

And then slowly got up and left the room. Out into the night. Leaving me in his kitchen.

I watch as he goes down to the bottom of the garden and stands by the hives.

I go down and join him. Braving the possibility of a sting or two.

(And this is actually where I was stung for the first time but let's not dwell on that because it derails the flow.)

You ok?

Eric   Have you ever heard of the trolley problem, Rob?

Rob   No.

Eric   A runaway trolley is heading towards five railway workers.

Rob   A trolley?

Eric   A train car. It's just an old fashioned . . . listen.

There is a runaway train car heading towards five railway workers. There's no time to warn them. They will die if it hits them. You are standing by a lever which, when pushed, will send the train car onto a siding on which there is a single workman. If you push the lever you will kill him but the five workers will be saved.

Do you push the lever?

Rob   Yes of course I do.

Eric   So why don't you fucking vote you fucking moron!

. . .

Rob   I didn't see Eric at all over Christmas. To be honest, after our weird night I thought our friendship might have run its course. Probably for the best.

But then one day in March 2016 I get a message on Twitter.

Rob! It's happening. Immigrants are moving in all over the fucking place. Nazis have planned a big protest in Aberdeen. I'm organising a counter-protest. Please say you'll come with me. See what I'm all about. The real me.

It seemed like he had forgiven me.

And this is where I should have left it. Politely declined. Simply not replied.

But even as those thoughts were circling in my mind my fingers were typing a reply of their own accord.

Because I wanted to fix what I had done. I wanted to be a part of the solution. I wanted to find hope.

And so my fingers typed: *See you there.*

Scene Four: Present Day

Rob   There is a runaway train car heading towards five non-violent Nazis (they hold the views without committing violence). There's no time to warn them. They will die if it hits them. You are standing by a lever which, when pushed, will send the train car onto a siding on which stands a normal right-wing/left-wing voter. If you push the lever you will kill the voter but the five Nazis will be saved.

The proposition is this . . .

This community would push the lever (and save the five lives).[19]

Rob   Before I went to Aberdeen I did some more research on the White Hand. Discovered that they were a non-violent organisation. Amongst the views I found on their website, they wanted to reintroduce Section 28, which prohibited the 'promotion of homosexuality' in schools, and limit immigration of non-whites to zero. They were kind enough to say that any legal non-whites currently living in the UK could stay. And as I say they emphasised the whole non-violent thing.

I became a little obsessed with checking his website, which he updated every day. This is a live website and Ralph still posts regularly. Let's see if he's sent anything today.

Its White blood traitors on the left who are threatening the safety of decent British people. Letting in these non-whites is tantamount to allowing genocide against youre [sic] *people. It's us or them.*

Yes. This is typical of his output. He never directly called for violence. Just insinuated it. Always keeping just within his free speech rights. But the intent was clear.

Eric had told me that people wanted to find out Ralph's real identity. So I went to work. He was well hidden but social media being what it is, after a couple of days of going down various rabbit holes I had found him.

His real name and even his address.

But I was torn on what to do with the information.

Ralph was a hideous human being. People deserved to know who he was.

And so . . . I composed the following message.

Rob *does this live.*

Dear Ralph, I know what you are and decent British people deserve to know who you are. Thomas Wright, 12 Quarryman Way, Elgin, Scotland, IV30 1AX.[20]

And I sat there. My finger hovering above the send button. Eric will love me for this. People deserve to know. It will benefit the community.

Do you think I should have sent it?

The proposition is this:

---

[19]   Early versions of this scene included a brief response or comment on the results as they came in, but we soon decided to let each of these moments simply hang in the air. It felt stronger just to let the audience decide what they meant in the context of what else was happening in the show, the world and their minds.

[20]   These details were fictional, and the doxing staged. This was partly because the National Theatre would not allow us to do it for real. We were careful not to choose a real address.

This community wants to send this message.

Please vote now.[21]

The result comes in. If it is YES **Rob** *presses send. The message appears on screen.*

Rob   My decision, back then, was not to send it. But it's interesting that you wanted to. You've obviously got more backbone than me.

Don't worry. It's his website. He deletes it every day.

If it is NO **Rob** *says:*

Rob   Yeah. Probably wise. I didn't sent it back then either. Didn't send anything. Always regretted that actually. Maybe I should send something now.

Rob *decides to type.*

Dear Ralph. I very much disagree with your views but I'd be fascinated to know why you hold them. Would you be free for a chat?

There. That will solve the Nazi problem.

Either way, **Rob** *looks around.*

I can see some of you are upset with the majority decision.

But remember you did choose this. This community understood and agreed with how the show would run.

And anyway, don't worry. None of this is real. It's just theatre.

Rob *pushes the laptop closed and the entire table disappears.*

Scene Five: March 2016

Rob   March 2016 and I've become what I think is referred to as a keyboard warrior. I'm no longer scared of confrontation, no longer apathetic to politics, quite the opposite. It's worked! Eric has re-activated me.

I'm engaged in ongoing Twitter feuds with dickheads of varying flavours. Anti-vaccination morons, right-wing racists, pro-life nutjobs.

And I'm slaying them left, right and centre. Fuck you! You have no idea what you're talking about! You're abhorrent! Wrong side of history! Scum!

---

[21]   The fact that a lot of audiences voted to dox Weiss is perhaps because of the licence to play and to make provocative choices in the context of a theatre show. But perhaps vigilante justice is alive and well in the left. We were surprised how many voted to do this – it either meant they knew we had faked it all or that they were happy to risk his safety because his views (he was non-violent remember) were abhorrent. From his position on stage, Rob remembers this being the tensest part of the show, and when he pressed send to dox Weiss, the atmosphere was thick with disagreement, disgust, disbelief. Rob felt wrong doing it, even though he knew it wasn't real.

Eric is right, these people have got to be told, they've got to hear the noise of condemnation or they'll never change. This is it. This is what I've been missing.

I'm getting extremely excited about Aberdeen. My wife is a little upset that I've been taking so many trips up north but I explain to her . . . it's important.

I arrive in Aberdeen train station and see Eric immediately. But he doesn't look happy. There's something missing there.

Eric   The Nazis salted the hives.

Rob   What?

Eric   The bees have gone. The majority. I think someone salted them out.

Rob   I'm sorry.

Eric   Don't get sorry, get even.

Let's go.

Rob   We head up to the high street and at first it seems like any other city on a Saturday afternoon. But then . . . slowly they emerge. The protestors. Looking exactly like you or me, but . . . different somehow. Hardened. Stern. No room for fun in their lives. Not until they've fixed this problem.

As we get closer to the high street the regular people begin to become outnumbered and as we turn the last corner I see it . . . the protest.

Eric   Fuck me.

Rob   Says Eric.

Eric   More than I thought.

Rob   It is alarming how many people have shown up to protest against the arrival of desperate immigrants from a war-torn country. But heartening to see that the counter-protest still outnumbers them around two to one.

Eric has made a bee-line to the front line. I remember thinking as he arrived and shook hands – *none of these people recognise him. He said he'd organised this.*

We stood there, looking across the main road, through the traffic, at the enemy on the other side. Placards hoisted high.

BRITAIN FIRST. WHITE MIGHT. KEEP SCOTLAND SAFE.

They can't all be Nazis, I say to Eric.

Eric   No. Some of them will be plain old right-wing bigots.

Rob   And before I know it Eric is screaming at the top of his lungs . . .

If you're right, you're wrong. If you're right, you're wrong. If you're right, you're wrong!

And our side are joining in. And I join in. It's my first political chant. I'm giddy.

The opposition retort with a chorus of 'Scotland first, Scotland first', but we hit back at them with . . .

Fuck off, bigots, fuck off!

It's not clever but it's to the point.

There is rage in the air but I've never felt safer. I can't explain it, I just thought . . . This is where I'm meant to be. Doing something. Standing up for something. Shouting about something. At this time on a Saturday I'm usually in my underwear watching football on TV. But now I'm out here standing up for immigrants. It felt great.

Eric spots a group of protestors who he seems to recognise.

Eric   That's them! That's the White Hand guys.

Nazi scum, Nazi scum!

Rob   He screams over and over again at them. So loud that some of the police who are surrounding the protestors actually turn and look over the road towards us.

This is great isn't it? I say to Eric.

Eric   It's pathetic. Standing here on two sides of a road. They've not even bothered to stop traffic. And they know what they're doing. Just standing there. With their signs. Those signs are incitement to hatred. Those signs are violent. And the police just stand there. They know as long as they don't do anything we can't raise a finger against them.

Rob   Would we want to?

Eric   Words are never going to change their minds.

Rob   He's probably right, I think.

I mean if you can't punch a Nazi who can you punch?

Rob   And so the day goes on. Three hours we stand there, taking breaks to head to the pub for pints and snacks. Coming back and chanting some more. Getting to know the anti-protestors. A nice bunch. Normal people concerned with stopping fascism.

By five o'clock Eric and I are pissed and the protest across the road is winding down.

And I can tell Eric is disappointed.

And to be honest, I am too. We just let them stand there all day spewing ignorance and hate. They'll be leaving now thinking they've won. Fuck.

The day has been a failure.

And as we're walking back to the station . . .

As dusk is settling in over the granite city . . .

We come upon a lone protestor.

Eric   He's one of the White Hand.

Rob   Whispers Eric.

He's holding a sign that reads, 'NO MORE IMMIGRANTS'.

He's on his phone and he's . . . laughing.

And joking.

He thinks his side have won the argument. But he can't have won because there were more of us! Why does he think he's won?!

And something inside me snaps.

A combination of rage, excitement, alcohol and . . . finally understanding why it's important to care . . .

Because it's not fake. It's not theatre. It's right here. It's real and it's in front of me.

I pick up my pace . . .

I position myself behind this guy . . .

And I just . . .

Swing.

From behind.

With my fist clenched.

And I punch him on the side of the head.

And it doesn't hurt.

And I catch him sweet.

And he drops to the ground.

And his phone smashes on the cobbled street.

. . .

. . .

Two policemen nearby have seen the whole thing.

I didn't even bother to check . . .

I was on autopilot.

And as I turned around, my hands held out before me, welcoming the arrest, I remember thinking . . .

Worth it.

I did the right thing.

But as they arrest me I realise . . .

To my surprise.

Eric has run away.

. . .

In the morning, when I had sobered up and I realised I was going to be prosecuted – I pled guilty and received a six-month suspended sentence – I didn't feel quite so good about myself.

I decided to cut ties with Eric. Completely.

He called me, twice a day, for three weeks straight. Sent me message after message on Twitter. I read none of them.

And then a letter arrived in his handwriting. I couldn't bring myself to throw it in the bin but I also didn't want to open it and risk being sucked back in to that world. I put it in a drawer and tried to forget about the whole thing.

Safer not caring about things, I remember thinking.

Act Three

A domestic scene. **Rob** *is home again.*

Scene One: Present Day

Rob   Now, I've noticed some of you squirming in your seats, which suggests there may be more than a few of you that require a toilet break. But I'll tell you now, we are building up a head of steam so to break now would not be wise.

But this is a democracy so let's find out if people want to have mercy on the people who are in pain – because it is painful, isn't it, needing to wee.

So, the proposition is this . . .

This community believes that we should deny the minority a toilet break.[22]

Please vote now.

The result is No. **Rob** *mouths 'sorry' to an individual he has already pointed out as needing to pee.*

Scene Two: June 2016

Rob   June 2016. The UK is in shock. Again. Brexit has triumphed. The majority have spoken. What did this community vote? In the Brexit referendum? Do you mind me asking? Why don't we do a rerun?

The proposition is . . .

This community believes that the UK should leave the EU.[23]

Vote now.

If only we could go back. Shout louder. Call more Brexiteers racist. Call more of them idiots. Maybe even punch a few of them. The result might have been different.

---

[22]   While most of the audiences voted for the show to continue, there were some votes to pause at this point. Anticipating this, we took the decision to rig this vote. This was because if there was a break in the action it would have completely derailed the rhythm of the show. Dramaturgically speaking we would have been mad to allow that. It was a perfect moment as it was both a nice lighthearted pause in the story and served to remind the audience that they were capable of anonymous tyranny against minority groups.

[23]   Predictably, considering the typical demographic of a National Theatre audience, the majority vote was *always* for Remain. Across the twenty performances the average level of support for Remain was 70 per cent, with a low of 61 per cent and a high of 77 per cent. Less predictably, as the results came in, during several performances the audience broke into a round of self-affirming applause, with the occasional shout of approval. This crystallised the problem: it was a bunch of people who thought the same way in a room together cheering for themselves. A similar point is made by the comedian Stewart Lee in his 2016 show *Content Provider*, as he mocks his audience after a pro-EU applause: 'That's right: clap the things you agree with. *Clap, clap, clap; agree, agree, agree.*'

If this was 2014 I wouldn't feel so bad about this.

I log onto Facebook. I've not been on in months. I check my messages. It's mainly my liberal friends, who've heard what I did, praising my choice to punch the man for what he thought.

I delete my account. Quickly, before I have the chance to reconsider.

And then I do the same with my Twitter account.

Better fingers in the ears than a fist in the face.

My wife chooses this day to tell me she's pregnant. My first thought is: shit. What have we done? What world is this child going to inherit? How can I teach them how to live when I've no idea myself?

Shit. I feel worse than I did at the beginning of all this. I need to speak to Eric. He got me into this mess. He can get me out.

But I've deleted my account. So instead I pick up my mobile and call his landline number.

It rings and rings and finally Lucy picks up.

Oh. Hello. It's Rob. I was looking for Eric.

Lucy   Oh fuck.

Rob   She says.

Lucy   You haven't heard.

Rob   What?

Lucy   Rob. Eric is dead.

Scene Three: July–November 2016

Between July and November of 2016 I visit Lucy three times.

Here's what I found out on the first visit.

Eric came home after Aberdeen deeply depressed.

They didn't see much of him for a while.

And then one day she came round to the house to drop off Morag and . . . he was gone.

There was no note. And all of his things were still there. But she knew something was wrong because there were bees, the ones who had remained, buzzing and dying all over the kitchen.

She called the police. They said there's not much they could do. He's a grown man. He decided to leave.

Lucy insisted he would never just leave. He must have thrown himself into the sea or something. Or . . . maybe the Nazis had killed him. He was always saying they would one day.

They said they'd keep an eye out for him. But there was no evidence of any crime.

But there was. Or so Lucy thought. Because on the kitchen table was a badge – the type you sew on – and on the badge was the emblem of a small white hand.

It had to mean something.

But no matter how much she complained the police insisted it was Eric's. He was obsessed with that group.

By the second visit she had sold the house. She needed the money. We sat in her living room with Morag colouring in in the corner.

Lucy   The badge on the table. It has to be a message. From the White Hand.

Rob   Maybe he just decided he needed some time away.

Lucy   Why would he do that to us?

Rob   He might have thought you were better off without him.

She looks at me in the eye for the first time and smiles.

Lucy   He'd be right.

Rob   I watched Morag colour in. She was good at keeping in the lines.

By the third visit Lucy had given up. It was November and Donald Trump, the host of the American *Apprentice*, had become the President of the United States of America.

I imagined Eric, wherever he was, hearing about that. I told you so, Rob. I fucking told you so.

Lucy must have been the only person on the planet who hadn't heard.

Lucy   What did you say?

Rob   I said Trump won.

Lucy laughs.

Lucy   That's funny.

Rob   Lucy I'm going to stop coming up here. Is that ok?

Lucy   Why wouldn't it be?

Rob   No reason.

You know, Lucy, I've suffered from depression too.

Lucy   You don't say.

Rob   And withdrawing isn't really the answer.

Lucy   I know that. What is the answer then, Rob?

Rob   Well . . . I tried being like Eric.

Lucy   Ha. That was your first mistake.

Rob   So now . . . I don't really know what to do. I know I care. I'm glad about that. I know I want to do something. It's just . . .

How do you care without hurting?

Lucy   I don't know, Rob. But you think you're going to find out sitting here with the likes of me?

The Message Reply[24]

Rob   Let's just see if we've got a reply from our message earlier.

Yes. He's usually replied by this point in the show.

Here we go.

Rob *reads out the reply. It's either . . .*

Rob, are you going to do this every night? The more people who see this, the more danger you put my children in. You just confirm what I've always thought about the left.

Or . . .

I'm ALWAYS happy to have a civil DISAGREEMENT. Ask me anything you like.

Scene Four: February 2017

Rob   February of 2017. I'm now living in Loughborough – my wife got a new job – and I'm reading an article online that's made my blood run cold.

In America, a neo-Nazi by the name of Richard Spencer was punched in the face by a protester during a live TV interview.

And the *Guardian* published an article that included the line . . .

A punch may be uncivil, but racism is worse. When criticising tactics against racism, it's important to prioritise.[25]

---

24   It is difficult to know how many audience members accepted this as a real time reply by a real person. We suspect that most understood it as a fiction. This is not something we would, or could, do for real as it would have genuinely been endangering someone's life. But by offering that chance to the audience we got to have our cake and eat it. They often voted to put someone in danger, which made the point clearly, but this was mitigated by the fictional and theatrical context.
25   Taken slightly out of context but nothing here is untrue (including the bit about Rob living in Loughborough).

A national liberal newspaper published an article that defended punching people for holding opinions.

But instead of feeling vindicated in my own actions, I felt sick.

I close the laptop as my mum enters the room holding her grandson.

Mum   Yes, yes you are, yes you are. Yes. Yes you are.

Rob   My son is something that much is clear. I'm just not sure what.

Mum   You are the cutest little boy. Yes you are.

Rob   Ah. Right. That clears that up.

Mum   He is the cutest little boy. Isn't he? Yes you are. Yes you are, Eric. Yes you are.

Rob   The TV is on in the corner. Donald Trump is on it. As is the new normal.

Mum   You know if I was American I think I'd have voted for Trump too. No-nonsense, all-action type of guy you know?

Rob   My baby boy stares at me. He's not smiling yet. Just looking. Checking shit out. Deciding whether or not this whole being born thing has been a good idea or not. He's on the fence so far. I can tell.

Mum, you can't be serious. You would vote for Trump?

Mum   Yes.

Rob   Then you're an idiot.

Mum   Robert. What do you want when you talk?

Rob   What?

Mum   When you talk. What do you want?

Rob   Different things.

Mum   Do you want to learn if you're wrong or just show how right you are?

Rob   I would want to know if I'm wrong. Would you?

Mum   Absolutely. And how does it feel like to be wrong?

Rob   It feels . . . you feel silly.

Mum   No. That's how it feels to find out that you're wrong. How does it feel like to be wrong.

Rob   Well. It feels . . . it feels exactly the same as being right.

Maybe my mum doesn't stumble into profundity. Maybe my mum is just profound.

Mum   Oh, and by the way, I was unpacking boxes and I found this. You've not opened it.

Rob   And she hands me a letter and takes my son up to bed.

The letter. I had forgotten all about it.

The letter Eric had sent me one week before he had disappeared.

The Final Trolley Problem

There is a runaway train car heading towards no one. There is no need to do anything. No one will die if the train continues. You are standing by a lever which, when pushed, will send the train car onto a siding on which stands one neo-Nazi. If you push the lever they will die.

What is the correct decision?

The proposition is this.

This community would push the lever.

Please vote now.[26]

Scene Five: Present Day

Rob *holds the letter in his hand.*

Rob   This is the actual letter Eric sent me. And its contents are . . . very interesting. Maybe not what you'd expect. It's kind of the key to everything.

But I'm afraid we have a problem.

Because also in this letter are explicit instructions from Eric that its contents never be divulged to anyone.

This letter was meant for me and me alone.

So.

Do you want to hear the letter?

This community believes the letter should be read aloud.

Please vote now.[27]

The audience vote.

Rob *either takes out the letter and looks at it himself or reads the letter aloud.*

---

[26]   For the final trolley problem scenario, 7 per cent voted for this option after it was made clear that the single neo-Nazi held beliefs that they had never acted on. This section of the audience therefore opted to murder someone because of their ideology. There were often a lot of gasps when the number of people who chose this course of action was revealed not to be insubstantial each night.

[27]   This was generally quite close, but audiences usually voted not to hear the letter read out. On these occasions, Rob would reflect on the words silently before moving on to address them. On one occasion, an audience member climbed up onto the stage after the show to retrieve the prop letter, desperate to know its contents.

Dear Rob

Fuck you. Fuck you for ignoring me. Fuck you for leaving me hanging on like this. What happened in Aberdeen. I had to fucking run away. I can't be involved in anything like what you did or I'll go back inside. If you'd bother to take my calls you'd know that. Fuck you.

(And then there's an illegible bit that's probably another insult.)

I get the picture. You don't want anything to do with me. I'll try to hide my surprise. You're just like all the rest. You talk the talk but then you run at the first sign of trouble. Fuck you. You punch one deserving twat and you get scared and crawl back into your hole of self denial. <u>FUCK YOU!</u>

(He's capitalised and underlined that one. I get the impression he'd been drinking.)

I killed someone you know. Told Lucy a few years back. When Morag was born. And she was just like you. She got scared. Insisted on living apart. Well guess what, the guy deserved it. He was a fucking despicable human being – fucking Thatcherite cunt – and it was self-defence anyway. And I did my time and I'd do it all again because you've got to do something, Rob. You've got to put yourself on the line for what you believe.

I hope one day you might realise that what you did was right. We all need to send a clear fucking message to the right by standing up and taking back control. And if that means attacking people who say things we can't tolerate then so be it. But somehow I doubt it will get through to you. Because you're a fucking lost cause, Rob. You're pathetic. I've left you something. On the kitchen table. Either become part of the solution or you may as well sew that to your sleeve and join them.

Don't worry, you won't hear from me again, nobody will. And don't think that me writing you this is permission to share it with anyone in one of your impotent fucking theatre shows. I explicitly forbid you from doing that, Rob. And if there's one thing I can appreciate about you it's that you're a man of your word. Even if that word is spineless.

Eric.

Rob *looks at the audience.*

Silence.

Rob *takes a deep breath and then.*

I drop the letter to the ground, I'm trembling. Fuck me, Eric. No. Fuck you.

Fuck you!

Wherever you are.

Wherever you've gone.

I mean, do you really think that we'd be better off if we were going around . . .

I mean, who's punchable? What ideas are . . . Who do we attack? What words are banned?

What opinions?

And where do they go those people, those ideas? They don't just disappear. They . . . they fucking . . . fester.

I mean is it every right-wing view? Because my mum, my mum's right-wing. . .

Because being left, being liberal is of course synonymous with being correct isn't it? And we know that because . . . Eh. How do we know that again? Remind me?

Is it through honest consideration of the opposing views or is it through . . . just knowing.

If you're right, you're wrong. Right? It's black and white. Yes or No. Nothing in between.

I mean for fuck sake, Eric, how did we get here? And how do we get out?

When did everyone who disagrees with us suddenly become a Nazi or a bigot or a racist?

When did nuance die?

Silence.

I liked the feeling of punching that Nazi.

I like the feeling of attacking the right.

Makes me feel good. In here. Because I know I'm right.

But the thing is . . . so do they.

Because the feeling of being right is exactly the same as being wrong And you know who taught me that, Eric? A Tory!

And I'm not quite clear on this yet but it's something to do with . . . I mean, how the fuck will either of us learn that we're wrong if it feels like we're right and . . . and we've killed the very thing that would let us find out? In favour of what? Virtue signalling and hyperbole.

We need to be fucking better than the thing we're criticising, Eric!

We need to disagree better!

Rob *gathers breath.*

You know what I'm going to do, Eric. The next time I hear some opinion that makes me want to . . . attack. I'm going to take a deep breath. I'm going to look the person in the eye. I'm going to . . . I don't know.

I'm going to . . . try to find out. If I'm wrong.

I'm not going to tell them they're wrong. I'm not going to insult them or roll my eyes or walk away. I'm going to . . . ask them, why they think what they think. Crazy, right?

And maybe, when they try to explain it to me, they might have trouble justifying it. They might realise for themselves that . . . Or maybe I'll realise. Whatever.

I'm not going to push the lever, I'm going to break the lever. And find another way.

Now does that not sound better than . . .

Better than . . .

This?

Rob *addresses the audience.*

I'm hoping that you might show up to one of these shows. Hoping it. And dreading it. At the same time.

Well, Eric. Are you in tonight?

Silence.

Why don't we take a vote.

Our last vote of the night.

The proposition is this:

This community believes that abusing someone for holding an opinion is a helpful thing to do.[28]

I hope you vote No. That might give me some peace of mind. Vote now.

The results come in. Some people are still pro-attack.

Could we just . . .

Can we have the lights up, please.

After the whole show. After my monologue just there . . :

That was meant to be the big moment of . . .

We were all meant to agree there and go out into the night and . . .

Fuck.

Who voted Yes? Some of you still think . . .

How the . . .

---

[28]   Rob clarifies that 'abusing' here can mean physically or verbally. It was such a tricky line to get right and we shifted from the ambiguous 'attack' in an earlier draft. The wording of this proposition was the most talked about thing in the post-show in the foyer and in many of the write-ups of the show. We never got it quite right and continue to debate it today. Perhaps we should just have been ultra clear. Is it ever ok to fight ideas with violence? But the ambiguity and confusion around the wording was also productive as it provoked a debate on these issues through the prism of a critique of the show.

   Across the twenty performances the average level of agreement with the final proposition was just 7 per cent, with a low of 3 per cent and a high of 15 per cent. Most people rejected the proposition (68 per cent) though a sizeable minority abstained (25 per cent).

Who voted Yes?[29]

I once asked Eric if we'd ever all get along. He didn't answer me but I know now that the answer is no. And I know now that that's ok. That's good in fact. Because total agreement is the death of conversation. It's the end of thought.

So please don't think this is the end of the show. This should continue.

I'm going to go down to the foyer now. Let's put down our voting pads and just . . . talk, shall we? Come tell me why I'm right. Come tell me why I'm wrong. I promise, either way, I'll listen.[30]

Lights fade. An image of **Rob** *and* **Eric** *appears.*[31]

---

[29]   On occasion, this became a brief dialogue but this was essentially the transition point where the rules of the show (no communicating apart from voting) were broken and an attempt at a better way was instigated, so this moment had to involve Rob genuinely listening to the reason that an audience member voted Yes (if they offered it) and then offering them the chance to talk to him properly about it at the end.

[30]   Rob loved and hated this part of the show. It was the section that took a good show and, at times, made it exceptional, must-see, vital theatre. A genuinely impromptu discussion/argument/heated debate in the foyer after every single show. People leaving into the night still talking and arguing, 95 per cent of it conducted in a civil way. It's the 5 per cent that was exceptionally difficult for Rob to deal with. He was exhausted, physically and emotionally drained and then he walked out and invited people to tell him why he was wrong. And, boy, did some people take that invitation. The worst was a Jewish woman who seemed to think he was a Nazi sympathiser and took issue with the 'snide and sneering' way he was insulting the left-wing in the show. She refused to talk to Rob in a calm way or listen to what he was saying. Other audience members jumped to his defence. Rob maintained his cool and never raised his voice (he couldn't – he had just laid out our mission statement not to do so on stage!) but she really got to him. She left, refusing to shake Rob's hand, with her friend insinuating that as he 'was an actor' he was trying to rile them up deliberately by being calm. Trying to get a reaction. Rob had genuine tears in his eyes after they left (still refusing his handshake) and some audience members saw that and stayed to try to comfort him. After performing for an hour and a half then standing taking a volley of abuse from someone who refused to listen or engage with a genuine attempt at reconciliation, it was impossible to remain unaffected.

   However, most post show interactions were entirely constructive and reasonable. Rob's position and his ability to articulate it got stronger as a result of these challenges and Rob sums them up simply: 'I don't think it's effective to shout at people with whom you disagree, no matter how much you feel that some of them might deserve it. I'm more interested in being effective than feeling righteous.'

[31]   This image was taken with Rob and a local beekeeper, who looked similar to how we imagined Eric. For those who assumed the whole thing was made up, our hope was to offer a final moment of doubt as they left the auditorium.

Top Table

Ross Allan as Ross Munro, Rebecca Benson as Michelle Munro, and Callum Cuthbertson as Sandy Munro in *Top Table*

Top Table was first performed at Glasgow Lunchtime Theatre's A Play, a Pie and a Pint at Òran Mór in 2011.

Master of Ceremonies   David MacLennan
Sandy Munro   Callum Cuthbertson
Ross Munro   Ross Allan
Michelle Munro   Rebecca Benson

Director   David Overend
Assistant Director   Anna Nierobisz
Stage Designer   Patrick McGurn
Producer   Susannah Armitage

A wedding reception.[1]

The top table is set for five people. A picture of the bride and groom is set centre stage behind where they should be sitting.

Five pies and five pints sit proud.[2]

A digital camera is pointed at the table.

The **Master of Ceremonies** *appears.*[3]

MC   Ladies and gentlemen, I know you're all here to share in the celebration of Craig and Michelle, but before we begin the speeches I hope no one will mind if I also point out that this venue is also used to present new writing . . . (*The* **MC** *can now feel free to go through any pre-show introductions.*)[4]

So without further ado . . . Ladies and gentlemen please be upstanding for the top table.

Music plays.

The audience stand and applaud but only two people emerge from the doorway – the father of the bride, **Sandy**, *and the best man,* **Ross**.

They make their way to the table where they have a heated discussion with the **MC**. **Sandy** *and* **Ross** *appear to be in disagreement.* **Sandy** *seems a little drunk. Eventually the* **MC** *addresses the audience.*

MC   Ladies and gentlemen, I'm afraid that the bride and groom are . . . indisposed at this time. However, by request of the bride herself we are going to continue with

---

[1]   Participating with the audience isn't just about literally bringing them up on stage and asking them to speak. It can also be about making them understand and feel comfortable from an early stage with their role in the show. In a traditional play with a fourth wall this is understood implicitly – you come and sit and watch and think. But when you shake the foundations by ripping down that wall you need to make sure that you put in some support beams or the whole thing will collapse. In this case, we made their role as the wedding party guests very clear by having the programme set out like an order of service and the venue entirely set up for a wedding reception.

[2]   A Play, a Pie and a Pint is a lunchtime theatre venture that produces the largest number of new plays in the UK every year. Each week the downstairs events venue of the Òran Mór pub in Glasgow's West End hosts a different lunchtime play, entry to which includes a pint of beer (or wine or a soft drink) and a Scotch pie (or veggie equivalent). Over the years working there we have come to know and love this venue and the regular packed-out audience it brings. This is a very eclectic audience of theatre industry professionals, students in training and older people who adore theatre in the good old Glasgow variety tradition: a tradition that very much involves playing with the audience and including them in the show – delighting in a more direct engagement with them than might be expected elsewhere. Rob grew up with this audience and David has come to know and love them. We know what they want, what works for them and what doesn't. They are perfectly capable of sitting down and contemplating a deep and meaningful philosophical discussion, but more often than not the plays that kill in this venue are ones that are written for them. That is to say, they do include deepness and profundity, but they are delivered in a variety style, where there is always a nod and a wink to who is watching. They come for the event. They come to have fun. They come to feel involved.

[3]   As discussed in the Introduction to this book, as with most of our work, an important way for us to very quickly and efficiently let our audience know what is expected of them is through the use of a gatekeeper – in this case a Master of Ceremonies. In all cases, A Play, a Pie and a Pint begins with a member of the production team introducing the play and letting the audience know what's on next week (a very variety trope in itself). We utilised the audience's knowledge of this conceit by twisting it and having this person playing a small part in our production: the Master of Ceremonies. The audience particularly lapped this up as the gentleman presenting our play is known for his flamboyant dress sense. So when the late David MacLennan – the venue's much loved artistic director – came out in tartan trousers to play his part it is almost as well received as the play itself.

[4]   These are quite specific at Òran Mór, almost to pantomime levels of anticipated predictability.

the speeches as planned. So, without further ado, ladies and gentlemen, the father of the bride, Sandy Munro.

The **MC** *claps with the audience then leaves.* **Sandy** *struggles to his feet. He takes a swig of the pint.*[5]

Sandy   I know most of you were at the church this morning and a lot of you saw and heard what happened after the service but . . . as the man said . . . we shall continue as normal. The show must go on. My perfect princess Michelle and her new husband Craig are sorting things out as we speak and those of you who know me best will know that there is nothing . . . I repeat . . . nothing . . . I would not do for my angel Michelle. If my princess wants us to carry on then guess what we'll do?

Go on, guess.[6]

That's right, we'll carry on!

He takes another swig of his pint.

She can always watch the speeches back on video. Sorry. DVD.

He points to the camera, gives it a thumbs up.

Or green ray or whatever it is now.

He focuses on his speech.

Ok. So.

Welcome. Thanks for coming and sharing in this most . . . perfect day.

Take a bite of your pie.

Oh.

He laughs at his error and takes a bite of his pie.

I hope you are all enjoying the gourmet wedding lunch.[7] Craig's choice, not mine, eh, not Michelle's. He wanted to add the common touch . . . to my daughter's one and only fairy-tale wedding.

Say what you like about Craig . . .

No, seriously, say what you like about him.

He laughs.

Just a joke.

---

[5]   On one afternoon the stage crew had neglected to set both Ross and Sandy's chairs – we sat in the audience in horror as we realised what was happening. Were the actors going to have to perform the entire show with no chairs? Thankfully not, as, with most of our shows, the ability to make a mistake seem like part of the show enabled the actors to simply ask for chairs (appearing to be acting annoyed when in fact they were legitimately annoyed) and the show continued as planned.

[6]   If the first rule is to establish the audience's role as early as possible, the second rule might be to reinforce this soon after with an invitation to engage at the acceptable level. In the Òran Mór, the audience always gets it – they chimed in every day with yells of 'carry on!'.

[7]   Again, this is a nod and a wink to the audience who know only too well that the pies at the Òran Mór, although tasty, are hardly haute cuisine. It's a joke but it also serves to blur the lines between the reality and artifice of the event.

He fumbles with his cards.[8]

Don't worry, there won't be many more. The real entertainment will be brought to you soon in the shape of my son and Craig's best man, Ross. The father of the bride's speech is traditionally heartfelt and teary eyed. I think I can handle that, but Ross . . . He's the funny one in the family, aren't you, son? Aren't you a funny one? In fact he's the one who introduced his sister, my princess, to Craig in the first place so if it doesn't work out we know who to blame.

Sorry, I . . . I wrote this before . . .

He laughs nervously and goes back to his cards.

Well, what an amazing day it's been so far. I'd like to commend the reverend on a very moving service. It certainly got to me and I'm not ashamed to admit I shed a tear or two. It was a lovely ceremony . . . until the end . . . obviously. And I'm glad to say the weather held up well or not even the bad weather could spoil the perfection of the occasion.

Sorry, I should have scored one of them out. It was nice weather. It was nice.

I'd like to thank Craig's friends for making the long journey up from Plymouth. Some of you may know that Craig has no family – his parents were lost under . . . tragic circumstances a few years back now so . . . But . . .

He reads from his card.

Craig has a family now. We are his new family and . . . while I cannot provide a surrogate mother for him, as my wife isn't . . . I would be honoured if Craig would call me 'Dad'.

A father is an important thing in a boy's life . . .

My parents got married in 1947. Same year as Liz and Phil. The big royal wedding . . . The Queen and the Prince . . . mum was pregnant within a month – we don't hang about us Munro men – and soon my little sister Sandy was born.[9] I never knew her of course – she died aged one and I came along years later but . . . she's still my sister. And I share her name. Shared a lot of her baby clothes too because my parents weren't wealthy people and . . .

Ross   Dad.

Sandy   Yes. Sorry. Thank you also to our side of the family who have turned out in force. It's a great . . . source of regret to me that my mother didn't live to see this day. She would have loved to have seen . . .

---

8   The participatory premise of the performance is well established by now and this will be reflected in the reduction in footnotes here. Now the audience are in role, the show does not rely on the same degree of interaction as the previous plays in the collection. As with *Wallace*, *The Majority* and even *Bullet Catch* to an extent, this is the norm in our work – improvised, open sections followed by sections where the audience can relax a bit before being brought back into the mix. We don't want to exhaust them. Much like a well-paced thriller you need 'breather scenes' in participatory theatre.

9   Sandy Munro is Rob's brother-in-law's name. This is another moment of surreptitious autobiography, as seen in *Bullet Catch* and *The Majority*. Elsewhere, Rob has even made a whole show about his dad (*Our Fathers*, 2018); and his mum has appeared in a few too. In all of these plays, there are a number of these 'Easter eggs' hidden in the script.

You see after I was born, and I wasn't a girl, dad ran off with some tart or other . . . that's what mum used to call her, some tart or other. Some tart or other and her adulterous husband. He could rot in hell for what he did . . . And so she was left to bring me up. Alone. And she did a wonderful job. I know a lot of the older members of the family, those who can remember it, I know you question it . . . the way she fawned over me, the way she brought me up . . . But. It couldn't have been easy for her.

Sandy.

Her new little Sandy.

I was named after a dead girl.

Ross   Dad.

He motions towards the cue cards which his father has laid down. **Sandy** *picks them up and goes back into speech mode.*

Sandy   *Ma maw.* She would have loved this. She was crazy on weddings. Especially royal ones. Even though her own wedding was less than grand, she still loved being married the same year as Liz and Phil. Years after I was born copies of the film became available on 8 mm. We must have watched it a hundred times. My hand would cramp up from cranking the projector but I'd never stop until it was finished. I'd fight through the pain. It was perfect. Liz arriving in the carriage. Phil standing waiting for her. Nervous as all hell. The eight bridesmaids. Liz coming down the aisle. Them making their sacred . . . unbreakable vows. Beautiful. Perfect.

No one would have had a clue that just that morning at Buckie Palace Liz's tiara had snapped and they had to rush the court jeweller to his workshop with a police escort to fix it.

Mum used to say to me that all she hoped for in life was for me to have a perfect fairy-tale wedding someday. Your dead wee sister never can so you'd better have her day for her.

Silence.

Well, sorry, Mum. It never happened for me – I married my Anne in a . . . grey civil service by a motorway. But I know Mum is beaming with pride now looking down on Michelle's happy day.

He pauses on this, looks at the deserted top table. Looks directly down the camera. Continues with his next card.

I'm equally sorry that my Anne, Michelle's mum, my wife – she's still legally my wife – couldn't be here today. But it's Michelle's big day and she gets to invite who she pleases.

I met Anne in 1980 through the Salvation Army. Mum and I volunteered with them – we would go into hospitals and visit victims of sexual abuse, offer them comfort and support – see if they wanted to come to church. From the moment I saw Anne lying there – a broken angel – I knew. Right there and then, I vowed to mend her wings. It might sound strange but when I saw her lying there, in her white nightdress, it kind of looked like a wedding gown and I thought this is the one I'm going to marry.

I didn't take advantage. I didn't. You can't help who you fall in love with. Anne wasn't sure about it at first – about me, but she soon realised what I could offer her and she fell in love with me right back. She agreed to marry me. On one condition. She didn't want a church do. Registry office. No fuss.

No fuss.

That's what a wedding's meant to be. A fuss. A big . . . perfect . . . fuss.

Mum always used to say it's the one day of your life that you're allowed to fuss.

But Anne wouldn't hear of it. She didn't want a church. See it turned out the guy who'd . . . done it to her . . . he was a member of her mother's church. It had *happened* in a church and she . . .

So we got married in a dank little registry office – more like a hut really – just off the M8. Mum didn't like that.

Anne did allow me one concession though. I could pick the date. And there was only one date I wanted. 29 July 1981. Yeah? Rings a bell doesn't it. Of course it does. Same date as Charlie and Di. Same time even. 11.20 a.m.

I weighed it up and in the end I felt it worth it, to be married at the same time as them, even if it meant not watching it live. And anyway, I could always watch it later on tape. Over and over to my heart's content. On VHS.

Mum . . . she stayed at home to watch it live. 750 million people watched it live. Me and Anne had about twelve.

Anne wore a grey pantsuit.

So even though the day wasn't quite as I had imagined it – no white dress, no church, no Mum – it still felt special to be married at the same time as Di and Charlie.

Pause.

Ross was born the very next year.

He stares at **Ross**.

Sandy   We were . . . very happy with him but . . . I won't lie . . . things were far from perfect . . . Mum always said if the wedding isn't perfect then how do you expect the marriage to be? We got off on a flat note and for the next eight years the tune just got worse and worse . . . but then . . . then Michelle came along to save us.

My perfect princess Michelle.

The reason we are all here today.

So . . .

He's almost crying. He gees himself up with a big grin and an intake of breath.

I've been told the father of the bride's speech should include humorous stories about the bride . . . Oh-oh! Look out, Michelle!

He laughs.

I remember the day Michelle was born – 12 August 1991. She slipped out her mother like a bar of soap and the midwife almost dropped her. I remember her looking up at me with those big brown eyes of hers and . . . I swear my heart almost stopped right there and then – and I'd have died happy if it had.

She was such an inquisitive child.

He laughs.

I remember when she was three she caught me watching the tape of Charlie and Di's wedding. Daddy. Is that you and Mummy getting married?

He laughs. Pauses.

I told her yes. Yes it is.

She said, you look different, Daddy.

I said, it's the lighting.

She said, does light make your ears grow then?

She was too clever. I had to tell her the truth.

It's a princess's wedding.

And from that moment she was hooked.

We'd watch that tape together two, three times a week. I'd tell her about Di's gown. A £9000 Emanuel puffball meringue made from silk taffeta decorated with lace sequins and over ten thousand pearls. She loved the look of Charlie in his full naval commander uniform.

Michelle said they didn't look very happy. In the video. Why didn't they look happy? Are they happy now? I told her that although Charlie and Di were going through a tough time, they would be alright in the end.

She'd ask me about my wedding and I'd lie and tell her how special it was; how perfect. Mummy in her flowing white gown. Daddy in his royal highland uniform. She asked about Granny – why she didn't have a husband. And I told her the truth – because he was a very bad man who did an unforgivable thing and ran off with some tart or other and we don't know if he's dead or alive nor do we care.

We'd talk about her wedding too. She wanted all the same things I did, apart from she wanted the minister to be a dog and her first dance to be to the Spice Girls.

Silence.

I bought her dolls. Fairy princess dolls. Dozens of them in the end. One of them looked a little like her and she called it Princess Michelle. She used to hold little make-believe weddings and it was always Princess Michelle getting married.

He laughs. Swigs his pint.

They were just perfect days those.

The divorce hit Michelle the hardest. I remember her mum sat her down and said to her, listen, sometimes two people just aren't meant to be together. Sometimes divorce is the right option. I didn't like her lying to Michelle like that but I let it go . . .

I remember Michelle looking up at her with tears in her eyes.

But where will Diana live now?

He laughs

I'm not ashamed to admit I cried myself when I heard they were divorcing. Charlie and Di. I always thought the separation would be temporary. After that perfect wedding and everything. It was wrong. For common people to divorce is one thing but them . . . they should be setting an example . . . they're meant to be better . . .

It tainted my wedding too. Our wedding. Mine and Anne's. It was the one thing that was special about it and now it was gone.

I destroyed the tape of course. It was ruined now. However beautiful . . . it was tarnished for ever and there was nothing that could change that.

I destroyed it of course.

He goes back to his cards.

I remember the next year when Diana died, Michelle lined up her princess dolls and told them all what had happened. Like they would be sad about it.

Michelle was always thoughtful and caring like that.

I couldn't help thinking, awful as it was, that Di might have deserved it. For the infidelity.[10] Charlie cheated too of course so that part didn't seem fair. It should have been both of them really, if we're being fair about it.

Anyway, I think the whole Diana thing . . . put ideas into Anne's head. I wonder just how many marriages that whole dreadful saga wrecked. Wives across the country thinking maybe if Diana wasn't happy in her fairy-tale marriage then maybe they weren't in theirs.

She left me the same year. That's not a coincidence is it? And so did you, didn't you Ross? You went with her.

Ross Dad, maybe I should take over /

Sandy / No. No, you'll have your turn. This is my time.

She took him and ran off with some sailor or other. Merchant navy. Met him at some . . . pub. I didn't know she was going to pubs but apparently . . . She went to Plymouth with him. Just about as far away from me as she could have got. Said she

---

10   We were often surprised by the audience's reaction to this line: either gasping in sacrilegious horror or whooping and clapping their approval. It's difficult to tell how much they were playing a role here.

couldn't take Michelle away from me – we had too strong a bond – but Ross was old enough to decide himself. Said she was sorry. She just didn't love me and . . .

How do you explain that one to a five-year-old?

Mummy's gone off with a sailor.

Is she on his boat?

Pause.

She's the only woman I ever . . . There was no one before her. No one since.

She broke her vows. She left me to bring up Michelle on my own. And let me tell you all – I did a fucking good job of it. I did.[11]

He looks at his card.

Another funny story about Michelle.

When she was fourteen she went off royal weddings and, to my horror, began focussing on celebrities. She wrote Jordan a letter asking to be invited to her wedding to Peter Andre and when she didn't get a reply she went on hunger strike. She lasted four days. It made the regional news. Wedding Obsessed Girl on Hunger Strike. They went so far as digging up dirt on me. Suggested my obsession had been a bad influence on her. Obsession? No. Respect. A healthy respect for the institution of marriage is what I have and if more people shared it then this world would be a better place. How does holding that view constitute being a bad influence?!

Here's another funny one.

When I started, and I'll admit this, maybe having one or two too many shandies of a . . . morning . . . she would . . . she was a pillar of . . . she never gave up on me. She sat with me for hours – she sometimes even stayed off school. And when it came time to think about university she said she didn't need to think. She wanted to stay with me. Look after me.

We got through it together.

He drinks.

What?

If you can't have a drink on your own princess's wedding day then when can you?

Silence. He looks at his cue card.

I'm meant to talk about Craig as well. That's traditional too. Say a little bit about him. About when I met him . . . and that . . .

Ross met Craig at Plymouth University. They became very good friends. Not that I knew of course. I never heard from him, did I son? Until he brought him home.

---

11   In all of our participatory work there are moments where the characters break the agreed contract with the audience, resulting in a feeling of danger in the room. We were very happy with the reaction this one got as we held it right back until now. Yes, Sandy had gone off piste before this, but this was the moment where he absolutely smashed the convention of a happy wedding speech by swearing angrily and it got the desired response from the audience, who were aware of the transgression and felt it in a way they wouldn't have behind a fourth wall.

You wanted to mend some bridges didn't you, son, and Craig needed a fresh start after . . . what happened to his parents . . . on that golf course.

We all went out for dinner – that little Italian place by Central.[12] And the moment Michelle laid eyes on Craig – a handsome lad, I'll admit – I knew I had lost her. A little bit of her. Her heart was not entirely mine any longer. The way she looked at him that first dinner. I knew. It was how I had looked at Anne in that hospital bed – she wanted to mend Craig. She wanted to marry him.

She played with her hair.

And you know what? I liked Craig. I did. I actually liked the boy. I thought, maybe this could work. Maybe Ross and Craig and Michelle and I will be a family. And maybe then Anne will come back and beg me to take her back. And I'll say, fuck off Anne, you adulterous bitch. You had your chance and you blew it. You ruined it. After all I did for you. It's gone now and it can never come back. It's spoiled for ever and nothing you can say will ever undo the unforgivable thing you've done.

He realises he has gone off script – fumbles for the next card.

And now we've come full circle. It's 2011. Another royal wedding. Hopefully this one will last. Pause for laughter. It says here. Pause for laughter.

Liz and Phil. Mum and Dad.

Charlie and Di. Sandy and Anne.

Kate and Wills . . .[13]

Michelle knew she had to move quick if she was to keep the family tradition going.

She proposed to Craig within a month. And he accepted. He needed someone. And I'm not afraid to admit as happy as I was for her I felt jealous and bitter. Jealous of her because I knew I would give her the wedding I always wanted. And bitter towards him. For taking my daughter away from me. Leaving me on my own.

But I was adamant that my bitterness would not affect them. I would be happy for her. And him. Never let them know how I felt. I paid for all this. I made it possible. I even went on the stag night.

I'm not used to nightclubs. It was . . . a new world to me. And I had a few drinks and . . . I actually found myself having a good time. There were people my age there. Honestly. I didn't know . . . I just didn't know . . . We were dancing . . . I was dancing and then . . . before I knew it we had all piled into taxis and back to my house.

And then . . . there she was . . . a girl . . . she looked like a young Jackie Bird[14] . . . and . . . I'm still technically married, I . . . guilt ran through me as I watched her . . . But it wasn't me she was there for. She had a ghetto blaster with her. She put on some music

---

12   Referring to Glasgow's Central Station. There are several Italian restaurants in this area, but this audience would all have their favourite one and be able to picture the specific location.

13   This production took place shortly after this wedding, so there was lots of chat about royal weddings at the time.

14   Jackie Bird is a much beloved Scottish news reader – the type everyone's dad had fancied for decades. As we hoped, the audience were highly amused by this reference, which is developed further in *Eulogy*.

and then . . . she was dancing with Craig. Taking her clothes off. While we all stood round in a circle and . . . leered. It was disgusting. I had to go outside for some air.

I must have passed out . . . when I came back inside an hour and a half later . . . they had disappeared. My living room was full of drunk sleeping shadows but . . . Craig and young Jackie Bird had gone.

I searched the house for them . . . this cannot happen . . . this is wrong . . . I can't let this . . .

I found them in an upstairs room. Together.

And then today . . . I mean, he was probably still drunk the boy, who holds a stag do the night before the wedding, Ross? You were asking for trouble.

When Craig broke down on the way out of the church – collapsed under the weight of the guilt and the alcohol – and admitted what he had done . . . with the young Jackie Bird lookalike . . . when I saw my perfect princess's face just . . . fall . . . I . . .

In my own house.

I tried to stop it.

This is all my fault.

Ross   You couldn't have stopped it, Dad. It's not your fault.

Pause. **Sandy** *breaths deeply.*

He laughs – manic.

Sandy   Maybe you're right. I mean, he didn't have to do it did he? Maybe it's no wonder he did what he did considering the example his parents set him. The sexual deviancy. The way they lived. The way they died /

Ross   / Woah, woah, woah. Not cool, Dad.

Sandy *goes for another swig.*

Ross   Maybe you've had enough eh?

Sandy   It's your fault I drink in the first place Ross. You could have convinced her to stay. She wouldn't have gone anywhere without you. You were her favourite. Her special boy.

Do you know what you did to me?

Where's Mummy gone with the sailor? Is Mummy on his boat?

She asked me that over and over again. Over and over. How do you answer that? How do you explain an act of betrayal like that to a five-year-old? I'll tell you how. You tell the truth. Because there's nothing like the truth. Nothing. I lied at first. I lied for weeks. Months. But then one night when I'd had a few and she asked me again, I just lost it. I told her straight what had happened.

I told her that mummy had done an evil thing and it would just be me and her from now on and when she grew up she must never do what Mummy did to anyone because it would make them cry – like Daddy. We survived together and Michelle came to agree with me. That what her mum had done was unforgivable. You do not do that to someone. And we agreed that I would never give her a divorce. Never. I wouldn't break my vows just because she had. I would stay single. I would keep my promise even if she hadn't.

I'm a fucking wonderful person . . . What I did for her. She should have counted herself lucky to be with me.

It was meant to be perfect.

Long awkward silence as he realises how off script he has gone. He wipes his eyes, drains his pint and picks up the last cue card.

But enough of the past. Now let's look to the future.

He turns and addresses the bride's seat.

Michelle, my darling, sweet, beautiful, perfect princess. I long only for your happiness and am so glad you have found the true love and had the fairy-tale wedding that passed me by. I look forward to the day when you introduce me to my first granddaughter so I can spoil another little girl all over again.

Like I spoiled you.

He turns to the groom's chair.

And Craig, please take care of my little girl and never cause her pain.

A toast to the happy couple! To Craig and Michelle.

He raises his glass. Waits for everyone to join in the toast.[15]

Craig and Michelle.

He sits down. Silence.

Sandy   On you go then, Ross. Your turn.

Pause. **Ross** *eventually stands up.*

Ross   Thanks, Dad.

I'm sure Michelle will love watching that back . . .

Silence.

Listen, this isn't about me and it isn't about him. It's about two amazing people – Craig and Michelle. Here's hoping they're back there sorting this mess out and in half an hour or so they'll be out here enjoying themselves and dancing like morons with the rest of us. And as crazy as this may seem, it's what Michelle wants, so I'm going to try to keep this light and fun. Yeah? Oh, and I've been asked by management if for

---

[15]   This is an important moment: as a lot of time has passed since the initial role-playing fun, the audience have relaxed into their usual mode of reception. Insisting on the toast brings them back into the game and gives them a moment to pick up the role of wedding guests again. We did this much more with the songs in *Eulogy*. We always look for ways to keep our audience alert to the fact they are active in the room, even in plays where the interaction is less overt.

health and safety reasons you could refrain from getting up on the chairs and tables during my standing ovation.

Now, I was nine when ma wee sister came into the world . . . and I was not happy. Who was this little alien coming into my house and taking up half my bedroom? Crying me awake every night. Hogging all my parents' attention. Especially my dad's. But soon I realised that she wasn't a monster. She was actually a pretty special little girl. And as odd as she was, as many times as she watched Princess Diana and Big Ears getting married, she was my little sister. And I loved her. Still do.

I didn't share my dad's strange passion for weddings, but she certainly did. I had more in common with Mum. I think it was a relief for him when she came along – finally someone to listen to him. I remember one time, I was about twelve and I couldn't find any of my He-men figures. After searching everywhere I went out into the back garden and there she was . . . marrying off He-man to Princess Jasmine! And all my other figures were in the congregation watching, all of them paired off with some princess or other. I was livid! He-man is not the marrying kind – he's too busy saving the universe. And if he was going to marry anyone it would be Teela, not a bloody Disney Princess.

Pause. He mimes finding another figure.

And Skeletor *would not* be in attendance! He'd maybe go to He-man's funeral but he certainly wouldn't attend his wedding.

Pause. He looks at his cue card.

Now it says here I've to thank the groom for his kind words about the maid of honour, but as neither of them are here . . .

I don't know if you know but the maid of honour, Shilpa, she's my girlfriend now actually – we got together a few months back – she's back there with Michelle now, making sure she's ok.

If listening intently with an upturned glass at a locked door counts as making sure someone's ok that is.

He picks up some greeting cards.[16]

Now bear with me as I read some cards from people too lazy to get off their arses and actually come here today.

Dear Michelle and Craig. Sorry we couldn't make it – we wish you all the best on this, your happiest day. Lots of love from Brian and Elaine.[17]

Dear Michelle and Craig. Sorry we couldn't make it today we hope your special day is perfect in every way.

---

[16]   This is another important section, which adheres to wedding speech protocol. We want to constantly keep our audiences invested in their characters – they are not the audience, they are guests at a wedding.

[17]   The names of Rob's parents-in-law.

Oh, bit of a rhyme there – that's from Colin and Justin. I don't think it's that Colin and Justin, but you never know.

Dear Michelle and Craig – gutted I couldn't be there to share your perfect day. All the best for the future. Love from Janice – your wee pal from Home Economics – chicken, chicken, mince pie, chicken! LOL!

I know Janice and it's nice to see her carers are finally allowing her access to pen and paper.

He laughs.

And the last one . . .

He opens it and stops short . . .

To my darling Michelle. I wish you and Craig a lifetime of happiness. Thinking of you always. Mum.

P.S. Ross, tuck in your shirt.

He smiles. His shirt is indeed untucked. He tucks it in.

Silence.

Right. So.

I feel now would be the right time to admit something.

I am in love with Craig.

Totally. Unequivocally. Irrevocably.

Heterosexually.

This bromance that has lasted longer than any relationship I have ever had and I feel that it may just last for ever.

As my dad said, he has no family of his own. But now . . . Now he is part of my family. Our family. And one mistake cannot and will not undo that. I won't allow it.

I met Craig at university in Plymouth. I didn't know anyone and I was still getting over the fallout from making the move down south . . .

He looks sideways at his dad, who seems lost in an emotional reverie.

Craig is the type of guy who just will not stand by and see someone standing awkwardly at a party. It's easier to leave them be and have fun with your own friends but he tends to take it upon himself to make sure they are ok. Integrate them into the group. It's thanks to Craig I had a social life at uni. I really believe that if he hadn't said hi, I might never have gone to another party. He brought me out my shell, introduced me to girls – lots of girls. Craig was definitely a big believer in free love but always practised safe sex. And by that I mean he made sure none of his girlfriends ever found out about each other.

He always said that sex was as natural as breathing. If you lock two people – any two people – in a room for long enough they will eventually end up shagging. Which made the time I accidentally got locked inside the bathroom in the student union with him just about the scariest night of my life.

Pause.

Basically, Craig gave me a life. And I thank him for it.

What I don't thank him for is the time he left me drunk and naked in the quadrangle handcuffed to a specially made solid wood cut-out of our politics lecturer, Dr Sullivan.

It was, as he put it, 'only a delightful quirk of fate, the cherry on the icing on the cake' that Dr Sullivan was the first person I passed on the high street as I dragged the thing bollock swinging naked to the safety of our student flat.

Craig's parents were just as free spirited as him – perhaps even more so.

Most of you will have heard how they died.

Because it's a funny story. It is. It's got it all. Sex, nudity . . . a random lightning strike.

Hilarious.

But they're still people. They've still died. And it's unfair that they be defined by the way they went. Reduced to . . . sexual deviants. Because although they were . . . free spirits . . . and didn't have a whole lot of hang-ups when it came to . . . that sort of thing . . . they were wonderful people.

He addresses his dad.

Kind, generous, loving . . . and it's unfair to think of them in any other way.

Craig was left alone.

And I saw it as my opportunity to repay him. For what he had done for me. He wanted to get out of Plymouth and I had been wanting an excuse to come home and see Michelle anyway so . . .

And besides, I had some bridges to mend.

He looks at his dad. Silence.

When Craig first saw Michelle his tongue hit the floor like a cartoon dog. He was smitten with her and it's the first time I've ever known him to be nervous talking to me.

Eh, I, eh, I kind of, like, really, fancy your sister so, maybe, if you wouldn't mind, I know it's weird, but, could I have your permission to, you know . . .

What, shag her?

No, no, no, I, er, well, maybe, but no that's not what . . .

I told him to relax and go for it. Couldn't think of a nicer guy for her to end up with.

And he is. A nice guy. No matter what he did . . . You know, you can do bad stuff and not be a bad guy . . . I mean, we let murderers out after thirty years or so, so surely we can forgive Craig for one moment of drunken madness.

I take responsibility. If it helps. I do. I organised the stag – I got him blootered. But honestly, he never stopped talking about Michelle the whole fucking night. At one point I even caught him texting her. He sent the text and I watched him wait – he timed it on his watch – about ten seconds or so and then he laughed. I asked him what he was doing and he said he was waiting till she'd read it so he could laugh at exactly the same time as her.

Is that a bad guy?

And I didn't organise the girl by the way. I knew Craig wouldn't be able to cope with that kind of temptation. It must have been one of the Plymouth boys – Hazmat or G-Had or Kendrick.[18] If I'd known they were planning it I'd have stopped it. Although I can't fault the choice – I mean, a young Jackie Bird – come on! Even Dad's eyes were on stalks.

He laughs.

But what he was saying – about it being his fault. That's rubbish. It was my fault. I should have got him out of that house but instead . . . I goaded him on.

And I don't blame my dad for being upset with me about how mum left. Because that was my fault too.

When she went she asked me to go with her and I said yes. I couldn't say anything else. We have a bond, Dad. Like you and Michelle do. If I'd have said no she wouldn't have gone. She wouldn't have had the strength. But she wasn't happy, Dad.

I couldn't let her turn down the chance to be happy.

And you know what? She is. With her sailor. He's called Simon by the way, Dad – and he's nice. She smiles, Dad. A lot. I know you find it tough but . . . you can surely take some consolation in the fact that she's happy.

Silence.

See, I know he's made a bit of a fool of himself today but the reason I don't have a go . . . The reason I cut him some slack . . . You see everything he's done. Everything. It's come from a good place. Yeah, he's a wee bit . . . different . . . but he's . . .

Silence.

Dad.

Before I came back up here.

Mum told me.

You see, my dad . . . he knew I wasn't his when he married her. He knew I was the result of . . . my mum's . . . assault . . . and he still . . .

---

[18]   All friends of ours.

Silence.

That's a wonderful thing he did. It was a wonderful thing, Dad, but it wasn't love. It wasn't what Mum and Simon have got. It wasn't what Craig and Michelle have got.

Shit, I didn't intend to do this – I've gone way off . . . what I'm trying to say is if you're going to blame someone, blame me. Not my dad. Not Craig. Me. I knew he wanted to stay faithful but I also knew how tough – how unnatural he found it. I should have kept an eye on him. That's the best man's job.

Silence.

Shit.

Light-hearted I think I said.

He laughs.

Craig hates himself for what he did. Fuck sake, he broke down – physically and mentally – on the way out the church and admitted what he'd done. In front of all of you. Are those the actions of a bad guy?

He looks at his cue card.

I'm meant to address the bride now so . . .

He looks down the camera.

Michelle, I hope to God when you watch this back you've decided to forgive him. You two have got to work it out because Craig loves you. I know he does.

I asked him last night . . . I said, Craig, are you sure about this? I mean, you've never believed in marriage. Are you absolutely sure?

He looked me in the eye and said . . .

Marriage isn't natural, mate . . . I always know he's drunk when he starts calling me mate . . . mate, marriage isn't natural. Over 70 per cent of people cheat – which kind of suggests monogamy isn't right. Staying with one person is against every natural urge in our being, mate . . . it's against nature . . . it's wrong, mate . . . but, he said, but, mate . . . after Mum and Dad died and I met your sister I realised . . . if you find someone who's worth *disobeying* nature for, worth sacrificing that instinctive desire for, someone you would turn down every other woman in the world for . . . *forever.* Mate, I'm giving up all women for ever for your sister. All women. For ever. That's a lot isn't it? I would die for your sister, mate. That's not logical is it? Love's not natural, but it's fucking brilliant.

And he meant it. He really did. But . . .

Silence. **Michelle** *has entered the room.*[19] *She stands there in her flowing white wedding dress, her face almost totally blank. Beautiful. Miserable. The room takes a*

---

[19]   These stage directions don't quite capture the full effect of her appearing at the back and walking slowly down the aisle. This was a genuinely chilling moment in some performances. And this wouldn't have been nearly as effective if we hadn't implicated the audience as wedding guests from the start.

collective breath as she walks down the aisle of the reception hall. How long has she been there? **Ross** *addresses her.*

Ross   He slipped. It doesn't mean he doesn't love you. It means he's human. Imperfect.

No one is perfect, Michelle. Perfection doesn't exist. But he does love you. That exists.

Michelle *has approached the table.* **Ross** *hands her her pint.*

Ross   A toast. To love.

He raises his glass with the audience.

To love.

Michelle *takes her place.*[20] *Looks at the photo of her and Craig.* **Sandy** *goes to see if she is ok. She is rather cold with him. She looks at her brother. Then the audience.*

Michelle   Hello. Hi. How . . . how is everyone? I'm sorry about . . . all this. Have they been . . . have they done their speeches like I asked them?[21]

Good, because everything's got to be . . .

Perfect – are you all enjoying your pies?

She laughs.

That was Craig's input. He's so down to earth and . . .

Ross, Shilpa's not coming out just now – she wanted to but her face is like a mascara graveyard from all the crying so I told her to go sort it first coz I'm not wanting her out here looking like that. Tears all down her face. You'd think it was her whose heart had been ripped out, eh?

She laughs.

I made a point of not crying and my make-up's fine – see.

Silence.

Fuckin' Jackie Bird.

Craig had never even heard of her before he came up here. Minute he saw her on TV he got this weird, freaky crush on her. She's old enough to be his gran.

Remember, Dad? He said, who's that?

And you said. That is Jackie. Bird.

She laughs.

---

[20]   We're not sure if anyone noticed it, but we were particularly pleased with her costume – a replica of Kate's wedding dress that we borrowed from a nearby clothes shop. Our assistant designer noticed it in the window and they were happy to lend it for the show

[21]   This was such a sweet moment. Most of the audience were too stunned to speak but there was *always* a member of the audience who, in solidarity, said, 'Yes', or 'Aye, hen'.

Sandy   Maybe we should /

Michelle   / No. Dad. I'm . . . We've got to keep going. We've only got the venue booked till . . .

Right. So. I'm going to do Craig's speech for him because . . .

She unfolds his speech – it's written messily on crumpled A4.

So.

On behalf of my wife and I . . .

That's meant to get a big response. That always gets a big response. It's tradition to give that bit a big response. Will we try again?

On behalf of my wife and I . . .

Audience respond.[22]

That's better. Thanks.

I would like to thank the many people who have helped make this day the huge success I think you'll all agree that it has been.

The maid of honour, Shilpa, has been amazing in keeping Michelle grounded through the meticulous process of putting her perfect day together. She also arranged the hen night and I'm assured she made sure the stripper wasn't too good looking as per my request.

Pause.

I'd like to thank my best man, Ross. Ross, mate, you are my best friend in the world – you introduced me to the love of my life and you supported me in the darkest time of my life when my parents died.

Mum and Dad . . . I don't believe in heaven so . . . But I do believe in honouring memories so I'd like to take the chance right now to say that there is nothing fucking wrong with having a threesome on a golf course as long as all the parties are consenting . . . and fully paid up members of the club.

And of course, make sure you pick a day when lightning showers aren't forecast.

That's meant to be a joke. He can't help it. Joking.

Mum. Dad. I love you. And I will always honour you by living life to the full.

I'd also like to thank my new father-in-law, Sandy, for his kind words. But most of all I'd like to thank him for the excellent job he's done in bringing up his daughter.

---

[22]   This was another small moment of participation, which had a really important function. The audience were really implicated now as they had watched and listened and revelled in the schadenfreude misery of the whole thing up to this point. These moments functioned perfectly – they audience played along, but in the same embarrassed, conflicted way a real wedding party would under these circumstances. The cheer at this point was expectedly loaded.

Sandy, rest assured I fully intend on taking care of her and remaining faithful to her for the rest of my life. I had no idea what love was before I met Michelle – no idea how powerful it could be.

She swallows hard.

I was kind of lost before I met Michelle. My family was just suddenly . . . gone and . . . She was there for me.

I remember the first time I saw her. I knew instantly. This is the girl who I want to spend the rest of the night with.

Sorry – I'm only being honest – she's sex on legs.

And to be serious for a moment . . . she saved my life and gave me back my smile.

On our third date she told me she wanted to fix my broken wings. Which to be honest was one of the worst chat-up lines I've ever heard . . .

Pause. She is hurting.

But it worked because three seconds later we were both naked.

That's not true.

At first I was a little taken aback being proposed to. I had never thought myself the marrying type but I certainly intended to do the asking if it ever happened.

To my surprise I said yes almost instantly. It just felt right. I wanted to be with her and only her for ever. Which was weird and rather unsettling but also . . . brilliant.

I didn't need a piece of paper to confirm that but I knew how happy being married would make her and making her happy had become my only goal in life.

Michelle . . .

I want you to know that I love you and that I will never do anything to hurt you. I will do all that I can to make you happy and to give you the perfect life you've always dreamed of.

Michelle you have turned my world upside down . . .

I'm not a poet but I wrote you this verse. I'm not a romantic, but I'd walk across oceans just to see your smile. I'm not a dreamer, but my sleep is full of you. I *don't* believe in marriage.

Please marry me today.

She is struggling not to cry. She composes herself then slowly, deliberately, burns the speech using the flame from a candle on the table.

You know, I looked at the stripper. Shilpa organised him. I didn't know anything about it. I looked at him and I . . . I felt so so so guilty just for thinking about him . . . in that way. I had to be sick. I had to be sick in the toilet.

Shilpa came and found me in the toilet. She was outraged because we had been asked to leave because she was a Hindu. She was going to go to the police.

She was livid.

And that was the moment I got his text message. It said . . . Kabab Foot.

And I laughed.

It's a private joke. One night . . . I dropped a kebab on my foot and . . . well, that's about it.

And I knew he'd be laughing too.

And then. Less than three hours later he was in bed with another woman.

Pause.

It turned out that what the bouncer had actually said to Shilpa was 'No *hen dos*', so we left and went somewhere else.[23]

Silence.

You know what my earliest memory is?

Princess Diana's wedding dress.

That massive train.

I was so unbelievably blissfully happy watching that tape with you, Dad. Over and over and over. Listening to you speak – planning . . . well, planning this . . . today. See that centre piece there? I've known what that would look like since I was four. We both have.

I always felt so bad for you having to get married to that miserable woman in a horrible little room. But I knew you wouldn't let that happen to me. I knew you'd help make my day absolutely perfect.

I met Craig and that was fine – he was great – he ticked all the boxes but I knew he wouldn't propose because he was a . . . hippy or something. And it had to be this year because of Kate and Wills. To keep up the family tradition. So I just did it myself.

I worried about that didn't I, Dad? I shouldn't have proposed – that's not traditional. That's not the perfect fairy-tale story. The prince proposes, doesn't he, Dad? Maybe that would bleed down and spoil everything else.

But you told me, it doesn't matter. It'll be fine. It can still be perfect.

And I trusted you. I've always trusted you, Dad.

Which is why . . .

---

[23] This was the best received line in any of our plays so far, and is unlikely to be surpassed. We still remember the newly appointed Makar (National Poet of Scotland) Liz Lochhead half standing with her hands above her head clapping and laughing with glee. That's like a rite of passage for a Scottish theatre maker. This felt like a full minute-long laugh on some days. It's actually the joke that the whole play began with. Rob wrote it for this specific audience and they reacted exactly like we knew they would. It's a variety joke – a Francie and Josie joke. It might not have worked as well anywhere else.

Why I can hardly believe what you've done.

Silence.

Sandy   We should get the DJ started.

Michelle   Craig's told me everything, Dad.

Sandy   He's lying. Whatever he said, I mean . . . You can't . . .

Michelle   You knew what he did and you told him to keep his mouth shut.

Sandy   Yes. Yes. I was trying to protect you. Is that all? Is that all he said?

Michelle   No, Dad. It's not all.

You hired her. He told me you hired her.

Pause.

You arranged it, didn't you?

Ross   Dad?

Silence.

Sandy   I did it for you.

Michelle   For me?

Sandy   I had to test him. To see if he was good enough for you.

She danced for Craig and he seemed like he was enjoying it but when she tried to kiss him he walked away. Got his phone out and sent a text. Probably to you I thought. He's passed the test.

Maybe he does love her. Maybe it's all for the best. Just accept it, Sandy. You've lost her. You've lost her too.

I felt myself begin to cry and I couldn't let anyone see that so . . . I went outside into the garden and sat there for half an hour or so.

And then I saw the light go on in the upstairs bedroom. I went down to the bottom of the garden to get a better angle and . . . I saw them . . . in the upstairs bedroom. In my bedroom. Mine and Anne's. Kissing. In our bedroom. Her . . . still . . . bare chested and . . . Craig . . . drunk and . . .

I thought about going right up there and stopping it. Saving him from himself. Stopping him before it was too late. But instead . . .

I stood at the bottom of the garden, in the mud, a branch of the little apple tree in my face, and I watched.

I let it happen.

All the while allowing the guilt to flow freely through me. Trading it off against the fact that at least I wouldn't lose you. Michelle.

But in the morning Craig came to me. Tears in his eyes. And he admitted it all. He confessed his sin and . . . I could see. I could see he did. He did love you.

I was ashamed. I told him what I had done. And he didn't . . . He actually hugged me. Told me he understood. He loved Michelle as much as I did. We just both needed to show it a little better.

I tried to fix it, Michelle. I did.

I told him not to say a word about any of it. It wasn't his fault – it was mine. I offered myself up . . . I . . .

He agreed. He did.

He agreed to keep his mouth shut but . . .

The idiot.

Silence.

You can move on. It can still be perfect for you. It can still be perfect.

Silence.

Michelle   No. It can't.

You've ruined it. It's gone now and it can never come back. It's spoiled for ever and nothing you can say will ever undo it.

It's tainted. It will always be what happened.

What once was special will never be special again.

Ross   Where is he?

Michelle   Gone.

Ross   Gone?

Michelle   I told him to go and he went. He walked into the street in his kilt.

Pause.

His left sock was down.

Ross   You need to find him.

Michelle   You know William doesn't wear a wedding ring.

Ross   What?

Michelle   Kate wears one. So why can't he?

Ross   Michelle /

Michelle   / He doesn't like to wear jewellery.

The prince.

Ross   Michelle. You have to forgive him.

Michelle   I have.

I have forgiven him, Ross.

But that's not enough.

It has to be perfect.

Doesn't it, Dad?

Silence.

It has to be perfect.

Silence.

It's time for the first dance.

Music plays.

Michelle *dances alone.*[24]

---

[24]   We didn't have time to do this sadly, as we were pushing at the allocated fifty-minute lunchtime slot as it was. Still, ending with Michelle's ironic assertion of perfection felt right.

Eulogy

Benny Young as Andy Munro, Joyce Falconer as Anne Munro, and Callum Cuthbertson as Sandy Munro in *Eulogy*

Eulogy was first performed at Glasgow Lunchtime Theatre's A Play, a Pie and a Pint at Òran Mór in 2018.[1]

Andy Munro   Benny Young
Anne Munro   Joyce Falconer
Sandy Munro   Callum Cuthbertson

Director   David Overend
Assistant Director   Cairan McLaggan
Stage Designers   Jonathan Scott and Gemma Patchett
Producer   Sarah MacFarlane

---

[1]   *Eulogy* was conceived as a sequel to *Top Table*, which is a pretty unique opportunity in theatre. It was the same venue and we knew some of the audience might remember *Top Table*, but if they didn't this worked as a stand-alone play as well. In this way we were participating with the audience across the pace of two different plays, five years apart, and asking them to play the role of friends and family members, who were at the wedding and now came to the funeral. Part three of this trilogy will be set at the christening of the reverend's new baby boy.

Act One: **The Reverend**

The audience are the mourners at a funeral.[2] *The* **Master of Ceremonies** *enters.*[3]

MC   Hello, welcome. Firstly, we here at the Òran Mór would like to extend our deepest condolences for your loss. Although today we host a service of remembrance, this venue is also used for lunchtime theatre and we have a wonderful play on next week called . . .

The usual spiel can now be delivered.

But now, I'll hand you over to the Reverend Andrew Munro who will be conducting today's service.

Thank you.

The Reverend **Andy Munro** *enters.*[4]

Andy   Hello.

I have in my time conducted some five hundred funerals. But this . . . this will be the hardest of them all.

My brother . . .

My little brother Sandy . . .

Was taken from us in the prime of his life.

Under such bizarre, almost surreal circumstances.

But we are not here today to dwell in misery. We are here to celebrate Sandy's life. His achievements. And even as I say these words, I'm sure that many of you may be asking yourselves . . .

What achievements?

---

[2]   As with *Top Table*, the venue for this play enhanced the setting of the drama. On entering the space, the audience encountered a coffin centre stage. We designed the programme as an order of service for a funeral, and filled the space with the sort of tepid, sentimental music that is usually played at such events. On the rear wall of the stage, there was a large projected image of the deceased: a photograph of Callum Cuthbertson playing Sandy in the same venue in *Top Table* in 2011. So a lot was going on to create an immersive environment, even before the opening line of the script.
    As the audience entered, they were greeted by Benny Young, improvising in character as the Reverend – a playful and informal opening, which he had also enjoyed when he played Edward Hammer MP in *Wallace*. On this occasion, for reasons that will become apparent, Benny had to decide which members of the audience to 'cast' early on. He also had to communicate their exact seating position to Callum backstage.

[3]   This time the venue producers shared this role and some of them relished the chance to perform. As the audience know them so well, this was a fun way to get started. It also serves as a clear and easy method for casting the audience – by telling them directly that they have suffered a loss and the venue are sorry for this.

[4]   At this point, the MC handed the microphone to the Reverend. This passing of the microphone-baton served effectively as a symbolic transition into a different register. The scripted play was now under way, and the audience instinctively settled into their role.

Well. Sandy may not have been the most successful. The most accomplished. The most celebrated. The most loved. The most handsome. The most sober. The most . . . emotionally . . . sane person who ever lived. But what makes a life well lived? Huh? Ask yourself that. What would you be happy with? What legacy do you wish to leave behind?

Sandy always wanted to be remembered. And so it is our duty to remember him. And remember him we shall do.

He turns to the audience.[5]

I see so many people here today that Sandy was so fond of.

Auntie Jeannie. So lovely to see you here today. How long has it been? Twenty years? The last time we saw each other was your wedding anniversary wasn't it, dear? Sandy got blind drunk and told everyone he saw your Jim kissing your neighbour Sally in the cloakroom. Of course in true Sandy fashion he'd gotten it wrong. It wasn't your Jim at all. It was just Sally's new boyfriend. But we only worked all that out years later didn't we? Anyway, I know Sandy's always felt bad about the divorce so he'd be glad to know you're here.

Cousin Frank. All the way from Australia. Strewth. Fair dinkum. Throw another shrimp on the barbecue. Sandy would be so touched to know you came all this way. Although, as I'm talking I'm remembering that he did owe you . . . how much was it?

The audience member can play along if he likes . . .[6]

Yes that's right. Although the flights must have cost a lot more than that. And he is dead. So.

Or:

Yes, that's right. An awful lot of money.

If it makes you feel any better I know for a fact that the money you loaned him was not idly squandered. In hindsight, yes, buying shares in Glasgow Rangers was the wrong investment at the time, but how was he to know that?[7] And how was he to know your Margaret would take it so badly? Anyway, I know he's always felt bad about the divorce so he'd be glad to know you're here.

---

[5] Benny enjoyed this moment, which he used to create a sense that he was about to involve the audience. Usually we try not to impose roles on audience members but, in this case, the job they had to perform was simply to sit there and be the character rather than do anything strenuous. Nevertheless, as you will see later, Jeannie is asked to come up on stage and do a reading. Part of Benny's job as he greeted the audience members was to choose someone who would be suitable for this task, and to ask them directly if they would be willing to read something out later in the performance. This was willingly accepted on every occasion, but had it not been, Benny would have simply asked someone else sitting near by. Again, we never demand participation.

[6] This is a very safe moment compared to a lot of the audience participation we have used. The understanding was that the audience member was playing a role but not really expected to say much at all. A few of them did and a few did not, but the moment worked well either way.

[7] This is a joke for this specific audience at this specific point in time. Years before, Glasgow Rangers had gone into liquidation and actually ceased to exist before being resurrected as a (technically) new club.

Someone who is not here today, although she was expected, is Sandy's estranged wife Anne who currently lives in Cyprus with their two children Ross and Michelle. And . . . well, it's not my place to say so but . . . I'm glad she's not here. That woman was nothing but trouble for my brother since the moment she lured him into her web. Sandy was not perfect. Clearly. But at least he's not . . .

Pure.

Unadulterated.

Evil.

He turns over his card.

Anyway, Anne sends her love and is sorry she cannot be here today.

However, someone who can be here today, and this may surprise you, is . . . Sandy himself.

No! He's not back from the dead, but he can join us now by the magic of . . . technology.[8]

He holds up a clicker and presses a button. Nothing happens.

Technology.

Oh Jesus Christ. Could someone please just hit play on that thing?

Thank you.

Sandy's *face appears on a projection screen.*[9]

Sandy   Hello.

If you are watching this then I am already dead.

Whhhooooooohooooooohoooooo!

No. In all seriousness, I knew the risks and, if I didn't make it, then I want you all to know I blame no one but myself and I take solace in the fact I died a hero's death. I died trying to make something of this short time here on earth. Trying to do something that would put me on the map. Something that would make people stop and say . . . he did what? Wow. That's something. Sandy Munro. He was something.

So do not be sad I am gone. Wipe away those tears. Turn those frowns upside down. Don't mourn me. Celebrate my life.

---

[8]   A cheeky, and rather blatant, hint at what was to come. By putting Sandy in the show here it actually covered well for the reveal later. This video link would explain why his name was in the programme and this would surely be the actor's only involvement in the action. Wouldn't it?

[9]   David remembers filming this in his front room with our assistant director, Cairan, operating his camcorder. It is often the literally homemade nature of the Òran Mór plays that goes down so well with the audience there.

Thanks go to my brother Andy for agreeing to officiate today. We haven't always seen eye to eye . . . because he's a lot taller than me! But seriously, throughout my life I've faced many, many, many, many, many, many, many, many challenges. My father running off when I was young. My wife deliberately and maliciously recording over my favourite VHS tape then leaving me for a Cypriot sailor named Simon. My children abandoning me to join her. My subsequent failed and unfortunately comical suicide attempt which, due to the combination of nudity, celebrity involvement and a slow news day, made the front page of nearly every newspaper in Scotland.

And now. My death.

Through it all my brother Andy has been there. By my side. Coming to live with me when my family left. Driving out to collect me from the police cells after that ill-fated night on the Renfrew Ferry. Paying for my rehab. Conducting this service here today.

Andy, you're the best big brother a little boy could ever have.

I have picked all of today's songs, poems and readings, and there's nothing religious about them – so if you don't like that . . . you can blame the guy in the box![10]

Andy, it is my wish – and you can't deny a dead man's wish – that you should kick things off by leading a rendition of my favourite song, the words of which I have cleverly adapted for this occasion.

Take it away, big brother. I'll see you on the other side.

An introduction plays. **Andy** *begrudgingly sings the following song – encouraging the audience to join in as he goes. Perhaps this is accompanied by a slide show of* **Sandy** *photographs.*[11]

Andy

>Goodbye Scotland's rose
>May you ever grow in our hearts
>You held yourself with grace and dignity
>While your life was torn apart
>You called out to your wife
>But she didn't care about your pain
>Now you belong to heaven
>And the stars spell out your name

---

[10]   Again, we're literally telling the audience the twist.

[11]   We were able to use rehearsal and production shots from *Top Table* here along with personal photos from Callum, which worked really well. The audience had the words on their order of service programme and many eagerly joined in. Far more did this at Òran Mór than the more reserved audience at the Traverse in Edinburgh the following week. This transfer to a more traditional theatre venue really significantly changed the reception of the play. Our work often plays well in standard theatre spaces, but here Rob was writing first and foremost for a Glasgow audience in the basement of a pub. He knows they will join in with the singing and the fact they are not in a formal venue actually aids in loosening them up – the rules are different in there. We're not in a theatre, we're not a theatre audience, we're guests at a wake, and we're bloody well supposed to sing. We know what's expected of us and we're going along for the ride.

And it seems to me you lived your life
Like a broken wheely-bin
Taking rubbish, dawn till sunset
When the rain set in
And the bin men won't collect you
Coz of your broken, shoogly lid
But while they may refuse you (I think that's a pun on refuse)
Your brother never did.

Loveliness we've lost
These empty days without your smile
Coz Anne fucked right off to Cyprus
And she took your darling child
And even though we try
The truth brings us to tears
All our words cannot express
The joy you brought us through the years

Because it seems to me you lived your life
Like a broken wheely-bin
Taking rubbish, dawn till sunset
When the rain set in
And the bin men won't collect you
Coz of your broken, shoogly lid
But while they may refuse you
Your brother never did.

The song ends. **Andy** *takes his place back at the lectern.*

Andy   Where were you when JFK was shot? Well, I was in the Borders General Hospital welcoming my wee brother into the world. On 22 November 1963, almost to the minute as Lee Harvey Oswald was shooting a bullet into the president's brain, Sandy Alison Munro was shooting right out of his mother and into this cruel world. He often lamented that this was a harbinger of his future. And each year, instead of a birthday party, our parents would insist on having a day of remembrance for the fallen president. But I made sure to slip him a bit of cake at some point during the day.

I was always there for my brother. And God knows he needed me to be. When our father left us he was an emotional wreck. He was too young to see that it was for the best. Simply felt abandoned. Unloved. Disrespected even.

Sandy often said he was cursed but if that's true then what does that make the person who has to clean up after the person who's cursed? Cursed once removed? Cursed-in-law?

Anyway, I took him under my wing and off we went to join the Salvation Army to help with works of charity and, truth be told, to meet girls. I courted a few lassies but never did manage to get very far with anyone because every time I got close Sandy would get himself in some sort of bother and I'd be needed. I remember the time he met a girl he liked and thought it would be a good idea to woo her by getting a tattoo. But he didn't have any money so he did it himself in the mirror with a fountain pen and a protractor from school. He thought the forehead would be the best place for it. To prove his love.

Only got two-thirds of the way through her name before he passed out and woke up with blood poisoning. Of course she was called Virginia so the misery was compounded and the next few years were a little bit barren for Sandy.

I mean imagine it. Going out to the dancing at the Barrowlands with the word 'Virgin' emblazoned on your forehead.

You can hardly see it now thanks to the skin grafts, but that experience was a bruising one for Sandy. Which was why I was so utterly delighted when he met Anne and she, almost inexplicably, found his least redeeming qualities endearing rather than outright irritating.

I thought he had found someone else to look after him so I could finally have my own life to live. Even got myself a steady girlfriend. Mandy. She worked as a chicken sexer on a Bernard Matthews farm a few miles from the church. That means she sorted the chicks into male and female, not that she did anything perverted to them.

I was her minister by this point so when we fell in love it was under the proviso that we couldn't do any, eh . . . sexing of our own, at least until we were married.

My life was on track as they say.

Until . . .

Look, I'm only telling you this because my job, as eulogiser, as Sandy's brother, is to explain his personality. I couldn't come out here today and tell you all he was a flawless man with no defects whatsoever. That would have been a sham. So I'm telling you the truth about him. But with context.

Anne seemed such a nice girl when he met her. A little spiky perhaps, but nice. Little did we know.

One night, in 1986, about five years into their marriage, Mandy and I, newly engaged, went over to visit them for Sunday dinner and found Sandy living in a tent in the back garden.

Turns out he had accused Anne of recording over his favourite VHS tape and she had flipped her lid and chucked him out the house. He'd been there a week. In January. She almost killed him!

I mean the man was surviving on Christmas shortbread he found in the shed for crying out loud.

Sandy was an obsessive. I freely admit. He used to be obsessed with weddings but shortly after marrying Anne, in a grey civil ceremony by a motorway, he became obsessed with funerals instead. Started collecting rare VHS tapes of funeral services from all over the world. Said if he couldn't have the perfect wedding he would damn sure have the perfect funeral. Considered it research. He had Stalin, Churchill, Gandhi, Elvis, Hattie Jacques, all the greats.

Anyway, on this day, we find him, blue, almost translucent with cold, and he stares up at us with frozen tears in his eyes and says . . .

She taped EastEnders *over Chic Murray.*[12]

I had to let him stay with me while they sorted the whole mess out. Put my own wedding back a few months. Mandy . . . got tired of waiting. Said I had my priorities wrong. She ended up going off with a cow inseminator from a farm in Dumfries. He got her pregnant shortly after. I always wondered if the best man was brave enough to make the obvious joke at the wedding but . . . I guess I'll never know.

I lost her.

Sandy always came first. Always.

Anne always maintained she never touched his stupid bloody VHS tape but that was the beginning of the end in hindsight. Over the next decade they tried to make it work for the children but . . . In 1996 Anne met a sailor named Simon, who whisked her off to live in Cyprus. His children went too eventually.

Ross and Michelle. Two kids. I never managed any.

I do sometimes wonder where Mandy is. What's she's doing now. How her child turned out. Did she have any more?

I've thought about finding her. On Facebook. But . . .

Mustn't dwell. Mustn't dwell. I've got God. That's enough for me.

Where was I?

Oh yes. After his family left him Sandy found himself more alone than ever. He had no one. Apart from me.

He got a little bit obsessed with Jackie Bird truth be told. Wrote her a lot of fan mail. Sent her a picture of him standing in a field in a kilt. Turned up outside BBC Scotland in a bird costume. Squawking. That sort of thing.

Squawk! I'm Sandy Bird. I'm Sandy Bird! Is Jackie Bird in? Squawk.

A restraining order soon followed. It was a new low.

He hit the bottle hard after that.

Went to a very dark place indeed.

---

[12]   *EastEnders,* also mentioned in *Wallace,* is a British soap opera produced by the BBC; Chic Murray was a popular Scottish comedian.

Lost his job, quality testing cat and dog food. *Hey, someone's got to do it*, he always said. *And there's only so much a dog can tell you. Even less so a cat.*

Now, suicide attempts are almost never funny. I say almost, because, well, Sandy managed it.

I was on a date when I got the call. November last year. I was making one last-ditch attempt to find someone. I should have known not to bother. Mandy was the one. It was always Mandy.

He was in a police cell. Completely naked from the waist down.

You see he'd tried to end it all by jumping from a bridge over the Clyde. But he was drunk and he tripped and his trousers got caught on the side of the bridge. So he squirmed out of them, boxers too it seems, and somersaulted downwards to the murky water.

Or so he thought.

For you see, Shereen Nanjiani was having her wedding reception on the Renfrew Ferry and, just before the first dance, Sandy plummeted through the darkness, testicles first, and landed, with an almighty plop, right on top of the wedding cake.[13]

The little groom figurine went right up his rectum.

It's undoubtedly funny but remember this is a man trying to end his life.

Anyway, to compound things, Jackie Bird was the maid of honour and so he had broken the restraining order. She recognised him as well. Maced him in the face and called the police.

It was in all the papers. A lot of paparazzi were guests at the wedding so the pictures were crystal clear. Sandy, sitting half nude aloft the cake. In tears. Sandy I mean. Not the cake.

The headline in the *Sun* was the most brutal I think.

Fanny Ruins Nanjiani Wedding Planny.

He was in a terrible state when I bailed him out. I took him straight home, sold my car – a vintage 1969 Ford Capri, my pride and joy – and used the money to secure him a place in a top alcohol recovery clinic in the Highlands.

And that is where, completely sober, he made the plan that would ultimately lead him to his death. In the most remarkable of circumstances. But of course, you all know about that so I needn't go over that again.

All of which is to say, Sandy was a hostage in his own life. A man trying to be good. Striving to find love. Desperate to be respected. But fate respects no man. He

---

[13]   Much like Jackie Bird before her (in *Top Table*) this is a kitsch reference to a beloved, if hardly A-list, Scottish celebrity radio presenter. Shereen Nanjiani is just a very pleasing name to say, especially in a Scottish accent. Again, little references like this help make an audience feel all warm and fuzzy – because they know you wrote it for them, and only them. It helps them feel they are a part of the story.

was a loving brother, husband, father and friend. It's just he rarely had the ability to show it.

So, Auntie Jeannie. Cousin Frank. Everyone in this room who was adversely affected as a result of knowing the man. I'm here to ask you all to forgive and forget. To be charitable towards a poor man who lost his way. So many times. In death I hope he can regain a sort of quiet dignity that he sorely lacked in life.

Auntie Jeannie, in that spirit, will you please come up and deliver for us Sandy's requested reading? A poem he wrote himself. So do be kind.

If **Auntie Jeannie***'s not up for it,* **Cousin Frank** *can be asked. If neither will do it, of course* **Andy** *can take charge.*[14]

Jeannie   What is death?

Death is my gift to a brother named Andy.

Death is a big tall glass of bitter brandy.

Death is a sweet shop full of poisoned candy.

Death, in actual fact, is pretty fine and dandy.

Death comes to all of us, to Stalin, Churchill, Gandhi.

Death is needed. Necessary. Handy.

Death is a long-lost love named Mandy.

Death is very scary, but never namby pamby.

It gets you when you're sleeping or even when you're randy.

Death is so many things.

And now . . .

Death is Sandy.

A round of applause and **Jeannie** *sits down.*[15]

---

[14]   In a lot of our work there are moments where we seemingly ask a lot of an audience member. Often, they will be asked to read out loud something they have never seen before in front of the rest of the group. Two things should be said about this. One: they never *have* to do it and there is always a back-up plan in mind if they don't want to. Two: we have worked so diligently to create an atmosphere of participatory ease and freedom that, in 99 per cent of cases the person gladly does the task in the knowledge that the entire room is willing them to succeed. And if they trip over their words, so what? We all know it's tough to sight read. It doesn't make the slightest bit of difference to the drama – in fact it adds to it if mistakes are made. As with Garth's letters in *Bullet Catch*, asking an audience member to read something unprepared always worked very well, regardless of ability. The audience come together in total support of their peer reading aloud on stage and it makes a valuable contribution to the sort of atmosphere we are building. On this occasion, it's also very funny because of the quality of the poetry, so in a way it makes it even better if the reader stumbles a bit or giggles as they read it.

[15]   In this case, the poetry was so bad that the joke wasn't on them but on the dead man who wrote it: Sandy. We were all laughing at him, not Auntie Jeannie, who always got a huge round of applause as she sat down.

Act Two: The Wife

Andy Thank you, Auntie Jeannie. Now is the time in the ceremony where Sandy would like the floor to be opened to anyone who wishes to say a few kind words about him.

He waits a beat and then continues.[16]

No one has anything to say?

A **woman** *shouts out from the back of the room.*

Woman I do!

Andy Jesus suffering fuck.

Anne?

Anne Andy.

Andy When did you get here?

Anne I've been here the whole time. I heard everything you said.

Andy Oh.

Anne *has come up onto the stage.*[17]

Anne Don't look at me like that, Auntie Jeannie, you hated him every bit as much as I did and no amount of poetry's going to hide that.[18]

Never namby pamby.

Andy Look, I think we should /

Anne / Don't take another fucking step or I'll grab you by your glandy.

---

[16] We were keen to avoid this becoming a moment where lots of audience members chimed in because it might hinder the flow of the show at this point. So we made a point of not labouring this or waiting too long before continuing. However, it's important to note that should someone have wanted to say something, the show would not have been compromised. Indeed, who knows what incredible moments might have happened if we had decided to actually seek input at this point. On balance though, it seemed not worth the risk. This highlights a very important aspect of participatory theatre – knowing when *not* to do it. We decided against it due to the pacing of the show. We sacrificed potential moments of poignancy for the safety of delivering a well-paced final third of the show. It was the right time for Anne to come in here and to delay it would (probably) have been wrong.

[17] We cast Joyce Falconer – a Glasgow Lunchtime Theatre celebrity – in this role for maximum impact. We always knew this entry needed to be dramatic – perhaps even a little over the top. This is another example of how we played with this particular audience and, mirroring *Top Table*, this was another dramatic entrance of a female character right through the audience to drive the play on to the final act.

[18] These small moments of interaction are important. They keep the conceit alive and keep the audience on their toes. In participatory theatre it's important never to leave the audience out of the show for too long. They should be relaxed but not switched off. They should be aware and reminded every now and then that they are in this play. They are characters in the room, not just audience members.

Andy *stops.*

Anne I've written my own eulogy for Sandy.

Anyone got a problem with that?

Jeannie?

Cousin Frank?[19]

Good.

Because Andy's left out a lot of important points.

So . . .

She takes out a speech written on random pieces of paper and napkins and lays it down on the lectern. **Andy** *takes a seat.*

Anne Hello, everyone.

I think I must be the only person in this room who was hated even more than the deceased.

But that's largely because of the way I've been painted over the years by his brother.

I threw him out the house, Andy?

I threw him did I?

I threw him out?

He left of his own accord. Refused to come inside even after I begged him.

I took him meals but he wanted to play the martyr. Eating that stale shortbread from the shed. That's why he did what he did for a living you know. Tasting pet food? Who chooses that for a career? I'll tell you who. A professional martyr.

Victim of circumstances. Fuck that. He had every chance to embrace life. He just chose to be a miserablist.

Right. Anyway.

Thanks to Andy for arranging today.

Ross and Michelle send their love. They wanted to be here – actually that's a lie – they didn't, they felt like they should, but I told them not to bother. They're living their lives. They don't need to be sucked back into Sandy's vortex of misery.

You know, the closer you were to Sandy the more misfortune befell you. I really believe that. Not in a mystical way. Just as a direct physical result of proximity.

---

[19]   Joyce was pretty terrifying here. Nobody would have spoken up!. There are different types of participation from an audience member. One is that they are to sit there and be a prop for the performer to play off. The other is that a verbal response can be offered. There's something in the way a line is delivered and the time you allow before moving on that indicates subtly which response is being sought. And audiences just tend to get it.

She looks at her notes.

You'll have to excuse me, I wrote this on the plane.

I wasn't going to come at all but then last night I had this dream where this lanky, spindly, sunken-eyed, half-spider of a man dressed all in black came in through my window and just stood at the bottom of my bed staring at me and smiling.

That was you, Andy, in case you hadn't noticed. My brain trying to remind me not to give you the last word.

Right. So. Meeting Sandy.

I met Sandy when he was volunteering for the Salvation Army.

And here's the thing you see. He appeared to be a nice, normal boy. Cute even, in a rodenty kind of way. Seemed to genuinely care about me. I'd never had any man care about me before. Never. It was a novelty. And I enjoyed his company. At first.

I thought, this is fine. And all I wanted from life was to be fine. I certainly didn't have any delusions of love, fame or riches. I could die happy just being . . . fine.

And life was fine. At first.

We had a little boy. Ross. Sandy was smitten.

But then . . . one day, when he was two . . .

You see, Sandy hated the fact that he wouldn't say Dada. It was always Mama, Mama, mama, but never Dada.

He would come to me for bedtime stories. If Sandy so much as picked up *The Very Hungry Caterpillar* he would wail his disapproval.

And when he was two. On his second birthday in fact . . .

Sandy gave him this big present with red paper and a bow. It was a little bike. And he tore this thing open and his eyes lit up when he saw what it was. We had never seen him so happy. Like his purpose in life was complete now he had this little bike.

He let out a huge shriek of joy and said . . .

Thank you, Mama!

And ran to me and gave me a hug.

And Sandy just . . .

Exploded. Like a cartoon character.

Mama? Mama? Mama? Thank you, Mama? Mama didn't buy this, Dada did. Dada did. Dada did. Dada did! Dada bought it. Dada carried it home from the shop. Dada wrapped it. But does Dada get a thank you? No. Dada doesn't. Dada doesn't. Well you know what, Ross?

Fuck.

YOU!

To a two-year-old. On his birthday.

And he picked up the little bike and went out into the front garden. We watched, Ross and I, through the front-room window, as he took the bike apart in the garden, bit by bit and started to lob pieces in every direction, hitting cars, neighbours' gardens, passing pedestrians. The police were called.

And do you know what Sandy said when they asked him what the cause of the disruption had been?

Ungrateful child.

And that's when I realised that the man I thought would take care of me for the rest of my life . . .

Was a psychopath.

We went to counselling. Sandy had always been very cagey about his childhood. I expected to hear great horrors to explain the man he was but instead . . . All he could come up with was that his dad abandoned them. That's it.

Anyway, in the end we had to stop the counselling sessions when Sandy became convinced the counsellor and I were having an affair.

And weirdly enough, that was what put it in my head for the first time.

The idea of an affair. The idea that I could have one. That it was a possibility.

But I didn't act on it. It was just a nice thought to have in my head. To walk about with. The possibility that the next man I spoke to could be in my bed by nightfall. Made life exciting again. I wasn't yet thinking about love but for the first time . . . lust was in my life.

And I liked it.

I tried dressing up for Sandy. He always had this fantasy about Jackie Bird. So one day, when he arrived home from work, I was in the hallway behind a news desk. And I said . . .

I'm Jackie Bird and here are the headlines. I'm not wearing anything under this desk.

He looked at me and he said . . .

You know, Anne, the allure of Jackie Bird is that she would never do anything as crass as that.

But our love life was non-existent. It didn't help that most days his breath smelled of cat food.

But . . . somehow, Michelle came along and for a while it seemed like she had cured him. She adored him. Her first word was Dada.

He mellowed. And, although I still didn't love him, I certainly saw a nicer side of him. I saw potential in him. Because he was loved. And appreciated. Unconditionally. Perhaps for the first time in his life.

Ross was older now. Too cool for hugs. And for the first time in my life I started to crave love. I wanted to know what it was like to be in love. For real.

And now, when I spoke to men in the street or at the shops I wasn't fantasising about sleeping with them, I was fantasising about waking up next to them. Being held. I'd never wanted that before.

Sandy never held me. He found human contact unnerving. His words, not mine.

It took the best part of seven years but, when I met Simon at a wine tasting – we were the only two people there on our own – I knew almost instantly that this was the one.

He was tall. Handsome. Had his own boat. He made me feel special. Asked about me. Deep questions. Not like Sandy. I think in all the years we were married the deepest question he ever asked was: do you prefer diarrhoea or constipation?

And then he got all annoyed because I said I didn't have a preference.

Simon was different. I'd only ever known two men. One who had taken advantage of me in the worst way. And another who . . . well, how do you describe Sandy?

Andy   Scared of happiness?

Anne   Prone to overreaction.

Andy   Obsessed with respect.

Anne   A total dickhead.

They laugh.

Simon was, and is, the first and only love of my life. And although I cheated. Although I hurt Sandy. Although I wasn't perfect in all of this . . . I think under the circumstances I can be forgiven.

Andy *nods.*

Anne   One day Simon told me he had to leave the country. For work. And he wanted me to go with him. I thought long and hard about it. I really did. But the question that ultimately did it was, *if I don't go will I regret it on my death bed?*

And the answer was a resounding yes.

So I had to leave.

Ross came with me and Michelle soon followed and . . . That's the part I do feel guilty about. Leaving him on his own. Taking his children from him. Especially Michelle.

If I hadn't left he'd probably still be alive.

But he's not.

He's dead.

Andy   Off to meet his maker.

Anne   Brown bread.

Andy   Passing through the pearly gates.

Anne   Coffin fodder.

Andy   At peace.

Anne   Finally kicked his oxygen habit.

Andy   Looking down on us.

Anne   Eaten his last soggy vol-au-vent from the buffet car on the train of infinite disappointment.

Andy   He's in a better place.

Anne   Back to the place he came from.

Andy   In the bosom of the lord.

Anne   Nowhere.

She is almost in tears.

Andy   Eh, Anne, I'm afraid Sandy has requested that you sing the second song but if you're not up to it . . .

Anne   No. I can do it. I'm fine.

She sings the following song.[20]

> Stranded at the drive-in, branded a fool
> What will they say Monday at school?
> Sandy, can't you see I'm in misery?
> We made a start, now we're apart
> There's nothing left for me
> Love has flown, all alone I sit and wonder why yi-yi-yi
> Oh why you left me, oh Sandy, oh Sandy
> Baby, someday, when high school is done
> Somehow, someway, our two worlds will be one
> In heaven forever and ever we will be
> Oh, please say you'll stay, oh, Sandy!
> Sandy, my darlin'
> You hurt me real bad
> You know it's true
> But, baby, you gotta believe me when I say
> I'm helpless without you
> Love has flown, all alone, I sit
> I wonder why yi-yi-yi,
> Oh why
> You left me,

---

[20]   She certainly did, bursting into song with gusto.

Oh Sandy
Sandy, Sandy
Why yi-yi-yi
Oh Sandy.

She finishes the song and stands with her hand on the coffin.

I blame myself for his death you know. I do. It was so obviously designed to get my attention. I mean, what else could it have been?

Trying to be the first man from Moffat to singlehandedly circumnavigate the globe. And me shacked up with a sailor. It doesn't take Freud does it?

Andy   No. It doesn't.

Anne   How far did he get again?

Andy   Salcoats.

Anne   Salcoats, that's right.

Andy   I mean what are the odds of hitting a naval mine off the coast of Salcoats?

Anne   One in a million.

Andy   A billion. Has to be. Boat went up like a firework. He never stood a chance.

Pause.

Anne   So what are you cremating then?

Andy   His VHS collection.

Anne   Of course.

Andy   I'll keep the ashes. To remember him.

Pause.

Should we wrap things up then, Anne?

Anne   Yes. Let me just . . .

I don't think Sandy was a victim of circumstance. I think everything that happened to him . . . he chose. He chose not to be happy. He enjoyed being miserable. Or at least, he didn't hate it. Not really.

I don't know. Maybe I did love him after all. In a way.

And that's why my final gift to him has to be the truth.

Andy   What truth?

Anne   The truth. About us.

Andy   Anne.

Anne   Sandy. Wherever you are. Up there or . . . down there or . . . nowhere. Sandy . . . one day, after the garden incident, after I deliberately recorded over that stupid video of yours, Andy came round and . . . Mandy had just left him for the cow inseminator and . . . one thing led to another and . . . we made love. We were just two people who had never experienced true passion, true intimacy and . . . We used each other in that moment. It only happened once and . . .

Suddenly, from nowhere the lid of the coffin springs open and **Sandy** *pops out.*[21]

Sandy   Ah-ha!

---

[21]   This was the crucial moment in this show, and the one that we were most concerned about. If the audience guessed that Sandy was in the coffin from the start, the whole thing would fall flat. This was the conceptual moment the show was written around: the first thought that led Rob to write the play. We were delighted, therefore, to find that every single audience reacted in exactly the way we had hoped: initial shock followed by communal hilarity. We fully embraced the unashamed theatricality of this moment, resulting in a real fusion of Rob's writing and David's direction, in the context of this lightly participatory format.

   Behind the scenes, the team worked hard to find a way to ensure that Callum didn't have to lie in a coffin for an hour as the audience entered and the play began. We removed the back panel from the coffin and built a route into it from backstage. This caused a lot of sleepless nights and worked a lot better at Òran Mór than it did at the Traverse the following week, when the stage was much more exposed with an audience on three sides and a very tight backstage area. The short time we had to transfer the show was almost entirely taken up with getting this to work and as a result the actors didn't get a rehearsal in the space before the opening performance. This is typical of the frantic, all-hands-on-deck approach that is required for these rough and ready shows. But on the whole audiences accept that not everything will be perfect, and the reveal still worked well.

Act Three: **The Deceased**

Andy Sandy?!

Sandy I knew it!

I fucking knew it!

I knew you taped over my video tape on purpose, you evil fucking witch!

Silence.

Andy What?

Anne Sandy. You're alive.

Sandy Surprised?

Anne Well, yes. It's your funeral.

Sandy *Oh no, it must have been one of the kids. I don't know how it happened. I don't even watch* EastEnders. Finally. We have it. The truth. The sordid truth is out. You maliciously and with forethought recorded over Chic Murray's funeral. You've admitted it now. And everyone here has heard you.

Well? What do you have to say for yourself?

I bet you're feeling a little bit foolish right now, eh?

Anne Sandy. How are you alive?

Sandy Faked it.

Anne You faked your own death?

Sandy Yes.

Anne To discover the truth about a video tape being recorded over?

Sandy Well, if you say it like that of course it sounds stupid. It wasn't just the video. I wanted to hear what you would say about me. All of you. If you thought I was dead. I wanted to hear with my own two ears exactly what my legacy would be. And boy did I hear some shit.

And by the way, Auntie Jeannie, your Jim was cheating on you, just not with that particular girl on that particular day, so don't come crying to me about me ruining your marriage.[22]

---

[22] Returning to Auntie Jeannie is always fun, as every time the audience member thinks she's got away with it, she's back in the play. During the pre-show set up, Benny had to 'cast' the person who would be playing this part and communicate her exact seating position to Callum as he waited backstage. This was the only way to ensure that Callum knew exactly who to direct this line to once he had entered via the coffin.

And cousin Jim. Nice to see you. Nice to see you're still spreading lies about me to anyone who'll listen! You wanted me to invest that money for you! I might have chosen badly but you were the one who trusted me to choose so why don't you make like Rangers, disappear for a while, think about what you've done then come back when you've changed.

Silence.

What are you all looking at?!

Dynamite. Obviously. If that's what you're wondering. Off the internet. I swam ashore then detonated it.

Boom!

See. Sandy's not inept. Could any of you have pulled this off? I think not!

Anne   Didn't you hear the rest?

Sandy   What rest?

Anne   The rest. About the affair I had with your brother.

Sandy   Oh that. He told me that years ago.

Anne   And you didn't mind?

Sandy   Of course I minded. But I forgave him. He's stood behind me my whole life. Which is more than you ever did.

Anne   I don't believe this.

Sandy   Right. Some more things.

He reveals he has a pen and paper.

Anne   You've been making notes in there?

Sandy *has just seen the picture of himself for the first time.*

Sandy   What the fuck is that? You couldn't have used a better picture?

Andy   There isn't one.

Sandy   Fine. Right. Never mind.

He turns back to his notes.

The tattoo.

I did not tattoo 'Virgin' on my forehead, it was 'Virg' and it was more like my temple.

I did not go out into the garden and strip that bike to pieces. I pulled off the handlebars and the tyres and that's it.

I was not eating shortbread from the shed. I brought it with me from the house. And it was five days, not a week I was in there.

I'm not an obsessive, I'm focussed, driven and passionate. And I've been saying that every day for the past twenty years.

Jackie Bird. Yes. I admit I had a wee bit of a crush on the woman but . . . and I say this in all humility . . . she led me on. And she'd be the first to admit that. She replied to my letter saying, and I quote, *Nice to hear from you. You look braw in that kilt.* Nice. Braw!

The Renfrew Ferry. Well, to be fair, you got that spot on. That was not a proud moment in my life.

He turns his notes over.

Ah ha! Yes. These continued attempts to belittle the noble profession of pet food quality control specialist. I'll say it again for you all to hear.

Someone's got to do it and there is only so much a fucking dog can fucking tell you! Even less so a fucking cat!

Andy Sandy. I mourned you.

Sandy Yeah, right, I'm sure you were very upset.

Andy I was inconsolable.

Sandy Right. Sure you were.

Andy Do you think so little of yourself that I wouldn't be?

Sandy You'll get over it.

Andy I'll get over it? I'll get over it? You made me believe my only brother had been killed in an explosion. That his body was blown into a hundred pieces half a mile of the coast of Salcoats. Where we used to holiday as children. I wrote my brother's eulogy.

Sandy Full of errors.

Andy This funeral cost me three thousand pounds!

Sandy *looks around the room.*

Sandy Really?

Can you believe that Anne?

Anne Listen, Scrooge McFuck, your brother went all out on this day. And you show up alive!

Andy We have cars booked to take us to the crematorium!

Sandy Yeah, well . . .

Andy There's a buffet arranged in the Cottiers.

Sandy What? Here to the crematorium then back west to the Cottiers? You've not thought that through.

Silence. **Andy** *is about to explode.*

Andy   I've not thought it through? I've not thought it through?

Sandy   Yeah, see what I'd have done is /

Andy   / You shut your mouth, you sniveling little hamster faced fuck. My whole life I've followed you from one disaster to another like your own personal Red Cross relief team, putting my own life on hold time and time again to emotionally support you in your latest attempt to purposefully bring ruin and misery to yourself and anyone unfortunate enough to be caught in your . . . What did you call it, Anne?

Anne   Vortex of misery.

Andy   Your vortex of misery.

I let the love of my life slip through my fingers because I put you first. Well, that's it. No more. This is the final straw.

Sandy   Do you not think you're overreacting just a tad?

Andy   Overreacting? You were dead!

Sandy   Aye, only for a bit.

Andy   It's over. We're done. You are dead. You are. I'm just going to keep believing it. You're dead. You're dead.

Sandy   I just wanted a little respect.

Andy   You want respect? Then maybe don't fake your own death and jump out the coffin at the funeral!

Sandy   I wouldn't have had to if people respected me in the first place!

Andy   I encouraged Anne to leave you.

Sandy   What?

Andy   You want respect. Well, I respect you enough to tell you the truth.

I broke your marriage up. Me.

Sandy   What are you talking about?

Andy   It wasn't a mistake. I seduced her. I made it happen. And then I told her to leave you and find someone new.

Sandy   Why?

Andy   You drove Mandy away. My last chance of happiness. You destroyed my life. So I thought I would destroy yours.

Anne   Eh, excuse me. No one seduced me. No one made anything happen to me. Like I'm some sort of pathetic little girl incapable of making decisions for myself. I shagged you because you were there. I went off with Simon because I wanted to. Not because you told me to. Do not try to cast me as the victim in all of this.

Sandy   Yeah. Don't do that.

I'm the victim in all of this.

Anne   And don't you just love it.

Sandy   Andy, listen. I know you had my best interests at heart. I forgive you, brother.

Andy   Why am I the only one you forgive? Why won't you just leave me alone?!

Sandy   Because you're the only one who will ever understand me. I'm sorry but . . . you're stuck with me.

Pause.

Andy   Michelle isn't yours. She's mine.

Sandy *stops short.*

Sandy   What?

Anne   Fuck.

Andy   It wasn't a one-off. It happened a few times. Over the years. Before she met Simon. Whenever you would have one of your . . . incidents. We would . . . comfort each other. Anne's right. No one seduced anyone. It was just . . .

Anne   Nice.

Silence.

Andy   I'm sorry everyone but I don't think we'll be having the final song so . . .

Sandy *has approached the lectern.*

Sandy   Sandy Munro was a simple man.

Some might say . . . an idiot.

Sandy liked . . . Princess Diana, musicals, knickerbocker glories with raspberry sauce. Dogs. And cats.

Once, when he was little he sat and wrote out a list of things he wanted to achieve in life so he could die happy because he had seen a film where the main character was on his death bed looking back at his life and realising it had been wasted.

He only managed to think of one single thing for his list, because, like I said, he was simple. His list of things to achieve before he died was this . . .

Get people to like you.

Sandy had a brother who liked him a great deal. And eventually he did find a wife and had children who probably liked him too. Maybe even loved him.

But Sandy's tragedy was that when he was loved he always felt it wasn't real somehow. He didn't have a clue why that was but . . . it was.

His brother meant the world to Sandy. And he hoped he knew how much he appreciated his patience.

Because Sandy was not unaware of his defects. In fact, if he had been, he may well have been able to be happy. Ignorance being bliss of course.

No. Sandy was self-aware. He knew what was wrong with him. But he couldn't for the life of him change. No matter how hard he tried. His personality seemed to be written into every fibre of his being. Built right into the DNA and any attempt to change it, like in some science-fiction film (which Sandy was also fond of by the way), only made the beast stronger.

But it wasn't all bad. He had good qualities too. He would always help old ladies across the road. He never played his music too loud on public transport. And if he had made dinner and one plate looked more toothsome than the other, he would always take the shit one for himself.

Sandy's favourite colour was blue. He thought it made him look handsome. He enjoyed hearing his children laugh. That made him as close to happy as he was capable of. He liked weddings. And funerals too. Positivity and doom, hand in hand.

Sandy sometimes, in moments when he found himself happy – like when he thought about the birth of his children – would sabotage that happiness almost instantly by thinking about their eventual deaths. He knew all this but could not stop it. On it marched. Relentless. Morose.

Sandy wanted to change. He really really did.

No matter what some people said.

He did not like being miserable.

He hated it.

He just simply couldn't help it.

He just did not know how to be, and remain, happy.

And so, the events of his life, the many varied, comical, surreal, tragic moments he created. While he cannot wholly disown them. While he must take some responsibility for them. Surely it can be said that he did not *fully* choose them.

He leaves the lectern. Hands **Andy** *a piece of paper.*

Sandy   Mandy's phone number.

Andy   What?

Sandy   I found her on Facebook. She's single again so I thought . . .

Andy   You . . .

Sandy   She's looking forward to hearing from you. I won't get in the way this time. Promise.

Andy *just looks at the piece of paper.* **Sandy** *approaches* **Anne**.

Sandy   Anne.

I just wanted . . .

I just want to be remembered.

And that's the thing you see. In an effort to defeat death, to try to be remembered. To be loved. And respected. For ever. Some of us . . . some of us are bound to go wrong.

I know I've gone wrong.

And I'm sorry.

A moment between him and **Anne**.

Sandy   I wonder. Maybe we could have the last song. Just to . . . end things. Feels wrong otherwise.

You only get to witness your own funeral once.

Andy   Some people not at all.

Sandy *addresses the audience.*

Sandy   Sometimes being miserable is just an emotional tactic, isn't it? I mean, if you're miserable already then no disappointment can touch you. But you've got to be careful that, over time, it doesn't become your personality.

Coz that's a problem isn't it?

So if you feel like joining in this song, maybe that will help.

Sandy *sings.*

> When you're smiling, when you're smiling
> The whole world smiles with you.
> When you're laughing, oh when you're laughing
> The sun comes shining through.
>
> But when you're crying, you bring on the rain
> So stop your sighing, baby, be happy again.
> Keep on smiling, keep on smiling baby,
> And the whole world smiles with you.
>
> Oh when you're smiling, keep on smiling,
> The whole world smiles with you.
> Ah, when you're laughing, keep on laughing,
> The sun comes shining through.

Now when you're crying, you bring on the rain,
So stop that sighing, be happy again.
Keep on smiling, cause when you're smiling,
And the whole world will smile with . . .

The whole wide world will smile with you.[23]

---

[23]   Like Joyce's song earlier on, Callum was really going for it by the end, and the audience joined in wholeheartedly. It was a great ending, which seemed to be exactly what the audience wanted at this point. This play is a real mixture of direct and indirect audience participation. It's pleasing that the audience literally get to sing the final line of the play with the characters.

Rolls in Their Pockets

Laurie Ventry as Norman in *Rolls in Their Pockets*

Rolls in Their Pockets was first performed at Glasgow Lunchtime Theatre's A Play, a Pie and a Pint at Òran Mór in 2012.

Norman   Laurie Ventry
Laurie   Lewis Howden
George   Jordan Young

Director   David Overend
Assistant Director   Kristin Davis
Stage Designer   Patrick McGurn
Music and Sound Designer   Harry Wilson
Producer   Susannah Armitage

Part One

Round One

In the darkness, a bell rings.

Lights up.

Early morning in the Toll Bell Bar.[1]

Norman *sits at a table with a fresh pint of Guinness.*

A pint of lager sits at the bar.

At the end of the bar is a telephone.

He puts his hand around his pint. Smiles. Waits for it to settle.

Long silence.

He notices a bottle of Bell's whisky on the table.

He picks up his pint and drinks it in five long satisfying pulls, placing it down for a few seconds between each gulp.

A bell sounds.[2]

He looks out at us . . .[3]

Norman   pintaguinesspleasebarman.

Lights down.

---

[1] *Rolls in Their Pockets* is the least participatory of the six plays in this collection and there will therefore be fewer notes here. However, it was included to indicate the range of work we create: from the highly participatory *Bullet Catch*, where the show is hugely dependent on the volunteer, to this play, which in its setting and socio-cultural context implicates this specific audience in the nightmare unfolding in front of them. This audience participate by sitting there drinking pints at lunchtime (before many of them might head upstairs to the bar and continue) whilst watching a play about people who sit around drinking at lunchtime. Rob wrote this play for the Òran Mór audience precisely because he knew they would have alcoholic drinks in front of them. And because he knew they would understand the very Glasgow-specific problem the play was investigating. In a traditional theatre this play would still work, but in this venue, in front of this audience, they are participating in the overall 'room picture', which is like a stage picture that encompasses the audience as well. They are on stage in a way, whether they like it or not, as the play opens out into the pub/venue to implicate us all in the action as it almost becomes impossible to tell where the stage ends and the audience begins.

[2] As research for this play we enrolled in Glasgow University and spent four years drinking at lunchtime. No, but really, we did go to some very dodgy bars open way too early in the morning and in one we witnessed a bell being rung every time a certain customer bought a pint. It was loving and mocking at the same time. A real bittersweet moment. This guy was a fixture in there so much so that they actually rang a bell for him when he ordered a drink. The bell was tolling for him. It was such a perfect metaphor we wondered if people would find it too convenient. But it was real.

[3] A moment of implication, if not interaction. In this opening scene Norman simply sits drinking and looking at us – the implication is clear. This is us. We are all here drinking together. At lunchtime.

Round Two

Lights up. **Norman** *has another pint in front of him. Next to him,* **Laurie** *has just arrived at his stool.*[4]

Laurie   Good morning, Norman.

Norman   monn.

Laurie   Is this for me?

Norman   aye.

Laurie   You shouldn't have.

Long silence. He drinks.

Norman   loari.

Laurie   Aye.

Norman   watyearzit?[5]

Laurie   What does the year matter to you?

Norman   fffff.

Laurie   How would knowing that help you?

If I said the year was 2065 what would you do?

Norman *shrugs. Drinks.*

Laurie   Exactly.

Norman *gestures with his head.*

Norman   yiweraloangtiminair.

Laurie   What?

---

4   David and our designer Paddy tried out various liquids to resemble Guinness but found that the only thing that really convincingly looks like Guinness is Guinness. Norman has to drink a great deal in this play, so this posed a problem if we wanted to avoid a drunk actor. Our solution was a clever mechanism that used a concealed central chamber to make quarter of a pint look like a whole pint. However, Laurie Ventry still had to drink a fair bit, diligently imbibing a couple of pints over the course of each forty-five-minute performance.

5   Norman is named after Rob's uncle, now sadly deceased as a result of decades of alcohol abuse. He was living when the play went on and the way Norman's dialogue is written is an attempt to replicate on the page the way he and many of his associates would speak. They're not exactly slurring their words so much as running everything together. The Glaswegian accent is impenetrable enough at the best of times, but add drunkenness to the mix and it can be almost impossible to follow. Our audience in this venue are only too familiar with this character and so, from context, everything can be deciphered. It was a real key to finding the character in the realisation that his lines would be written on the page like this. Any local actor would look at the lines as written and know exactly who this guy was. And while these lines may appear impenetrable – even for most Scottish readers – they were delivered with such clarity of intention that there never seemed to be an issue in performance.

Norman   yi.werea.loang.timin.thair.

Laurie   Aye, well . . .

Norman   ayjees.

Laurie   So you've said.

Norman *points to his Guinness.*

Norman   amwanaheed.

Laurie   I'll catch up.

Norman   illbeflaa.

Laurie   What?

Norman   flat.

Laurie   I prefer it flat.

Norman   bubblesnoagreewiyi?

Laurie   Bubbles?

Norman   well.

yiwereafuckinlongtiminthair.

Pause.

almostsentabarmaninaifteryi.

Laurie   Oh for fuck sake, Norman, can a man no have a wee jobby wi'out a search party bein' sent out for him?

Silence. **Laurie** *notices the whisky.*

That yours?

Norman   ahwish.

Laurie *picks it up. Stares at it.*

Laurie   I don't remember it bein' . . .

Silence.

Norman   tribblesumjoabiewisit?

Laurie   What?

Norman   tribblesumjoabie?

wisitatuffwan?

Laurie   I'm no discussin' my every movement wi' you, Norman.

Pause.

Norman   wisitaeeasiortaehard?

Laurie What?

Norman wistheretaemuchortaelittle?

Laurie Can we leave it?

Norman ahedgehogwisit?

Laurie A hedgehog?

Norman aye.

ajaggywan.

Laurie Why do you need to know?

Norman sgoodtaenohings.

Laurie Is it?

Norman ahmjusconcernd.

Pause.

cozyiwereintherafuckinloangtime.

Laurie I know I was, Norman. It happened to me. You don't need to keep telling me what happened to me. I lived it. I canny fuckin' help how long I'm in there. It takes how long it takes. Fuck sake, I've no had ma first sip and you've got me shoutin' like a maniac already. I canny help it, ok?!

Now let's just have a drink and forget . . .[6]

George *has entered. He has blood on his top and is bleeding from the head. He walks up to the bar.*

George Pint of Tennent's please.

Blackout.

A bell.

Round Three

The three men sit at the bar, fresh pints in front of each of them. **George** *has mopped up most of the blood with tissue paper. He holds the pint against his temple.*[7]

---

[6] Delivered with just the right balance of frustration and melancholy by Lewis Howden (whose character name is confusingly the same as the actor playing Norman).

[7] These were very quick scene changes, covered perfectly by Harry Wilson's beautiful accordion soundtrack, which was appreciated by *The Scotsman*'s Joyce McMillan, who praised these 'strains of pensive accordion in the style of that greatest of Scottish absurdists, Ivor Cutler'. We were delighted with this comparison. Rob's main influence in writing a play like this though is always Beckett. We read a lot of Beckett at university and were really drawn to the absurd, cyclical situations and the residue of human connection in the face of catastrophe. Rob loves plays written in one location with limited characters philosophising about life – and these are perfect for this venue.

Laurie *and* **Norman** *are staring at him.*

George   Alright, boys?

They nod.

Laurie   Who the fuck are you?

George   Oh. Sorry. George. I won't shake your hand.

Laurie   What . . . why have you come here?

Pause.

George   I'm having a drink.

Laurie   I've no' seen you before.

George   No. I didn't know it was open this early actually. I'm usually in here in the evenings.

My flat's just on the corner there.

Silence.

Laurie   Nasty cut.

George   I'll be fine.

Laurie   You been fightin'?

George   I believe I had a bit of a set-to.

Norman   astramash

George   Yes.

Laurie   How's the other guy?

George   I . . . eh. Funny thing actually.

Funny thing.

I don't really remember . . . to be honest.

Norman   totilblakoot.

George *laughs.*

George   Indeed. Total blackout.

You ever had so much to drink you can't remember a thing you've done?

Laurie   We try.

Norman   forgetforgetforget.godpleaseletmeforget.

Silence.

Laurie   What the fuck are you doin' here?

George   I'll move seats if you want.

Laurie   No. I mean . . . Is it no' a bit early to be fightin'?

George   I think . . . I think it was last night. I must have passed out in the street or . . . Actually last thing I can really, clearly remember is . . . walking through that door.

He laughs.

Laurie   Well there must be a woman involved.

Pause.

George   Deborah.

Laurie   Deborah?

George   Debbie.

Norman   debbiedoesdallas.

George   She's from Trongate actually.[8]

Norman   debbiedoesthebarras.

He laughs.

Laurie   Norman.

She your girlfriend?

Pause.

George   Fiancée.

Norman   ohdaeahhearweddinbells?

George   Met her at university.

She's expecting actually.

Norman   espectinwit?

Laurie   Pregnant.

Norman   ahcongratulashuns.

Laurie   What you doin' getting someone pregnant at your age?

George   Always wanted a child.

Norman *raises his glass.*

---

[8]   This is another very specific reference to a Glasgow location that this audience would know well. These plays suffer sometimes from their audience and time specificity, in that a second life for a production – or indeed a tour of a production – feels undesirable, as the moment has gone. That audience in that venue on that week of the year will never come again. This is not to say the plays would not do very well in a remount, just that they are created with the spirit of the moment and/or a specific audience in mind.

Norman   herestaetheweeyin!

Pause.

Laurie   What you studyin'?

George   Medicine.

Norman   ohadoacter.we'veadoacterinahoos!

Laurie   A doctor.

George   In a few years all being well. Touch wood.

Laurie   So you're pretty clever then? You know a lot about . . . how things work and . . .

Pause. **George** *has noticed the whisky. He picks it up. He weighs it in his hand.*

Silence.

Laurie   George. You ok?

George *puts the bottle down.*

George   Yeah. Just . . . You know when you can't remember something. It's often the brain's way of protecting you. Blocking out harmful information.

But more often it's just mild brain damage caused by excess alcohol!

He laughs.

Laurie   What's the last thing you do remember?

Pause.

Norman   shit!

Laurie   What?

Norman   hesnogoataroll!

George   What's that?

Norman   yineedarollwiyurbeer.

He takes a roll from his pocket and places it beside his pint.

George   It's ok, I'm not hungry.

Norman   yirnogoanieatit.

George   Then why /

Laurie   / It's quicker not to argue.

Norman   hereavgoataspare.

He takes a roll from his pocket and gives it to **George.**

yougoatyoursloari?

Laurie *pulls a roll from his pocket and places it on the bar.*

Laurie   You happy now?

Norman   yineedarollwiyurbeer.

Silence

George   I was in here. Last night. I remember now.

Laurie   In here?

George   Med student night out.

Laurie   Definitely in here?

George   Yeah. Why?

Laurie   No . . . nothin'. No reason. You need another drink?

Pause.

George   It was one of those nights you just need to get as hammered as you can in as quick a time as possible. You know?

Pause.

I was sitting in on a psychotherapy session with a lad who had tried to kill himself. He put stones in his pockets and walked into a loch. Nearly died. Didn't have a reason. Just . . .

I was standing at the bar over there. We were playing a drinking game.

Norman   here.drinkinsnoagiymson.

George   It's stupid but it gets you hammered.

It's called 21s. You go round the circle counting up to 21 and the person who says 21 makes up a new rule.

Norman   yecannyjusgoarunmakinuprulz.

George   Yeah, like, instead of the number five you've got to say the name of an animal or numbers eleven and three are switched. And then you do it all over again and if you get it wrong you have to down your drink.

Laurie   yicinonlydrinkifyegitsumhinrang?

Geogre   It's fun. The rules add up and up and up until there's just too much information in your head. I'm rubbish so I was pretty drunk by the end of it and /

Laurie   / Aye alright. We get the picture. You got drunk and had a punch-up. We've all done it. You want another pint?

George   I was totally bladdered.

Norman   wasted.

George   Paraletic.

Norman   miroculous!

George   Indeed.

Laurie   Will you have another drink? George. Another drink.

Pause.

George   Why not. Are you boys getting drunk?

Laurie   We don't get drunk, son. We are drunk.[9]

George   Oh.

Laughs awkwardly.

Aahhh!

I just hate that. A blank night. And the more you try to remember the more it's . . . pushed away.

I like to know.

You know?

Laurie   No.

There's a lot to be said for remaining . . .

Silence.

Norman   amstillwanaheed.

Laurie   What?

Norman   amstillwandrinkaheediyi.

Laurie   No Norman. You're selling yourself short there.

Norman *bangs his empty glass down on the counter.*

A bell sounds.

Norman   pintaguinnesspleasebarman.

Round Four

Laurie *is arriving back to his seat.* **George** *and* **Laurie** *have fresh pints.* **Norman** *is finishing a Guinness.*

Silence. **Norman** *and* **George** *exchange looks.*

George   You ok?

Laurie   I'm fine.

---

[9]   Possibly Rob's favourite line he's ever written. So economical. So true. The Glasgow audience totally got this. They laughed and sighed in regret at the same time.

George   Coz you were in there a long time.

Laurie   For fuck sake!

George *and* **Norman** *laugh.*

Laurie   Aye, very fuckin' funny.

George   Sorry, he made me.

A bell sounds.

Norman   pintaguinnesshpleassshbarman.

George *lowers his voice.*

George   Have you noticed that?

Laurie   What?

George   Every time that bell rings he orders a pint of Guinness.

Laurie   Aye.

George   Why?

As he talks **Norman** *drinks.*

Laurie   When Norman first started drinking in here the bar staff were so impressed with the frequency and fluidity of his Guinness drinking that they started ringing that bell every time he ordered a fresh one. And every time the bell went he got a wee cheer from the staff and the clientele. Condescending pricks that they were.

Anyway, the bell thing went on for years and years and got more and more frequent because he had taken this God-given skill and gotten it down to a fine art.

I didn't notice it happen at first. Whether they did it deliberately as a joke or as a way of making sure he put his hand into his pocket or whether it happened organically I don't know, but at some point . . . they started ringing the bell *before* he ordered.

George   Pavlov's dogs.

Silence.

He was a scientist who /

Laurie   / Fucked about with the subconscious minds of dogs.

Aye. I know.

You're not the only one who went to uni.

Silence. They smile.

George   Fuck.

Laurie   What is it?

George   Oh fuck.

Laurie   You ok, George?

George   I feel sick.

Laurie   You're remembering aren't you?

George   I think . . .

Laurie   Take a deep breath, George. Block it out. Take a nice big drink and forget it. Whatever it is.

George   No. I need to . . . It's important.

Laurie   You don't need to. Sometimes it's ok to just . . . let it go.

George   She . . .

Laurie   Don't try to remember, George. Don't force it.

George   She . . .

Laurie   Will I get you a wee whisky? Will we open this bottle?

He picks up the bottle.

George   She broke it off.

Laurie   What?

George   She broke up with me. She called off the engagement.

Laurie   Well. She'll just have been angry.

George   Yeah, yeah she was angry. I came home really really drunk. She must have seen the cut. She hates me fighting. She says I'm nothing but a wee boy. She . . .

Laurie   It's ok.

George   It's not ok. She's carrying my child. I need to sort this.

Laurie   Well, you can't go sort it lookin' like a character from a horror film. Smellin' like /

George   / I need to fix it.

Laurie   You can fix it later.

George   I love her so much.

Laurie   Finish your pint first at least. It's a sin to waste it.

George   I need to get her back.

I need to go to her.

Norman   gofiritjorj.

Laurie   Norman.

Norman   awyineedisluv.dadadada.awyineedisluv.luv.luvisawyineed.

He tips the end of his pint down his throat.

Laurie   Norman, shut your fuckin' mouth you don't know what you're doin'.

George   I appreciate your concern Laurie. But I need to sort this out. For my child's sake. For the future of my family. For my future family. For my family's future families. My entire lineage depends on /

Laurie   / George. Just . . .

George   I'll see you later maybe?

Pause.

Laurie   We're always here.

George *exits.*

Laurie   When he came in here Norman. I thought he was special. Different. Here to save us maybe. But he's not. He's just the same as us. We're all of us the same.

Silence.

You don't remember a fuckin' thing do you, Norman?

Norman   ahremumbrevryhin.

Laurie   No you don't. You don't know what I'm talking about.

I envy you that.

Maybe I'll drink enough to join you in your bliss.

He raises a hand to signify the order of a pint.

That boy. He can't find out.

Norman   fynootwit?

Laurie   I know what it feels like to know everything and be able to do nothing.

Norman   noewhit?

Laurie   Nothing, Norman. Just forget.

Norman *finishes his drink.*

Laurie   I think it's about time for you to have your fall now.

Norman   What?

He turns and falls backwards off his barstool.

A bell sounds.

Part Two

Round One

In the darkness, a bell rings.

Lights up.

Early morning in the Toll Bell Bar.

Norman *is wearing a bandage on his head. A fresh pint of Guinness has just been delivered.*

A pint of lager sits at the bar.

At the end of the bar is a telephone. It starts to ring. He just stares at it until it stops.

He is holding a bottle of prescription medication. He holds it up to read the label then puts it into his pocket.

He puts his hand around his pint. Smiles. Waits for it to settle.

Long silence.

He picks up the whisky bottle and looks closely at it. He picks at the curve of the bottom edge with a fingernail and examines what he has found.

He picks up his pint and drinks it in five long satisfying pulls, placing it down for a few seconds between each gulp.

A bell sounds.

He looks out at us . . .

Norman   pintaguinnesspleasebarman.

Lights down.

Round Two

Lights up. **Norman** *has another pint in front of him. Next to him sits* **Laurie**.

Laurie   Good morning, Norman.

Norman   monn.

Laurie   Is this for me?

Norman   aye.

Laurie   You shouldn't have.

Long silence. He drinks.

Norman   loari.

Laurie Aye.

Norman whosinchairj?

Laurie Who's in charge?

Norman aye.

Laurie Of what?

Norman oavthecuntri.

Laurie You mean who's the prime minister?

Norman aye.

Laurie What does that matter, Norman? How would knowing that help you?

Norman amjustabit . . . muddld.

Laurie It's the concussion. It's your brain trying to protect – trying to heal – by blanking out useless bits of information.

Norman oh.

Laurie Just drink up and forget about it.

Norman *takes some pills from his pocket.*

Norman ahthinkyidroapedtheez.

Laurie *takes them*

Laurie They're not mine.

Norman soakayloari.

Laurie I've never seen them.

Norman ahwizoanthemanaw.bakwhenahwizstilltriyin.

Laurie They're not mine.

Norman goatyirnameoanthim.

Laurie Norman, stop it.

Silence.

Norman dyihinkthatboayllcumbak?

Laurie What boy?

Norman jorj.

Laurie There was no boy.

Norman ayethirwiz.

Laurie Norman, just drink up and forget it.

Silence. **Norman** *picks up the bottle of whisky*

Norman   seethisboatl /

Laurie   / Would you shut the fuck up, Norman!

I'm sittin' here trying to forget and you're on at me all the time about who's prime minster and what year it is and do you think some student's going to come back, would you please just sit the fuck there and drink your fuckin' Guinness and give us some fuckin' silence for a while so we can just feel safe for a bit. If I'm lucky I can have ten wee minutes of peace before I remember the fuckin' situation we're in.

Just . . .

Please.

Silence.

Norman   ahwisjustsiyin.

sgotbludoanit.

theboatl.

Pause. **Laurie** *picks it up and looks at it.*

Laurie   Oh fuck.

Silence. **George** *has entered but is standing frozen.* **Laurie** *hurriedly puts the bottle down.*

George   I can't find her.

Debbie. She's gone.

Laurie   Oh. Well, it's maybe for the best.

George   The battery on my phone's gone so I can't even . . .

What time is it?

Laurie   It's early.

George   No, what time exactly?

Laurie *shows he doesn't wear a watch.*

George   Have neither of you got a mobile?

Norman   witsamoabyel?

George   What day is it? I've lost track of . . . What's the date?

Laurie   No idea.

George   Is there a newspaper?

Laurie   Barman doesn't like them. Too much bad news. Hard to clear your mind being bombarded with all that /

The phone rings again.

George   Is anyone going to get that?

Laurie   It's not time yet.

George   What do you mean it's not time?

Wait. Was I . . .

When was I last here?

Pause.

How long have I been gone?

Laurie   Oh dear.

George   What?

Laurie   I think you've got what Norman's got.

Norman   lice?

Laurie   No. I think he's a wee bit concussed.

George   Yeah. Yeah, that's it.

I probably am. My head . . . I mean . . .

What happened to you?

Norman   drink.related.mishap.

Laurie   Come and sit down and I'll get you a pint.

George   No. I'm quitting. I've quit. I've got to show Debbie I'm serious.

Laurie   Well, she's not here is she?

George   I'm shaking.

Laurie   What?

George   My hand. Look.

Laurie   Ah. That's the alcohol leavin' you.

George   Withdrawal from alcohol can be fatal if not carefully monitored by a health professional.

Laurie   Is that right?

George   We had a whole lecture on the irony of medicine the other day. The same substance that's killing you is also keeping you alive.

Laurie   Well, if that's true, you'd better have another drink, eh?

George *isn't listening.*

George   Cirrhosis, pancreatitis, cancer, polyneuropathy, epilepsy, septicemia, apoplexia . . .

Norman   wevawgoataedieo'sumhin.

George   Impotence.

Norman   yeacannydieo'thatkinyea?

George   Alcohol withdrawal syndrome is also known as the DTs or delirium tremens, which is Latin for shaking frenzy.

Norman's *hands start to shake as well.*

Norman   thehorrors.

George   Jazz hands.

Norman   spiritfingers.

George   The paint mixer.

Norman   gieintheinvisiblemanahaunshake.

George   Seasoning the veg.

Norman   gieinthedwarfashampoo.

Silence.

George   I've never heard that one.

Norman   fuckintoniblayir!

George   What?

Norman   thaswhozincharj.

Laurie   George, I really think you should have a pint. Just one. To settle your nerves.

Norman   hezwun.ahcanseehimoanmatele.smiyilinprik

Laurie   Just one pint. Then we can work out how to get Debbie back. Ok?

George   You mean that?

Laurie   I mean it.

He gives George his pint. **George** *drinks long.*

George *starts to cry.*

George   Sorry. I just . . . What if she doesn't come back?

Laurie   Maybe it wasn't meant to be.

George   But she's got my baby inside her.

Laurie   What's a young lad like you want a wean for anyway?

George   I don't know. Maybe it's selfish.

I've just always felt like there was something missing. A kind of . . . you're going to laugh.

Laurie   Maybe I will, maybe I won't.

Pause.

George   A kind of sadness that I couldn't explain.

Pause.

You're not laughing.

Laurie   No.

George   We found out it was a wee girl. The other day. You know, statistically if you . . . enjoy the odd tipple of an afternoon . . . you're more likely to father a girl? We don't understand why but . . . I mean all we are is a series of chemical reactions so anything's possible . . .

Fuck. Look at me. Crying. Embarrassing.

Even after I found Debbie. I still felt it. But when she said she was pregnant I thought, this is it. This is what's going to fix me.

Laurie   It wouldn't have.

George   What do you mean, wouldn't have? I can still get her back.

Laurie   Yeah. Sorry. Course you can, son.

Silence. **George** *picks up a roll.*

Laurie   Do you want to know why we need these?

George   Why?

Laurie   Because back in the day they made it legal to sell drink before 11 a.m. so long as it came with an order of food.[10]

But see, the landlords didn't want to have to go to the fuss and expense of preparing food every morning. So they came to an agreement with their punters. B.Y.O.R. Bring your own roll.

And so it came to pass that all over the city every dawn an army of alkies with rolls in their pockets marched towards their chosen vessel of safety to satiate their undying thirst; to drink and to forget the many and varied things that they wished to forget.

Norman and I were two such pioneers.

---

[10]   This is absolutely true, but we forget which specific pub it refers to. It certainly wasn't every pub, so the army of alkies is an exaggeration, but it's a powerful image.

Norman *salutes.* **Laurie** *laughs.*

Laurie   In all the years we've been drinking here no one from the licensing's ever checked up on the place. But Norman likes going by the book. Don't you Norman?

Norman   ahdoindeed.

Laurie   Makes him feel safe.

Silence.

That sadness you're on about George. We're no strangers. I don't remember what came first. If I feel it coz I drink or if I drink coz I feel it. It doesn't matter anymore.

I lost a wife, a son, my job. You name it, I've lived it. And the thing about that is . . . when something becomes a cliché, nobody believes it anymore. That's when it's safe to laugh or roll your eyes. Look at the drunk. Come have a laugh as he falls off his chair.

Because it's somehow too real to be real.

We're too real.

Pause.

We started the same as them. Out there.

We just reacted differently to the biggest burden of all.

Knowing we exist. Knowing we're doomed but not being able to do a thing about it. It's not the dying that's scary. It's the knowing.

Pause.

George   But you'd still rather know, right?

Laurie   Everybody talks about the weather. No one can do anything about it.

George   Yeah, but the more we learn about it /

Laurie   / The more helpless we feel when we still can't do a fuckin' thing about it.

George   Don't you want to know how things work? Don't you want to know how you work? What you are? What makes you a person?

Laurie   You need to stop thinking.

George   I don't like not thinking. If you stop thinking then what's left of you? I like thinking. I like knowing things.

Pause.

Laurie   The Church says that the acquisition of knowledge is actually *supposed* to bring pain. And they're right. The further I get from God – the more I learn, the more I interrogate and question – the further from happiness I get.

Ignorance is indeed bliss. And forgetting, a blessing.

And until you showed up . . . I was beginning to forget.

George   Forget what?

Laurie   I wouldn't dream of burdening you with that knowledge, son.

The phone rings again. **George** *stares at it.*

George   Shit.

I called her. That night.

She was drunk when she answered the phone. Not just a little. She was wasted. Like me.
I remember.

Laurie   You might not like what you remember, George.

Pause.

George   I was mad.

How could she risk the health of our child like that?

Laurie   We all make mistakes, George.

George   There's something else.

Laurie   Never mind all that.

Let's get nice and drunk, eh?

Pause.

George. What do you say?

Pause.

George   Ok.

Laurie   We're like your lad with the stones in his pockets, George.

Only we don't use stones.

We use rolls.

A bell sounds.

Pause.

Norman *looks around. Then remembers.*

Norman   pinta.

pinta.guinness.pleasebarman.

Round Three

As we re-join them, **George***,* **Laurie** *and* **Norman** *are enveloped in an air of drunken concentration.*

George   One.

Norman   Two.

Laurie   Eleven.

George   Four.

Pause.

Norman   titmouse!

Laurie   Well done, Norman. Well done. Shit, what are we at?

George   He's just said an animal.

Laurie   Eh . . . six.

George   Seven.

Norman   Eight.

Laurie   Fuck . . . eh . . . subdural . . . haema . . . toma!

George   That's it, Laurie. Spot on.

Eh. Ten.

Pause. Then they start to pick up pace.

Norman   Three.

Laurie   Twelve.

George   Thirteen.

Norman *puts his roll on his head and does a Hitler salute.*

Norman   ziegheil!

They're flying now.

Laurie   Scotch pie.[11]

George   Forfar Bridie.

Norman   chipsancheese!

Laurie   Eighteen.

George   Nineteen.

Norman   jackieburd!

Laurie   Twenty-one!

They all cheer and drink.

---

[11]   Remember that most of the audience would have just eaten one of these.

George   What's your rule, Norman?

Laurie   My rule is . . . no more rules – I canny handle any more.

George *laughs.*

George   I told you it was fun though, eh?

Laurie   Aye, George, I'll give you that much. It was fun.

Norman   thatwispurebrilliant.jackieburd.

He laughs.

Ahwidneymindgieinhurariytgid /

Laurie   / Aye, alright, Norman. Alright.

Pause.

George   Here, what was your first drink?

Laurie   Ma first?

George   Yeah, what was your very first alcoholic beverage?

Laurie   Jees-o, now you're askin'.

George   Mine was a bottle of Babycham I nicked from my sister's room. It was awful.

Laurie   How old were you?

George   Fifteen. What about you?

Laurie   Younger than that George. And it wasn't a Babycham.

Norman   maoldmantookmefurmafurstdrinkwhenahwiznine.

butitwizok.

cozalookedaloatoalder.

anitwizoanlyahaulf.

He laughs. The others don't.

Laurie   And now, If you'll excuse me, I'm going to point the pink python . . .

All   At the porcelain potty!

He stumbles off. **George** *and* **Norman** *laugh.*

Norman   ahtherulztherulzahlivefirtherulz!

Silence.

George   He's alright, isn't he?

Norman   mmm?

George   Laurie. He's a nice chap.

Norman   best.

Silence.

yino.ahcanaestontoniblare.

George *laughs.*

George   Well, you're not alone there. I mean, he kind of lost the plot after 9/11.

Norman   whisnynalivin'?

Silence.

George   You know, I can't even remember what I was worryin' about.

Norman   gid.

George   No. Really. How long have I been here? What time is it? Is it dark? Fuck. It's dark. It's night-time. Where is everybody? Why's it so quiet? I can't remember . . .

Noman   he'llbepleased.

George   Who will?

Norman   Loari.

George   Why?

Norman   well.

dontellimahtoaldyithis.

George   What?

Norman   heshidinsumhin.

George   Hiding something?

Norman   fraeus.

George   What's he hiding?

Norman   henossumhin.

George   What does he know?

Norman   ahvgoathisimage.inmaheed.

George   Norman, what does he know?

Norman   ahcanseeitclearasdiy.tonifuckinblair.

George   Tony Blair?

Norman   smilinanshakinhauns.he'sjustgoatintaepower.ahdonlikeim.

eventhoahmlaburthruanthru.ahjusdontrustim.

George   What's that got to do with Laurie?

Norman   hedisnaewintyitaeremimberher.

George   Who?

Norman   thegurl.

George   What girl?

Norman   debbiedoesthebarras.

Silence.

George   Debbie. How could I have forgotten about her?

Norman   seasytifirgetinhere.

George   Is she in trouble? Does he know where she is?

Norman   ahdonojorj.ahdono.theboatlsthekey.

George   The bottle?

He picks up the bottle and looks at it.

I bought this in here. Just before I rang her that night.

I grabbed it off the bar and went home and found her on the couch. Wasted.

She.

She was crying.

And laughing.

She said she was trying to get rid of it.

She didn't want to have a kid with a drunk.

I . . .

Oh my God.

Pause.

I put the whisky down on the coffee table and . . . I hit her. I . . . Her face. With my hand. My . . .

I honestly didn't mean to. I . . .

I need to go. I'll see you later, eh.

He exits.

Norman   we'realwayshere.

Laurie *enters*

Norman   yiwerealoangtiminthere.

Laurie   I'm not going to let you get to me, Norman. I'm havin' too good a time. I feel like my brain's switched off for the first time in . . .

Where's George?

Norman   left.

Laurie   Left? Why?

Norman   ahtoaldhimyiwereuptaenaegid.

Laurie   You did what?

Norman   ahhinkyoornotellinussumhin.

Laurie   Fuck. What have you done?

Norman   no.ahwillnotstoapdrinkin'

Laurie   What?

Norman   ahmnostoapin'.

Laurie   No.

Norman   ahdoncareifahhivbingedmaheed.

Laurie   No. Wait. No. I'm not having this argument.

Norman   fuckyoo'naw.

Laurie   Barman. Don't serve him anymore.

Norman   ah'vegoatasixpacathame.

Laurie   Well, fuck off home then, Norman, see if I care.

Norman   whitdidyousiy?

Laurie   No. I'm sorry, Norman. I can't help it.

Norman   fuckoffthen.

Laurie   Not again.

Norman *gets up and stumbles out.*

Laurie   Not again.

The lights flicker. The phone rings.

He puts his head in his hands.

It's suddenly morning again.

George *enters.*

Laurie   Good morning, George.

George *stops dead. Horrified. Confused.*

George   Morning? It was just . . .

Laurie   Sit down.

George   You going to tell me what the fuck is going on?

Laurie   Sit down, George.

George   Did you drug me or something?

Laurie   What?

George   Have you been putting something in my beer?

Laurie   Don't be ridiculous.

George   I've just walked out that door and ended up back in here.

Laurie   Sit down.

George   Is this my bottle of whisky? From my flat?

Laurie   I think so.

George   What is it doing here? And why has it got blood on it?

Laurie   Sit down.

George   No I won't sit down. Tell me. Did you . . . Have you done something to Debbie?

Laurie   No.

George   Norman told me. Told me you were hiding something.

Laurie   I know.

George   You know?

Laurie   Yes.

George   Where is he?

Where's Norman?

Silence.

You killed him too have you?

Laurie   George, don't be silly.

George   Well, where is he?

Laurie   He's at home. We had a fight.

George   About what?

Laurie   He was drinking too much. I told the barman to stop serving him. He went home in a huff.

George   Shouldn't we check on him?

Laurie   No. I don't do that.

George   What are you talking about?

Laurie   That's not what happens.

George   You're off your fuckin' head. You broke into my flat, hit me on the head, kidnapped my girlfriend, Norman found out so you killed him.

Laurie   George /

George   / And you've been drugging me. To . . . to wipe my memory.

Laurie   No.

George   Well, let's go check on Norman then. Right now.

Laurie   I don't check on him. I'm angry with him. I drink instead.

George   What the fuck /

/ The phone rings.

Laurie   Answer it.

George   You answer it.

Laurie   It's about Norman.

George   What?

The phone rings.

Laurie   Answer it.

The phone stops ringing.

They'll call back. They always do.

Pause.

George   Laurie, what is going on here?

Laurie   The brain represses painful memories for a reason, George. To protect you. It's for your own good. Ignorance is bliss.

George   Laurie, just tell me.

Pause.

Laurie   I don't know for sure but I'm betting you got in a fight. With your girlfriend.

George   I hit her.

I honestly didn't mean to. I . . .

Laurie   You'll find no judgement here, George.

What happened next?

George   She . . .

She picked up the whisky from the table and . . .

She was the one who . . . She hit me with the bottle.

Hard.

Silence.

What is this place? Where am I?

The phone rings again.

Laurie   We're all in the same boat George. That's for me. Norman had me down as next of kin.

Pick it up. Go on.

Pause. **George** *picks it up.*

George   Hello.

Laurie   They can't hear you. I've tried. Just listen.

He listens. He hangs up.

George   Lying on the floor of his flat for three days. The concussion floored him. The alcohol withdrawal killed him. It was the lack of alcohol that killed him.

Laurie *laughs.*

George   But I only saw him/

Laurie   / Time is meaningless here.

George   I left. I came back.

Laurie   We only leave so we can come back again.

George   What?

Laurie   You only think you left.

Silence.

George   Norman didn't know about 9/11. Why didn't he know about /

Laurie   / When Norman died, Tony Blair had just been elected. His TV was on when they found him.

George   This is a joke.

Laurie *takes out his medication.*

Laurie   Look at the date on the prescription.

George   1996. It's not 1996. It's /

Laurie   / It's both. It's neither. It's meaningless.

George   No. This is /

Laurie   / I was embarrassed taking these. Funny that. How a wee pint's ok but if you take these you're a nut job. I went to the toilet to take them. And every time I was in there I used to look at the bottle. Stand there for ages. Thinkin' about just taking the whole fuckin' lot of them. Ending it. Right there and then. Finding peace. Nothingness. But I never did.

Until that phone call. Until Norman . . . My best friend. My only . . .

And when I took them all, in search of peace, instead, I woke up here. Again.

George   Where? Where are we?

Laurie   I don't know, George. I don't know.

When you arrived I thought you might be here to save us. But you're not. You're just the same as us.

I don't know where we are or why we're here, George.

I don't know if this is real.

There are no answers.

That's what I wasn't telling you.

That's what I was protecting you from.

That knowledge.

George *places a hand to his head wound.*

Laurie   Shall we have a drink and forget about it George. Every now and then I manage. To forget about it. Norman hasn't quite got it yet and I'd appreciate if you didn't tell him. He's happy as he is. As long as they keep ringin' that bell, eh?

Silence. **George** *sits at the bar.* **Laurie** *pushes a pint towards him and picks up his pills.*

Laurie   Now, I've got something I need to do but don't worry. I'll be back.

We're always here.

He exits.

George *puts his head in his hands.*

Long, long silence.

Norman *enters and sits at the bar. He nods to* **George***.*

Norman   mornin'

He picks up his Guinness and drinks it in five long satisfying pulls, placing it down for a few seconds between each gulp.

A bell sounds.

He looks out at us . . .

Norman   pintaguinesspleasebarman.

Lights down.

Appendix

Optional script for Act One of *Wallace*: Arguments and positions

A NICE LINE FOR THE MP TO DEPLOY WHICH LINKS TO ACT TWO

MP I must say I was rather enjoying listening to the children squabble.

CAMERON'S LEGACY

Comedian It's over. If not this time then the next. It's coming to an end. You just don't want to be the ones who lost us, that's what it's really about. Cameron doesn't want that on his tombstone. The captain on duty when Scotland jumped ship.

HINT AT CHAIR HATRED OF JOURNALIST

Journalist Come on, Roberta, don't let your personal feelings for me sway you here, I think the credibility of our elected officials is totally on topic.

Chair I can assure you I have no feelings towards you whatsoever.

APPEAL TO HISTORY

MP The UK is the oldest and most successful economic union in the world. For 300 years, Scotland has bought and sold goods in other parts of the UK without having to worry about borders or trading with a different currency.

SHINING BEACON ARGUMENT

MP And say you're right, and I'm not saying you are. Say we do succeed. Is it right to do so at the expense of the rest of the UK?

MSP I am not advocating that we abandon the rest of the UK, merely that we govern ourselves whilst continuing to enjoy a fruitful relationship with our neighbours. Now what is so unusual about that /

Journalist / Come on, Sarah, you can't say that you want out and then say you want to keep enjoying all the benefits of being in.

MSP We can exist as an example /

Journalist / Oh not the shining beacon argument, please, Sarah, we both know that's just a means of assuaging guilt. I'm not leaving you behind, I'm setting an example for you, to inspire you. Cut the crap, if we leave, we're leaving the rest of the UK high and dry. Now, as an argument, I don't mind that, but please just be honest.

THE ABUSIVE HUSBAND METAPHOR

Comedian The problem is, not all unions work. This union of ours is broken. We just don't love you anymore, Eddie. You've wronged us too many times. Don't get me wrong, we want to still be friends. It's just you can no longer bend us over and shaft us whenever you feel like it.

Chair   Bruce, watch the language.

MP   I understand that but if you leave there will be no coming back.

Comedian   Jesus, could you sound any more like an abusive husband? If you walk through that door you're not coming back. You'll regret it. Don't come crying back to me when you run out of money.

OIL IS NOT FOR EVER

MP   Oil cannot pay for everything. Even with oil Scotland has run at a deficit for twenty out of the last twenty-one years. Nobody knows exactly how much oil is left but we know it is running out. Independence is for ever, oil is not.

EXAMPLES OF BRUCE'S HUMOUR

Journalist   First of all, Bruce doesn't care about Scotland, he's spent his career mocking it.

Comedian   Mocking?

Journalist   Welcome to Glasgow, don't forget to set your watch back twenty-five years?

Comedian   Social commentary.

Journalist   Welcome to Glasgow, Commonwealth athletes; thanks for temporarily dragging our average life expectancy above that of Fallujah?

Comedian   Concerned satire.

THE RISK OF DOING NOTHING

MSP   You know what's a risk? Remaining as we are with the dismantling of the NHS and the welfare state, the privatisation of /

Journalist   / A bigger risk than changing everything? Of course not.

PETRA'S LIPSTICK EXPERIMENT

Journalist   See this lipstick? It was tested on animals. I don't care – makes a better lipstick that way. But I bet a lot of people in the audience do care. Put up your hand if that bothers you. Cosmetics tested on animals.

A number of hands go into the air. **Journalist** *focusses in on one of them.*

You're ideologically against testing cosmetics on animals?

The audience member responds.

Right, so ideologically you would never put this on would you?

The audience member shakes her head.

Right, but what if I offered you a tenner to do it?

She takes out a tenner. The audience member shakes her head. **Journalist** *takes out more money.*

Right. So. How about putting the lipstick on for thirty quid?

The audience are encouraged to get involved with the debate.

Wallace (*shouts*)   Don't do it love! Stick to your principles! Show them we can't be bought!

Journalist   *Negotiates the audience member up to three hundred pounds to put on the lipstick. The audience member gives in.*

The audience member puts on the lipstick.

Journalist   You see. Ideologies do not really exist in any real way. It's all about the money whether we like it or not.

Comedian   Go on, then, pay up.

Journalist   Oh, the money? Sorry. You see, I was mistaken about what I could afford so I'm going to have to go back on my promise. Nothing I can do about it I'm afraid. I of course apologise unreservedly.

Comedian   That's bull.

Journalist   Yes. It is. And I hope you learn from it. You see, with both sides making up figures as they go, it's clear that the safest thing to do, the practical thing, is not to take the risk and just say, 'No thanks'. That way you won't end up covered in lipstick with nowhere to go.

THE CONVENIENT FINDINGS ARGUMENT

MP   We are not making it up as we go along, we have select committee reports, we have experts /

Comedian   / These select committees and experts they bring in – why do the findings always seem to match the party line? They never publish the results of the reports that don't come out their way do they? There must be some.

MP   Not that we have found.

MSP   Every report we have commissioned has shown a financial benefit to independence.

Comedian   You must be picking your experts very carefully then.

NOT A VOTE FOR THE SNP?

Journalist   Alex Salmond simply wants to write his name in the annals of history, he doesn't care if this is good for Scotland or not: he wants a statue alongside Donald Dewar /

MSP   / May I remind you that this is not a vote for Alex Salmond or the SNP: this is a vote for independence /

Journalist   / Of course this a vote for the SNP. Who do you think is going to implement independence and negotiate the terms and conditions with Westminster?

Comedian   Aye but once we get independence the SNP are screwed. I'm sorry Sarah, yous are. Folk only voted for you because they wanted independence. Once we get it we'll all go back to our natural parties. I know I'm going back to Labour. I can't stand Big Eck – the puffed-up prick. He has the self-satisfied air of a man who every day beats his own record for the best dump of his life.

MAKE SURE TO KEEP THE FRICTION GOING BETWEEN COMEDIAN
AND CHAIR WHEN IMPROVISING

Chair   Can we watch the language please, Bruce.

Comedian   Yeah, of course, sorry, sweetheart.

Chair   Don't call me sweetheart, Bruce.

EDWARD'S QUIRKY ANSWER

When a question about unity or separation is asked **Edward** *replies thus . . .*

Edward

> Who ever loves, if he do not propose
>
> The right true end of love, he's one that goes
>
> To sea for nothing but to make him sick.
>
> Love is a bear-whelp born: if we o'erlick
>
> Our love, and force it new strange shapes to take,
>
> We err, and of a lump a monster make.
>
> Were not a calf a monster that were grown
>
> Faced like a man, though better than his own?
>
> Perfection is in unity.

EU HYPOCRISY?

MP   Sarah, what is the SNP policy on the EU?

MSP   An independent Scotland would seek membership of the EU.

MP   So in that case you would say that we are what? Better together?

ON ACCUSATIONS OF RACISM

Journalist   It wasn't racist when Nigel Farage came up to Edinburgh and was told to get back to England?

Comedian   No. It wasn't. It was just an example of incredibly good taste on the part of the people of Edinburgh. For once.

Journalist   I say it was racism pure and simple.

Chair   Petra, you were caught going online under a pseudonym and trolling Yes voters in order to mine anti-English quotes for your articles.

Journalist   I was online asking genuine questions of Yes voters and the racist replies I got were astounding. Of course I used a pseudonym, that's undercover journalism.

Chair   I have a transcript here. You said, 'Fuck these English pricks, get them to fuck, we don't need them, never have.' Do you call that asking genuine questions?

Journalist   Did you see the replies? No one forced them to agree with that statement, did they?

CAN THE PUBLIC BE TRUSTED?

Chair   You said that trusting the public to vote on an important issue is like trusting your dog to choose your outfit. What did you mean by that?

Bruce   Well, again it was just a joke but I guess what I meant is that people tend to make choices without a valid reason. Like a dog picking a sweater.

1979

MSP   In 1979 when a majority of the turnout voted yes for devolution it was George Cunningham's 40 per cent rule that kept us from getting our own parliament. And this time you wouldn't let us have a devo-max option on the ballot because from the very beginning you've been using scare tactics – go all the way or not at all. You're playing chicken with an entire nation, but guess what? We're not moving out the way. We got our assembly at the second attempt in 1997 and we won't need two attempts this time to finish the job because we're not scared of you anymore.

MP   I can't believe you are this naïve, so you must be intellectually dishonest. Both sides use sneaky tactics to sway the vote their way. You're no better than we are. You lowered the voting age to sixteen thinking you would get a surge of young impressionable patriotic lambs to flock to your side. But you know what? That backfired on you because they're not as stupid as you thought those school kids, are they? They recognise their futures are at stake and they don't fancy being led to the slaughterhouse so that King Salmond can cement his legacy. They're all voting No!

ON BRUCE'S RESPONSIBILITIES AS A STAND-UP

Comedian   I push boundaries as far as I can in order to make an ironic point about our limits as human beings.

Chair   Do you think your audience gets the irony?

Comedian   I'm not responsible for why people are laughing.

Chair   No, but you are responsible for what you choose to say. And if I had a platform to talk to millions of people like you do I sure as hell know I wouldn't use it to make jokes about disabled children.

It's about what you chose to do with the power you find yourself with.